STRAITJACKET OR FRAMEWORK?

BUSINESS BOOKS INDUSTRIAL RELATIONS SERIES

GENERAL EDITOR : BRIAN TOWERS

E G A Armstrong

Straitjacket or Framework?

THE IMPLICATIONS FOR MANAGEMENT OF THE INDUSTRIAL RELATIONS ACT

BUSINESS BOOKS *LONDON*

First published in Britain in 1973

ISBN 0 220 66224 X

Set in 10 on 12 point Times and printed in England by
Ebenezer Baylis and Son Limited, The Trinity Press, Worcester, and London
for the publisher: Business Books Limited
Registered office: 110 Fleet Street, London EC4 A2JL
Publishing office: Mercury House, Waterloo Road, London SE1 8UL

Contents

Foreword

The study and practice of industrial relations have become, in recent years, areas of outstanding interest and significance. This process has been sharply accelerated by the Donovan Commission Report of 1968 which put the analyses, controversies and polemics of the sixties into an orderly framework and provided a springboard for further academic analysis and industrial and political debate. The most important development in the post Donovan era—although fundamentally contrary to its findings—has been the formal introduction of the law into the substance and procedures of industrial relations at the place of work. The implications of this development for the conduct of industrial relations at the place of work is a theme of wide interest. It seems natural, therefore, to begin a new industrial relations series with a practical analysis of the first effects and likely future impact of the Industrial Relations Act.

BRIAN TOWERS
University of Nottingham

Preface

Whatever the Industrial Relations Act 1971 has or has not done, may or may not do to our system of industrial relations, this controversial law has undoubtedly given fresh impetus to the study of the subject and prompted a greater measure of managerial involvement in industrial relations policies and practices.

Whatever changes are made to the Act (and it is a fairly safe prediction that even the Act's repeal would be followed by replacement legislation) a greater number of managers and would-be managers than in the past will need to concern themselves with the law's intervention into the untidy, spirited world of industrial relations. The belief that "the primary responsibility for the promotion of good industrial relations" should be accepted by management is likely to remain with us. It is with these considerations in mind that this book has been written.

Although a great deal of material has been published on the Act, a large part of this production, particularly in the early stages, has been, appropriately, of the "guide to . . ." character with the emphasis on succinct technical explanations. At the weightier end of the literature, lawyers have compiled voluminous compendia and detailed commentaries set in a legal context.

Straitjacket or Framework? is designed to occupy a position between the short guide and those much lengthier works which are indispensable for reference but daunting to the manager and student who wish to know both in general and reasonably specific terms what the Act is all about and what it appears to be doing to the industrial relations system. Although technical explanations do appear in *Straitjacket or Framework?* the presentation perspective is that of industrial relations rather than the law. To this end the attempt has been made to create a narrative flow, comment and appraisal of the Act accompanying the technical explanations so that the total result hopefully provides a sound synoptic view of this law, even allowing that changes to the Act are likely to be made.

Given that the Act contains 170 sections and 9 schedules, given that a variety of regulations have been made under the Act and that a swelling volume of case law is developing, the permutations of possible presentation in structural terms are legion. With the ideas of systematic development and narrative flow in mind, the Act has first been placed in a historical setting. Institutions serving as change agents are then examined. Whether trade union members or not, we are all individuals and the next cluster of chapters therefore examines individual rights. The bridge between this area and the collective aspects of industrial relations is built by section 5, a complete chapter being given, because it is so important, to a consideration of Hamlet's right to be or not to be a member of a trade union. Chapters on industrial conflict follow, to be succeeded, after considering registration rules and the Code of Practice, by a final chapter of appraisal of events to the end of February 1973—and some thoughts on the future.

Within this broad pattern, detailed attention has been paid not only to issues of great and self evident concern to industrial relations (Hamlet's right is a case in point) but to features which, though significant, have perhaps received less than their due from some commentators. Here the Act's effect on the wages council system and the modified role of the Industrial Arbitration Board come to mind.

In the preparation of this book especial warm thanks are owed to a number of people. Mr T G Whittingham and Mr B Towers made valuable, constructive comments and suggestions. Manchester Business School is well blessed with pleasant and competent typists, a number of whom worked on the manuscript. From among these Miss Jackie Jones must be singled out for particular mention. My wife, too, deserves praise for her good humoured encouragement of my literary endeavours.

These endeavours may reveal mistakes, not unlikely with a law of such complexity, but such mistakes are my own responsibility.

Note: In the text, references in parentheses ( ) are to sections of the Act; references in square brackets [ ] are to source materials, a list of sources being given at the end of the book. In some quotations I have used italic, that was not in the original, to emphasise the point being made.

Acknowledgements

I wish to thank the following for permission to quote copyright material:

BBC Publications and E J Robertson, *Disclosure of Information : A Management View, in Conflict at Work*

British Journal of Industrial Relations, "The Redundancy Payments Act in the Practice of the Industrial Tribunals" by C E McCormick, and "Labour Law and Labour Relations in Britain" by K W Wedderburn

Butterworth & Co (Publishers) Ltd, *Industrial Relations* by R J Harvey

Conservative Political Centre, *Fair Deal at Work*

Electrical, Electronic & Telecommunication Union—Plumbing Trades Union "Matters of Principle" by F J Chapple, in *Contact*

Engineering Employers' Federation and Kogan Page Ltd, Appendix 2 : "Application Concerning Sole Bargaining Rights"—from *Industrial Relations Problems and the Industrial Relations Act* by D J Hall

Faber and Faber Ltd, *The Waste Land in Selected Poems* by T S Eliot, Penguin Books, 1948

Fabian Society, *Laws Against Strikes*, O Kahn-Freund and B Hepple

HMSO, with the permission of the Controller

Donovan Report
In Place of Strife
Report of Chief Registrar of Trade Unions and Employers' Associations, 1971
Industrial Relations Handbook,1961
Code of Practice, 1972
Dismissal Procedures—a Report
Industrial Relations Bill—Consultative Document

A Guide to the Industrial Relations Act 1971 (also, Appendix 3 : "Unfair Industrial practices and Breaches of Duty")
Industrial Relations Act, 1971 Registration
Industrial Relations Act, 1971 Rights of the Individual
Industrial Tribunal Reports
CIR Report number 31, *Disclosure of Information*
Department of Employemnt *Gazette*

Incomes Data Services Ltd, "Industrial Relations Act," *IDS Report Supplements*, numbers 1 and 4

Johnson Publications, Ltd, *A Giant's Strength*

Praeger Publishers, Inc (New York) *International Labor Relations Management in the Automotive Industry : A Comparative Study of Chrysler, Ford and General Motors* by D Kujawa

Socialist Commentary, "Getting in on the Act" by P Plouviez

The Financial Times

Times Newspapers Ltd, *Times Law Reports* ,various articles and *The Times Guide to the Industrial Relations Act* by I Macbeath

Trades Union Congress, excerpts from *TUC Handbook on the Industrial Relations Act* and *Good Industrial Relations—A Guide for Negotiators*

E G A Armstrong

1

Genesis and Purpose of the Act

O it is excellent
To have a giant's strength; but it is tyrannous
To use it as a giant

Measure for Measure, SHAKESPEARE

Shakespeare can generally be relied upon to provide an apt quotation and the above aphorism prefaces *A Giant's Strength* published in 1958 [1]. This pamphlet contained "Some thoughts on the constitutional and legal position of trade unions in England"—a study prepared by a Committee of Members of the Inns of Court Conservative and Unionist Society. "Thoughts" expressed thirteen years earlier are to be found in greatly elaborated form in the *Industrial Relations Act 1971*. For example, in its "Summary of recommendations," *A Giant's Strength* advocated: "That in future the privileges given to trade unions under the *Trade Union Act 1871* (and other trade union laws) . . . should only be available to trade unions that have been registered. . . ."

[1, p54] As is well known, it is central to the purpose of the *Industrial Relations Act, 1971* to bring about the registration of trade unions partly by placing at greater legal risk unions which decide not to register. In 1958, as in 1971, a basic purpose of registration was to ensure that trade unions conformed to desirable standards of behaviour, as determined by government, not least in relation to their own members.

Explicit in Shakespeare's words is the belief that legitimate power is sometimes used unjustly and implicit in the Conservative lawyers' use of the same words is the conviction that in the post Second World War period the trade unions have abused the powers they self-evidently possess, particularly in relation to industrial action. Corrective measures are therefore needed. *The Industrial Relations Act 1971* is much concerned with proscribing alleged abuses of power and prescribing ways and means for improving industrial relations. The Act (and for convenience this term will be used henceforward unless otherwise stated) thus stands in direct line of descent from the ideas discussed in *A Giant's Strength* in 1958. The Act, although much more complex and detailed than the study paper, remains very much the product of Conservative lawyers. This assertion will be supported with evidence as this book progresses, but it is appropriate at the outset to indicate the authorship of the Act not with a view to passing judgement on the Act's possible efficacy—it is too early to do that anyway—but in order to point out that in its content and philosophy, the Act does not embody in any major consensus form, the flux of opinions and values held by those actually involved in industrial relations, namely management, the trade unions and government. The trade unions remain largely hostile to the Act and managements can hardly be said to have welcomed the new law with enthusiasm.

Perhaps no industrial relations legislation which was to be influential in the sense of giving a sharp jolt to our industrial relations system could be worked out on a tripartite basis. By the time of the next general election, we may have a better chance of knowing whether the jolt has been of the right kind.

Largely because of shifting political fortunes, more than a decade elapsed before the 1958 "Giant's Strength" ideas became transmuted and translated into the complicated legal provisions of 1971. Throughout this intervening period the unsatisfactory state of British industrial relations remained a fairly constant theme of public debate. Assertions and counter-assertions abounded. "The shop-stewards with their wildcat strikes are ruining the economy." "Inefficient managements are ruining the economy." "The Government with its timorous (or aggressive) policies is ruining the economy." For much of the time the debate lacked a focus and adequate facts. Focus was provided and fact-finding begun in 1965 with the appointment of the Royal Commission on Trade Unions and Employers' Associations. This Commission was charged with considering:

> . . . relations between managements and employees and the role of trade unions and employers' associations in promoting the interests of their members and in accelerating the social and economic advance of the nation, with particular reference to the Law affecting the activities of these bodies; and to report [2, p1].

Four major reasons may be identified for the appointment of what came to be popularly called the Donovan Commission after its chairman, Lord Donovan, a law lord. The volume and rising trend of unofficial strikes (see *The Donovan Report*) was causing considerable public irritation and resentment. Consequently, pressure had been exerted for some time on governments "to do something about strikes and unions." (Governments so far, had refused to grasp this nettle.) Legal privileges that the trade unions enjoyed in 1965 had, for the most part, been fashioned by Acts of Parliament between 1871 and 1913. Since that time trade unions had become very much more powerful and the economy, through advanced and interlocking technologies, much more vulnerable to dislocation by wildcat strikes. There was a case therefore to examine whether the laws of fifty and ninety years ago were relevant to the needs of an increasingly finely balanced society. It will be noted in the above terms of reference that the Donovan Commission was instructed to pay: "particular reference to the Law."

Not since the Whitley Committee had reported in 1917 had there been an analysis at public policy level of British industrial relations. The last Royal Commission on labour relations had reported in 1906. Clearly in 1965 it was high time for another authoritative, independent and systematic review of the total operation of industrial relations. Given a Labour Government in power in 1965, with its known heavy dependency on the trade union movement for support, and given the Government's awareness of widespread public dissatisfaction with trade union "misbehaviour," the Labour Government may well have deemed it expedient to set in motion the process of trade union and industrial relations reform thus pre-empting what an alternative Government might be tempted to do in the way of taking a harder line against the trade unions.

By one of the many ironies of history, this Labour Government strategy did not come to fruition. The harder line is now in operation and the subject of this book. At the time of writing, the Labour Opposition are committed to the complete repeal of the Act and also to industrial relations reform essentially on a voluntary as distinct from enforced basis. (Some replacement law would be needed, however, as will be indicated later.)

In June 1968, the eagerly awaited Donovan Report appeared. Essentially, the report consisted of a diagnosis of the patient's ills backed by prescriptions and some ideas on how the patient might be persuaded to accept the cure. Criticism of the diagnosis has been marginal not fundamental. The prescriptions have provoked some controversy.

At the heart of the Donovan diagnosis lies the concept of the "two systems"—the formal and informal systems of industrial relations. By "formal," Donovan means the national industry-wide forms of collective bargaining, carried out by joint industrial councils (JIC) and similar bodies. Alongside this system there has developed, in prevailing conditions of full employment (it was 1968 remember), the second or "informal" system, that of workplace bargaining. In many workplaces, bargaining by shop-stewards over incentives, bonuses or lieu payments and overtime, commonly takes wages well above the first system, JIC determined wage rates. In short, in the past twenty years power has increasingly gravitated from industry-wide to workplace bargaining.

Unfortunately, this power shift has not been accompanied by adequate institutional and procedural change. An industry-wide grievance procedure designed in conditions of unemployment when little, if anything, was paid locally above the nationally determined rate for an industry, can become a source of frustration, an irrelevance even, when work people, conscious of their new strength, naturally wish to strike the best bargain they can in their immediate local circumstances. The exercise of such strength might well entail a strike in breach of the outdated procedure. Fragmented, sectional bargaining had become commonplace.

In the Donovan view, it had become imperative to harmonise the two systems. The people who could do most to this end were management, or, more particularly, boards of companies, for it was they who were in a position to devise comprehensive and thoroughly professional labour relations policies for their undertakings. On a wider front, to promote and provoke the necessary reforms of institutions and procedures, Donovan recommended the creation of a change agent. This recommendation was accepted by the Labour Government and in March 1969, the Commission on Industrial Relations (CIR) was formed. (The CIR has, of course, very important functions under the present Act as will be seen in Chapter 3.)

As instructed, Donovan examined trade union law carefully, and at length. Possible sanctions against trade unions and particularly unofficial strikers received close analysis. Although there were some reservations by individual commissioners, the general position of Donovan on sanctions may be stated thus. Sanctions against unofficial strikes will not work and will do no good. In fact, they may do harm. Many, perhaps most, of the unofficial strikes result from the operation of deficient procedures and institutions. Reform these, by voluntary exertions, and where suitable, under the stimulus of a probing and educative CIR and the unofficial strike problem should be largely resolved. If this should not prove to be the case, then would be the time to consider very seriously the application of sanctions against misbehaviour.

It is, of course, quite possible and perfectly reasonable to advance arguments against the liberal and essentially optimistic Donovan view. Voluntary exertions over the years have achieved signally little by way of reform. Society cannot afford to wait for another indefinite period before industrial relations are significantly improved by voluntary endeavour. Sanctions and their potential rather than actual use are likely to move us in the desired directions more quickly. People who enter into agreements should be required to stick by them—or face disagreeable consequences. Agreements broken frequently and with impunity constitutes a formula for chaos.

In January 1969, the Labour Government made known its thoughts on Donovan with the publication of the White Paper, *In Place of Strife* [3]. This document clearly accepted much of the Donovan analysis and voluntary reform philosophy. But—and this is a highly significant but—because:

> The growing interdependence of modern industry means that the use of the strike weapon in certain circumstances can inflict disproportionate harm on the rest of society [3, p8].

—the Government proposed to take powers to impose a "conciliation pause," when deemed necessary, in cases of serious unconstitutional strikes. Additionally, where a major official strike was threatened but there was: "doubt whether it commands the support of those concerned" [3, p30] the Government proposed that a union should be required to conduct a strike ballot.

The Labour Government may well have seen political advantage flowing from their proposals to take a tough line with the unions. But the unions reacted by taking their own tough line with the Government seeing in the above proposals, which it was proposed to incorporate in a short anti-strike Bill, serious threats to the right to strike and the internal affairs of unions, which if not nullified would encourage that and future governments to curtail still further trade union "privileges." Under intense political pressure from the unions and in return for a "solemn and binding undertaking" by the TUC to try to reduce the strike problem, the Government gave up the idea of sanctions.

The *Industrial Relations Bill* which appeared in April 1970 contained no reference to compulsory cooling-off periods or statutorily imposed strike ballots. Perhaps because the atmosphere was still sour, the Bill was not warmly welcomed by the trade unions although it contained many features helpful to them—provisions for facilitating trade union recognition, safeguards against unfair dismissal, duties placed on employers to disclose more information, even the proposed availability of public money to develop trade unions, for example, by way of improved training and research facilities.

In the run-up to the general election of 1970, little was heard of the *Industrial Relations Bill* but a great deal was heard about unofficial strikes. It is impossible to establish—but still tantalising to speculate—whether if the Labour Government had persisted with its *In Place of Strife* limited sanctions policy, it might not have lost, and so unexpectedly at that, the general election.

The eighteenth of June 1970 brought an alternative industrial relations policy to the forefront of public discussion. By this time the ideas expressed in *A Giant's Strength* had been considerably developed. In *Fair Deal at Work* published in 1968, the Conservative Party presented its "considered set of proposals" for the reform of industrial relations. To this end the proposals included the creation of a new Registrar, special industrial courts, a Code of Practice, a push in the direction of establishing legally binding collective agreements, safeguards against unfair dismissal—all now familiar features of the Act.

The authors of *Fair Deal at Work* are open to the criticism that they had made up their minds about what should be done about Britain's industrial relations problems before an independent and authoritative Royal Commission on the subject had completed its work. *Fair Deal at Work* appeared in April 1968 and the Donovan Report in June of that year. Quite apart from its political origins, in the view of its critics, *Fair Deal at Work* was therefore likely to be prejudiced and inadequate.

Against this view it can be stated, as Robert Carr did in the Foreword to *Fair Deal at Work*, that: "the published evidence submitted to the Royal Commission . . . has also been studied and taken into account" [4, p7]. It can further be argued that the Conservative Government was under no special obligation to implement the findings of a "liberal" Royal Commission, appointed by a Labour Government. Had a Conservative Government appointed a Royal Commission on industrial relations its membership might well have been seen by the Labour Party and trade unions as "reactionary" and such a Commission's findings would not be particularly acceptable to a Labour Opposition.

Whatever the merits of the political ping-pong instanced above, it is beyond question that, *A Giant's Strength* (1958), *Fair Deal at Work* (1968), *Industrial Relations Bill Consultative Document* (1970), *Industrial Relations Bill* (first version December 1970) and the *Industrial Relations Act 1971* (August) are consistent with one another. Whether it is consistency of the kind best calculated to bring about "good industrial relations" is another matter and one which will be considered in succeeding chapters.

Once returned to office in 1970, the Conservatives lost no time in redeeming certain election pledges and, within a few weeks, the *Industrial Relations Bill Consultative Document* [5] was made widely available. This document presented in a more formal and detailed way proposals for "the improvement of industrial relations" [5, p1] by legislation. Although a consultative document, little time was allowed for effective consultation and it is doubtful whether much effective consultation took place. Trade union hostility to the proposals was predictable, managers were worried rather than enthusiastic about the Government's intentions but the Government was clearly determined to press ahead with its projected reforms. The first version of the *Industrial Relations Bill* appeared in December 1970 and ran to 150 sections, 8 schedules and 139 pages.

The label of "National Industrial Relations Year" might well be attached to 1971. The battle against the Bill was fought at length and with great acerbity in the House of Commons, with urbanity and greater constructiveness in the Lords, with "Kill the Bill" demonstrations in the streets, with national one-day strikes in the engineering industry. The TUC convened a special meeting of union executives and resolutions were passed committing affiliated unions, in effect, to a policy of non-co-operation and non-registration. A massive educational campaign was undertaken by the TUC to alert trade unionists to the "dangers" the Bill threatened to trade union and shop-steward functions. The mass media enjoyed not one but several field days of discussion about the Bill. It was almost with relief on everyone's part when the Bill became law, if not fully operative on that date, on 5 August 1971. The measure was by now swollen to 170 sections, 9 schedules and 187 pages.

By its opponents the Act is seen as a severely constricting straitjacket around our voluntary system of industrial relations. Its supporters, on the other hand, regard the Act as a legal framework in which the voluntary system can be helped to work more effectively. It is too soon to say which viewpoint is correct (both may prove to be inaccurate) but both clearly agree that the voluntary system will be altered. So what has come to be understood by the voluntary system? This issue must be examined if the Act is to be placed in an adequate context and its controversial nature appreciated.

It was long a source of pride to many British people, particularly trade unionists, that this country had developed a system of industrial relations that, for the most part, was regulated by the unions and employers themselves and very little by the law. Where the law intervened it did so principally to protect weaker groups in the community, as with the Wages Councils Acts, or to point the way forward out of industrial conflict, as with the *Industrial Courts Act 1919*, and not to impose solutions on quarrelling parties. Even in these processes of determining legal minimum wages and arbitrating on wage claims, the employers and unions themselves were closely involved and the relevant institutions could not have worked without their co-operation. At a general level, therefore, "voluntary" has been equated with "minimum intervention from the law."

In more specific terms the word "voluntary" could be attached to the following constituent elements of collective bargaining, the key process in our industrial relations system. For many years, people have been free in our society to associate with one another for all kinds of sensible or bizarre purposes. Mass media demonstrate this fact to us daily—with demonstrations. Workers have enjoyed freedom of *association* to form themselves into trade unions for the past one hundred years. Restrictions on the exercise of this freedom have had far less to do with the law than with social and economic constraints, fear and prejudice.

To achieve and maintain viability, associations need to organise. People who have joined those organisations that are known as trade unions have done so "voluntarily" in the sense that the law has not compelled them to join. Social, economic and moral pressure may well have been applied to people to join up—sometimes it is alleged unjustly so—but a union has not been able to go to court and say: "Compel this man to join our union." The law has not intervened in any general way in the operation of the closed shop (100 per cent organisation) or at the other end of the scale (0 per cent organisation) where an employer has made it a condition of employment that his workers do not join unions. *Organisation* has rested essentially on voluntary exertions and wishes as distinct from legal requirements.

Recognition by employers of trade unions is a pre-condition of collective bargaining. Recognition has come about in the past essentially on a voluntary basis as shown by the absence of a general law requiring an employer to recognise a union in stated circumstances. Public policy as expressed through the Nationalisation Acts, the practices of governments as direct employers, has been to encourage recognition and collective bargaining but there has been no general law (until 5 August 1971) on the subject.

Even where recognition has been conceded, there has been no law requiring an employer to *bargain* effectively or, in American terms, "in good faith." Where employers have bargained effectively, this has resulted essentially from commonsense accommodation to voluntary pressures.

The purpose of collective bargaining is to establish *collective agreements*. As is widely understood, British collective agreements have been voluntary agreements, gentlemen's agreements, binding in honour only and not in law. This non-legal enforceability of our collective agreements has perhaps been the most distinctive characteristic of the British voluntary system, standing in sharp contrast to the contractual nature of collective agreements reached in some other countries.

In a free society it is right and healthy that there should be disagreements arising from collective bargaining. *Disagreements* may result in strikes or other forms of industrial action, such as refusing to work overtime and working to rule. The law has only been able to help people towards a resolution of such conflict. Settlements have depended much more on the exertions and the consent of the parties in conflict than on an imposed ruling from an external legal authority.

Into all these features of our voluntary system—association, organisation, recognition, bargaining, agreement, disagreement—the Industrial Relations Act intervenes, or makes provision for potential intervention, in ways that will be later explained. Is, therefore, the voluntary system, much prized for its flexibility, to be strapped tightly into a legal strait-jacket or set within a legal but reform-promoting framework? A bold, assertive answer to that question is likely to be more exciting than helpful. Much will depend on how employers and unions and the government of the day make use of the variety of sticks and carrots the Act contains, to bring about or thwart the changes that the authors of the Act see as desirable. Allowance must also be made for the influence of case law, for intervening variables such as a prices and incomes policy, the level of employment and the inevitable ebb and flow of support for particular political policies.

Whatever its precise practical effects, as a piece of legislation the Act does represent a massive intervention by the state into the procedural aspects of industrial relations. Such intervention from a Conservative Government has its own special ironical flavour because industrial relations (apart from sporadic forays by most post-war governments, particularly with income policies) has long been a major bastion of *laissez-faire* activity.

What then are the stated purposes of this interventionist Act? Section 1 sets out to tell us something of these.

The Act's purpose is to promote "good industrial relations." Unlike many other terms in the Act "good" is not defined. Such an omission is understandable, given the complex nature of industrial relations processes and the variety of value judgements inherent in them. For example, what is seen as intimidation by one person may be seen by another as legitimate pressure. However, "good" in the Act is related to four general principles and in plain terms has something to do with "collective bargaining freely conducted" but "with due regard to the general interests of the community." "Good" is also associated with "developing and maintaining" orderly bargaining and grievance procedures, again "with due regard to the general interests of the community." It is quite clear, therefore, that collective bargaining is to be seen not as a bipartite but a tripartite process, the third ever-present member at the bargaining table of the employers and unions being the "public interest."

Although almost anything can be justified by government as being "in the public interest," if it has a mind to do so, the Act in many of its provisions clearly represents an attempt to redefine some of the boundaries of power, to have the wielders of power identified, to have power authorised constitutionally and used in a constitutional way—all of this with trade unions particularly, but not exclusively, in mind. The underlying premise, if not expressed in these terms, appears to be that a firm, sector of industry, an industry, or the community should not be held to ransom by irresponsible trade union behaviour. (Sentiments of that nature echoed loudly during the railway dispute in the spring of 1972.) It is largely because the trade unions see the Act both in its philosophy and in many of its detailed provisions as an attack upon trade union strength that they are so bitterly opposed to the legislation.

The third general principle enunciated in section 1 is that of "free association" of workers and employers into their respective organisations which should be "representative, responsible and effective." Having dealt with group activities the fourth general principle is concerned with the rights of individuals, with "freedom and security for workers, protected by adequate safeguards against unfair industrial practices, whether on the part of employers or others."

These four general principles are to serve as the "guiding principles" for those with public responsibilities for the operation of the Act namely the Secretary of State for Employment, the Commission on Industrial Relations, the Chief Registrar of Trade Unions and Employers' Associations, and assistant registrars, the National Industrial Relations Court and industrial tribunals.

Certain of the terms employed in the past few paragraphs are defined with some precision in the section on Interpretation (s167) and elsewhere in the Act. (More will be said later about interpretation—see Chapter 3.) The definition of "trade union" is an important illustration of this arrangement. However, other terms used in the same paragraphs are not so defined. What, for example, is to be made of "due regard" in relation "to the general interests of the community" or for that matter of "to the general interests of the community"? When does an "orderly procedure" become a disorderly one? How fast is an *expeditious* settlement of disputes? (s1(1)b). What sort of "freedom" and what sort of "security" can we expect for workers? (s1(1)d). Case law will often be needed to tell us.

Case law, using the term in the broadest sense, will be made for us by the individuals appointed to the institutions and offices who will be under a statutory duty to follow the "guiding principles." Whatever the stated guiding principles, individual judges, adjudicators, officials have their own individual styles. Some judges by temperament, persuasion and experience are conservative and may interpret the law restrictively—others may be liberal, occasionally radical and expand the law by extending the limits of the permissible. American history is rich in examples of how particular individuals or small groups of people involved in the judicial processes of industrial relations can bring about significant shifts in the operation of an Act of Congress. It is, therefore, important to pay close attention to those institutions whose responsibility it is to further the purposes of the Industrial Relations Act, to the composition and powers of those institutions, paying "due regard" to the men, and possibly a few women, who will be guiding us in some form or other.

Before passing to a consideration of the institutional apparatus of the Act one other form of guidance must briefly be mentioned—*The Code of Practice*. Under section 2 of the Act the Secretary of State for Employment is placed under a statutory duty to prepare a code of "practical guidance" that will "be helpful" for the promotion of good industrial relations. The code has been prepared, is operational and forms the subject of Chapter 14.

2

Change Agents—I

Members of the Donovan Commission acknowledged that perceptive as their analysis of Britain's industrial relations ills might be, the patient was unlikely to accept the variety of prescribed medicines unless prodded to do so by some external authority. Prodding entailed increased intervention by the state into industrial relations and Donovan made recommendations to that effect. The Labour Government accepted this general case and the Conservative Party had anticipated it as *Fair Deal at Work* illustrates. Despite their differing political philosophies, both major political parties have, therefore, committed themselves to modifying the *laissez-faire* character of collective bargaining in its structural and procedural forms.

Thus, a wide measure of political agreement exists on the need for state intervention. Sharp clashes of opinion arise, however, over the nature and extent of that intervention. While this is not the place for a detailed comparison of the Labour and Conservative legislative packages, it does need to be said now, and later observations will reinforce the point, that both packages contain some common change agent features.

Under the Act, six institutions enjoy prodding powers in the sense that the purpose of their existence is to stimulate people to behave differently from how they would otherwise behave if such institutions did not exist. Two of these change agents exercise judicial functions: the National Industrial Relations Court (the Industrial Court for convenience) and the industrial tribunals. Two institutions are essentially administrative in character, not having the power to make orders like the Industrial Court and the industrial tribunals; these administrative agencies are the Chief Registrar of Trade Unions and Employers' Associations and the Commission on Industrial Relations. A fifth institution is the Industrial Arbitration Board the purpose of which will be examined after first mentioning the need to keep in mind that the Secretary of State for Employment is also given considerably increased interventionist authority in ways that will be later examined. Many and sometimes subtle are the links that connect the six institutions.

INDUSTRIAL ARBITRATION BOARD

The Act confers a new name—Industrial Arbitration Board—on a long serving institution, the Industrial Court, an arbitration tribunal established by the Industrial Courts Act 1919. The new name is obviously necessary to avoid confusion with the newly established court of law, the Industrial Court, creation of the 1971 Act. This change of name is not only technically necessary but also sensible because the 1919 Industrial Court was never a court of law. It was, and remains as the Industrial Arbitration Board, an arbitration tribunal on wage claims and related matters.

For more than fifty years, what is now called the Industrial Arbitration Board has been our most authoritative arbitration tribunal on industrial relations problems. Its work has been of the steady rather than spectacular kind as few major wage claims have been settled by this process of voluntary arbitration. "Voluntary" is the key word. Except in a limited and a special class of cases, the tribunal could only be used provided *both* the employer and union/s sought this form of help and provided that any negotiating procedures established by the parties themselves, for settling the problem, had been fully exhausted. The application for arbitration, therefore, rested on joint consent—as did acceptance of the arbitration award. The Act does not disturb these voluntary arbitration procedures. What it does do is to extend the range of "limited and special class of cases" referred to above. This requires explanation.

Deriving from the Second World War emergency legislation [6] compulsory arbitration in peace time was preserved and modified in 1951 [7] and again by section 8 of the Terms and Conditions of Employment Act 1959. Henceforward, and until the operation of the Industrial Relations Act 1971, the position was briefly as follows.

A trade union or employers' association (but not an individual employer or worker) could make a claim, to what is now the Industrial Arbitration Board, that a particular employer was not observing, in the sense of measuring up to, the terms or conditions of employment established in the industry in question and that the employer should be required to observe these employment standards established by collective bargaining. In practice, unions, particularly white-collar unions, and not employers' associations, have used this opportunity to lever-up a resisting (undercutting) employer to the level of the prevailing employment standards for the relevant sector of employment. Unions have made successful claims on behalf of individual members or groups of workers where, for example, and a not infrequent one, a financially hard-pressed (stingy to some) local authority had incorrectly graded and so under paid some of its officers.

Section 8 has thus provided our only form of compulsory, as distinct from voluntary, arbitration. The compulsion contains several elements. Initiation and completion of the arbitration process rests not on the joint consent of the contending parties but on unilateral application. The tribunal's awards on section 8 claims are explicitly legally binding, the new terms of employment becoming part of the individual contracts of employment of the workpeople concerned. To give a simple illustration: as the result of an award, the new contractual rate for one or many individual employees could be £21 a week instead of £20. Non-observance of the award—that is, the new contractual rate of £21—by an employer would constitute a breach of the contract of employment giving rise to a claim for damages.

From what has been said, it will be realised that an employer can be compelled to observe conditions not of his making. In practical terms, a non-federated firm could be brought into line with federated firms' conditions. The maintenance of reasonable collective bargaining determined standards is considered, as a matter of public policy, to be more important than the freedom of a maverick employer to negotiate with or determine for his employees employment conditions below widely agreed norms. His freedom to contract out above the agreed norms is unimpaired by section 8.

Having said all this, before the Act some 3 to 3½ million workers remained outside the operational scope of section 8. Exempt workers (and therefore exempt employers) were employed in wages councils trades such as retail distribution, catering, clothing manufacture and many small manufacturing trades employing a high proportion of women. Wages councils, of course, establish legal minimum employment standards and the earlier thinking was that it would be inappropriate to have, for example, two legally binding wage rates in some sectors of these trades—one determined by a wages council and the other, which would be a higher one, by section 8. Unions were thus prevented from levering up a particular firm's wages structure to that established on a *voluntary* basis by unions and employers for a *section* of a particular wages council trade. (In a number wages councils trades two-tier bargaining operates—that is, a voluntary negotiated superstructure of rates and conditions has been built above the statutory minima.)

Section 152(2) of the Act states:

"Claims shall not be precluded from being reported under that section (section 8) by reason only that they are in respect of workers whose remuneration or minimum remuneration is fixed under the Wages Councils Act 1959."

In short, USDAW, for example, might now be able, through the Industrial Arbitration Board, to require a particular multiple grocer that is not a member of the Multiple Grocers Federation, to observe the levels of pay established by that Federation and the union as these are above the rates set by the Retail Food Wages Council. In other words, section 8 can now be used to strengthen voluntary collective employment standards and possibly as a consequence, voluntary collective bargaining in trades hitherto generally dependent on the statutory machinery of wages councils. This enlarged scope for the operation of section 8 is consistent with other sections of the Act which, it can be argued, are concerned with fostering collective bargaining. This change is particularly important to the plain intention of the Act that wages councils shall wither away more rapidly than hitherto. This point is amplified in Chapter 10.

But—and it is a very big but—there is a snag—a very thorny snag—to the possible future use of the Industrial Arbitration Board for compulsory arbitration purposes. Section 152(1) of the Act reads:

"No action under section 8 of the Terms and Conditions of Employment Act 1959 . . . shall be taken on a claim unless it has been reported to the Secretary of State by a trade union or an employers' association."

As is well known, trade union, under the Act, means *registered* trade union. The vexed issue of registration will be considered in a following part of this chapter. For the moment, we may consider two new areas of activity conferred on the Industrial Arbitration Board by the Act.

As other parts of the book will make clear, after the completion of a lengthy procedure, the Industrial Court could issue an order requiring an employer to recognise and bargain seriously with a particular union or unions as sole bargaining agent (see chapter 8). If the employer concerned committed the unfair industrial practice of refusing to comply with such an order, then section 125 coupled with sections 101 and 105(5) establish a right by order of the Court for the (registered) union/s concerned to present a claim to the Industrial Arbitration Board.

The nature of the claim is interesting. It is not a claim for recognition. Recognition has already been "won" if not technically or practically conceded. The claim is for new, obviously meaning better, terms and conditions of employment. The claim is presented not to the employer, who refuses to recognise and bargain with the union/s as sole bargaining agent, but to the Industrial Arbitration Board, which makes an award. Presumably the award will bear some reasonably close relationship to the wage increases, for example, the employer might be presumed to have conceded that had he bargained (which entails recognition) with the union. This, of course, is another aspect of compulsory arbitration initiated on unilateral application.

Similar arrangements (ss126)(102)(56) apply where an employer has refused to comply with his statutory duty (s56) to provide representatives of *registered* trade unions with information for collective bargaining purposes. (See also Chapter 10.)

But what are we to make of the Industrial Arbitration Board's powers (s127) in relation to these "bargaining seriously" and "disclosure of information" issues? In both cases the nature of the *registered* unions' rights is expressed in identical terms (see ss125(3) and 126(2)).

"Any such claim . . . shall be a claim that (for employees concerned) . . . the terms and conditions of employment to be observed by the employer . . . should be, or should include, such terms and conditions as are specified in the claim."

Section 127 states:

"If . . . the Industrial Arbitration Board determines . . . that the terms and conditions of employment to be observed by the employer should be, or should include, either:

a Those specified in the claim, or

b Other terms and conditions which are considered by the Board to be more appropriate than those so specified

the Board shall make an award under this section."

Presumably a union may not always achieve the "wages and conditions" improvements the union itself claims it would have achieved had the employer bargained seriously or voluntarily given desired information. "More appropriate" could conceivably mean better, worse or different conditions from those specified in the union claim. It seems obvious, however, that the Board must make such awards as will convince recalcitrant employers that if they are going to have to pay more money and/or improve conditions as a result of union activity, they might just as well make such concessions to the union directly as to the union indirectly through the Board's awards.

"Any such award . . . shall require the employer to observe those terms and conditions . . ." (s127(2)).

And "in so far as they are not expressly included in the contract of employment of any employee of a description specified in the award, shall be implied in that contract" (s127(3)) from a date specified in the award. Such terms will remain in the contracts until superseded or varied by agreement between the employer and employees concerned or by subsequent Industrial Arbitration Board award. (Professor Wedderburn has pointed to a possible weakness in this arrangement [56, p274]). It seems an implicit expectation of section 127 that once an award has been made, an employer will henceforward see the sense of "bargaining seriously" or "disclosing required information" as the case may be.

It could, of course, be argued why shouldn't an obstructive employer be fined for his unfair behaviour in refusing to "bargain seriously" or to "disclose collective bargaining information"? The answer would appear to be that imposing some of the preconditions (disclosure of information) and the product (terms and conditions) of collective bargaining on the reluctant employer is a better way of promoting collective bargaining than fining an employer in the conventional sense.

Enforcement of awards of the Board under the Act, as with the Board's other awards, is still by the route of the individual contract of employment, alleged breach of such a contract and consequent claim for damages.

From the preceding discussion, it will be realised that the scope of unilateral compulsory arbitration has been considerably expanded by the Act—to wages council trades, to the "bargaining seriously" and "disclosure of collective bargaining information" type of cases. But, as pointed out above only a *registered* union can initiate section 8 claims and by the nature of the "sole bargaining agent" and "disclosure of information" provisions only *registered* trade unions are able to seek legal redress against stubborn employers in the circumstances and ways indicated.

For these and many other reasons, registration is a key issue of the Act and will therefore be considered next.

THE REGISTRAR

It will be remembered (see page 1) that in 1958 Conservative lawyers expressed the view that legal privileges should only be attached to registered trade unions. The 1970 *Consultative Document* on the Bill [5] developed this theme:

"At present (1970) . . . legal status as a trade union, and many associated advantages, are available equally to registered and unregistered bodies. In the Government's view, the substantial *new* rights which it proposes for trade unions should only apply to those which" [5, p11] . . . *register* under the new arrangements.

Before considering the rights and privileges of registration it must be mentioned that the first change agent to be appointed under the Act was the Chief Registrar of Trade Unions and Employers' Associations on 1 September 1971.

"The Registrar has four main tasks:

1 To maintain a register of those organisations which wish to enjoy the rights and privileges of registration
2 To ensure that the rules of registered organisations conform to the minimum requirements set out in the Act
3 To see that registered trade unions and employers' associations satisfy certain other statutory and administrative requirements
4 To investigate complaints by members of registered organisations that their rights have been denied by the organisation" [8, pages 3–4]

Of these four main tasks: (2) and (3) are further examined in Chapter 13; (4) is also referred to in that Chapter and in Chapter 5; (1) will now be briefly discussed. Item (1) refers to "a register" but in fact, there are or have been three: the Special Register, the Provisional Register and *the* Register, the Permanent Register.

Sensitive and sympathetic to the needs of professional workers, the Government via the Act created a Special Register. Organisations such as the British Medical Association and the Royal College of Midwives, although not trade unions, certainly pursue trade union and industrial relations objectives among their other activities. Entry on the Special Register confers broadly the same rights and immunities and establishes the same obligations as for registered trade unions (ss84–6) [9, p39, 40] without making such special organisations trade unions. Nonetheless, if midwives went on unofficial strike, section 96 would technically apply to their militancy as would the Code of Practice, in a rather special way (see Chapter 14, page 163).

Most of our important trade unions were registered under the Trade Union Act 1871. All such unions were automatically transferred to the Provisional Register unless they deregistered. It is open to a union to deregister at any time from the Provisional or Permanent Registers but such action must be consistent with its own rules. Many union rule books required unions to be registered—1871 style. To deregister, therefore, consistent with TUC instructions, some TUC affiliated unions had to change their rules, which sometimes meant convening special rules revision conferences—one reason for the delay in deregistering.

The Provisional Register closed on 4 February 1972. By that time an unregistered union such as NALGO could have applied to be entered on the Provisional Register on the basis that it was a "trade union" within the meaning of the old Acts. After 4 February, therefore, a union seeking registration would make application for entry on the Permanent Register.

It is important to stress that registration *precedes* the Registrar's examination of a union's rules. Registration is conditional upon *eligibility*. A workers' organisation is eligible for registration as a trade union if it has the power to alter its own rules, to control the application of its own money and property and is independent—that is "not under the domination or control of an employer" (s167). Independence is of particular significance for staff associations seeking to become registered trade unions. In his first Report the Registrar had some interesting things to say on this matter [50]. An organisation seeking registration must have among its principal objects "the regulation of relations between workers . . . and employers" (s61).

Unions on the Provisional Register will be placed on the Permanent Register, if considered eligible, within six months of their provisional registration. If not considered eligible, the Registrar will so inform the organisation and allow time for the necessary steps to be taken by the organisation to meet the eligibility criteria. In certain circumstances before the Registrar removes the organisation from the Provisional Register, the organisation may appeal to the Industrial Court.

Once a union is on the Permanent Register, having cleared the eligibility hurdle either by the Provisional Register route or direct application route then the Registrar begins to examine the union's rules, "as soon as practicable" after the issue of a registration certificate (s75). The purpose of the examination is to ensure that the union's rules conform to the behaviour standards required by the Act as expressed in the "guiding principles" and schedules 4 and 5 (see Chapter 13). If the Registrar considers the rules to be deficient, he will so inform the organisation and allow time and, if necessary, more time for the required remedial action to be taken. If these opportunities are not taken by the organisation the Registrar may apply to the Court for an order cancelling registration. The Court may allow the organisation further time to amend its rules before such an order is made. Other grounds for the Registrar seeking a deregistration order exist—for example, that registration was obtained by fraud.

If a registered union so requests the Registrar has no choice but to cancel registration. The Court is not involved.

A registered union before and after its rules have been vetted remains under scrutiny from its past, present and prospective members—and from the Registrar. As indicated in Chapter 5, individuals can complain to the Registrar that principles or rules have been broken. The Registrar investigates and tries to promote a settlement on a voluntary basis. If the Registrar fails in this attempt, he may present (as champion of the individual against arbitrary union bureaucracy) a complaint to an industrial tribunal or the Industrial Court. Tribunal and Court are empowered to issue orders determining rights and/or award compensation. The Court may also make a restraining order against the offending organisation. Alternatively, the complaint may be made direct to an industrial tribunal.

If the Registrar has reason to believe that a registered union is persistently or seriously breaking the rules or principles, he may initiate an investigation into the matter with a view to remedying the situation. If his diplomacy fails, he can, as a last measure, complain to the Court seeking "an order specifying what the organisation must do" [8, p9] to put matters right.

So much in sparse terms for the Registrar's technical functions. The rules and guiding principles to which these functions relate are discussed in Chapter 13. Given the nature of the functions, the rules and principles, and the character of the Act itself, it could reasonably have been expected that the Registrar would be a lawyer. Mr Robert Keith, the first appointment to Chief Registrar was a civil servant. The choice of a layman may well have been deliberate as an attempt to mollify, if only slightly, union hostility towards the invasion of voluntary industrial relations by "excessive legalism."

VEXED ISSUE OF REGISTRATION

"Rights and privileges" attach to those unions which register. Registration is conditional upon conformity with good behaviour criteria. Given that the architects of the Act are much concerned with good industrial behaviour, it is no surprise that the Act contains numerous sections ingeniously biased towards the encouragement of registration and discouragement of non-registration. In plainer terms, sticks and carrots are used to stimulate unions into registering. Let us look at some of these. First, some of the sticks.

It has constantly to be kept in mind that as a result of the Act trade union funds have become vulnerable in law in a systematic way for the first time since 1906, when, under The Trade Disputes Act, union funds were given almost complete protection from claims for damages. Whether the authors of the Act are right or wrong in now weakening trade unions in this manner, only history can determine but the unions' anger over the removal of their 1906 "rights and privileges" is perfectly understandable.

Vulnerability of funds is now related to registration. Both registered and unregistered unions can be required by orders of the Industrial Court to pay compensation from their industrial disputes funds to "injured parties." For a registered union an upper limit, dependent on the size of the union in membership terms, is set to the compensation it may be called upon to pay (s117). No such limit is set for unregistered unions. In short, an unregistered union puts itself at greater financial risk than does a registered union. (It is, of course, both feasible and lawful for a union to run down its dispute funds in order to reduce the amount of money available for "compensation.")

Similarly, section 96 which, in simplest terms, is concerned with inhibiting unconstitutional strikes, gives in the case of such strikes some legal protection to the registered union and its members but none to the unregistered union and its members. (Unconstitutional strikes are strikes in breach of an agreed avoidance of disputes procedure—that is, in breach of the "constitution." Unofficial strikes are strikes which lack the approval of trade union authority. Unconstitutional strikes are nearly always unofficial. Unofficial or wildcat have tended to become the popular terms for unconstitutional strikes. Almost invariably all such strikes entail a breach of the contract of employment by the individual strikers.) Although, as will be seen later, the practical application and practical implications of section 96 have been very materially affected by a House of Lords ruling [52] it remains true that in the form of words employed in section 96 the unregistered union remains at a legal disadvantage compared with the registered union in situations where leaders of industrial action induce other workers to break their contracts of employment.

This disadvantage may inhibit not only unconstitutional strikes but the emergence and development of union leaders, particularly in the workplace—a weakening, as some unions would see it, of the unions in a double sense. A counter argument would be that such consequences could be averted if the unions concerned registered and played by the constitutionally agreed rules. Among its other objectives, section 96 undoubtedly includes a firm push in the direction of registration.

Within the thickets of this new law, various carrot patches are to be found marked "*positive* rights and privileges of registered unions." Some of the more important rights will now be identified but only briefly discussed as the focus is on registration.

Only a registered union can apply to the Industrial Court to become the "sole bargaining agent" (see Chapter 8). Although an employer is free to concede sole bargaining rights to an unregistered union, an Industrial Court order *requiring* an employer to recognise a particular union can only be made in relation to a registered union. In other words, statutory as distinct from voluntary support for the agent is restricted to registered trade unions.

Provisions in the Act which affect union security are designed to help the registered but not the unregistered union. Probably, it is now universally realised that under the Act the closed shop, the traditional form of union security, is "out" and the "agency shop" and "approved closed shop" are "in" (see Chapters 5 and 8). But agency shop and approved closed shop agreements can only be made between an employer and a registered trade union. As far as the Act is concerned, union security is dependent on registration. In this context, section 5 is highly pertinent.

Union security is partly a function of the degree and nature of union organisation which is largely dependent on the strength of membership. The law can help or hinder the recruitment and retention of members. Section 5, among other things, establishes the statutory right of every worker to be a member of a trade union—provided that the union in question is registered. Workpeople remain free to join (in the sense of there being no legal prohibition against their joining) unregistered unions but they have no statutory right to do so. Only a registered trade union, therefore, can encourage the employees of the firm to exercise their *statutory* right to join if they wish to join that union. The appeal of this arrangement and related parts of section 5 to all unions with interests in the growth sector of employment, the white-collar sector, is obvious.

The effectiveness of collective bargaining, the promotion and maintenance of good industrial relations, are partly dependent on the disclosure of adequate information by employers to trade unions. Section 56 of the Act imposes a statutory duty on employers to disclose such information to trade union representatives—provided those representatives are members of a *registered* trade union. While the Act does not prohibit the employer from providing such information to representatives of an unregistered union, only the representatives of a registered union can claim such information as a statutory right.

If a union subsequently considers that an employer has not carried out his section 56 duty then the union concerned—*provided it is registered*—can seek redress through the compulsory arbitration procedures already outlined.

Although the Act does not specifically say so, the trade union that decides on non- or deregistration could "fine" itself for pursuing such an independent course of action:

". . . the Income and Corporation Taxes Act 1970 continues to restrict that tax relief" (in respect of provident benefits expenditure) "to registered trade unions" [9, p37].

In a House of Lords debate (26 May 1971) [10] it was estimated that the loss of such tax reliefs could cost the T & GWU £750000 annually and the AUEW, £500000. Ways of avoiding such "fines" have been suggested [11]. Some union leaders have argued that although such tax losses look large when expressed as total sums, when related to "per head of membership" £0.50 extra per person a year in increased subscriptions is a small price to pay for refusing to take out "the State (registration) licence to operate."

Enough has been said in this chapter to indicate that a detailed balance sheet in strategic, financial and legal dimensions, can be drawn up to establish where the balance of advantage lies, for the unions, on the issue of registration *v* non-registration. On any such dispassionate technical assessment, even allowing for the resentment felt by the unions, the unions and their members stand to gain by registration and to lose by non-registration. But this is to ignore the political dimension of the registration equation. The technical balance of advantage may well be the siren song, as the TUC Odysseus hears it, luring unions to registration and, therefore, to acceptance of the Act and all it represents. The trade union movement, by and large, is opposed to the Act as a total package because they believe this new law is an attempt by their traditional opponents, the Tories, to weaken the trade union and working-class movements. Registration therefore, whatever its surface advantages, places a seal of union approval on the Act. TUC policy has consequently been to instruct affiliated unions not to register and to call to account those who do for whatever special reasons they may have for registration.

In January 1972, the TUC issued a Handbook [12] to its affiliates which, in effect, is a guide on how to operate effectively under the Act as an unregistered union. The stance to be adopted by a union is not one of defiance of the law but of non-co-operation. Even non-co-operation brought acute legal difficulties as was seen in the Spring of 1972. (See Chapter 3.) Non-registration brings risks but, if unregistered unions follow the detailed TUC advice, such risks can be minimised.

Union hostility towards the Act, if understandable, may be misplaced. Factual as distinct from tendentious information on registration may eventually gain a greater influence among rank and file trade unionists. Certainly one of the most fascinating areas of political manoeuvring within the trade union movement in the early stages of the Act's operation has been the area of registration. Ideological opposition to the Act has been yielding ground in some cases to pragmatism, to the realisation that a union may be doing a disservice to its members by not registering and also losing potential members to unions which do register. At its 1972 congress the TUC suspended (significantly a lighter "sentence" than expulsion) from membership thirty-two unions which between them represented half a million workers.

Importance lies less in the number than the nature of the registered unions and the reasons why such unions, sometimes after agonising debate, have put the interests of their members before loyalty to the TUC and the wider trade union movement.

The NGA (National Graphical Association), a major print craft union, chose not to deregister as such action would entail, for technical reasons, virtual dismemberment of the union.

For its own survival as a union, the National Union of Seamen consider achievement of the "approved closed shop" a necessity. This form of security is available only to a registered union. Similar concern to protect their already precarious security prompted Equity (the actors' union) to remain registered. "At any given time at least three-quarters of our 20000 members are out of work" [58, p30]. In such circumstances Equity considered an approved closed shop agreement to be essential to maintain any semblance of reasonable employment conditions.

NUBE, the bank clerks' union, sees registration as essential to offset the competition of the staff associations which enjoy negotiating rights with the banks.

ASTMS, the union perhaps best placed to use the organising and bargaining opportunities deriving from registration, finally decided, at a rules revision conference in November 1972, to deregister. Reasons for this reversal of an earlier decision to remain registered were no doubt mixed, but loyalty to the TUC deregistration policy would seem to strengthen the claims of Britain's fastest growing union for a greater say in TUC counsels.

From what has been said in the latter part of this chapter it is apparent that the operation of important parts of the Act will be inhibited, perhaps almost completely thwarted, if the great majority of unions maintain their anti-registration position. Such a position carries considerable significance for the industrial relations policy of the next Socialist government.

3

Change Agents—II

Subtle wits find obscurity in what is not obscure,
and refuse to understand what is perfectly plain

La Bruyere, 1645–96

"It all depends what you mean by . . ." Older readers will recall that Professor Joad of the radio Brains Trust fame prefaced many of his answers to questions with those remarks—and he was right to do so. The Act also expresses views on what is meant by—"trade union," "strike," "worker" and many other conventional industrial relations terms.

It is appropriate to remind ourselves that much of our law derives from two main sources—common or judge-made law and statute law, the law made by Parliament. But litigation arising from the operation of statute law is a matter for the judges who need to interpret words used in Parliament-made law. Was the employee injured on "factory" premises or just outside? The answer may well affect the injured worker's chances of recovering damages. Parliament gives some help by providing, under the Factories Act 1961, a three-page definition of a factory. Similarly, the Industrial Relations Act in Section 167 (Interpretation) in particular, provides many definitions which must constantly be borne in mind whenever we see the defined terms used in other sections of the Act. As is well known, "trade union" means registered trade union (s61(3)).

Section 167 tells what a "worker" is. It takes only a moment's thought to realise that a "worker" within the meaning of the Act covers many more people than fitters, dustmen, clerks, typists. Managers and accountants, for example, of lowly or exalted status are "workers" and, as such, enjoy the same rights as other workers under Part II of the Act. One such right is to join a trade union, i.e. a registered trade union. An employer who deters a manager from exercising this right would be committing an "unfair industrial practice." But what constitutes deterrence? The Act does not make this clear—but the judicial bodies operating under the Act certainly will if called upon to do so. Case (judge-made) law will develop and round out statute law, clarify some of its ambiguities and probably sometimes compound them. The principal judicial body for this purpose is, of course, the National Industrial Relations Court.

NATIONAL INDUSTRIAL RELATIONS COURT

The authors of the Act intended that of all our law courts, the newly created Industrial Court is the one to be used for the handling of those industrial relations problems which require judicial rulings. Such a specialist court is without precedence in this country. The court's membership and powers are therefore of the greatest interest and importance.

High Court status is conferred on the court and, as a consequence, High Court judges, one of whom is appointed President of the Court. But lay expertise is blended with legal expertise. Persons deemed by the Lord Chancellor and the Secretary of State for Employment "to have special knowledge or experience of industrial relations" (s99(3)) are appointed as lay "judges" and although the numbers may vary the court, which may sit in Divisions, in London and elsewhere must consist of a High Court judge and usually two appointed members in order to be properly constituted.

"Special knowledge or experience of industrial relations" merits some attention. The key phrase reads, "special knowledge *or* experience" and not "special knowledge *and* experience" or even "special knowledge *and/or* experience." What weight therefore should be given to "special knowledge" and what to "experience"? These two factors can be inter-related for the "special knowledge" may arise from particular "experience." But a person's experience if confined to one or two firms, or to a particular industry, could result in narrow rather than broad experience. "Special knowledge" could be very special even esoteric or much wider ranging.

Assuming they were willing to serve, should there ever be among the seventeen lay members a preponderance of professors of industrial relations? By definition, they are surely the persons with "special knowledge" of industrial relations. Some among them have appreciable experience in the practical world of industrial relations. The appearance of knowledgeable academics in large numbers on the "bench" is a remote, if imaginatively tantalising possibility.

None the less, the appointment criteria do seem to encourage the selection of some mixture of "ideas men" and "sound practical men." In the event the Government have essentially gone for sound practical men. They may have had little alternative choice.

Given the myriad ever-changing complexities of employment life, it is undoubtedly sensible to harness industrial relations expertise with legal expertise in the membership of the Court. Even so, the Court's composition does constitute a marked departure from the long-established tripartite approach to the resolution of industrial relations problems as evidenced by the independent members (lawyers, academics), employer members, trade union members structure of wages councils, the Industrial Arbitration Board, Courts of Inquiry and, until recently, industrial tribunals.

Although the Act does not debar employer representatives or trade union representatives from membership of the Court, it does not guarantee their presence as does the Industrial Arbitration Board. It may well be that the Conservative Government foresaw the dangers inherent in a tripartite structure for the Court, given intense trade union "kill the Bill" hostility and the subsequent TUC non-co-operation instruction to its affiliated unions not to provide members for the Court if so invited. A formally constituted tripartite court from which one of the parties was missing would be off to a very bad start, assuming it could start, in terms of credibility. As it is, the appointment criterion being "special knowledge or experience," the way is still open for the eventual appointment of trade union members to the Court if union policies should change to co-operation with the Act's institutional apparatus. In the first critical stages of the Act's operation, it is obviously of crucial importance for the Court to have as balanced a composition as circumstances allow.

Confirmation of the prediction that the Court, because of trade union non-co-operation, would be lopsided in character came in November 1971, when the names of the first nine lay part-time members of the Court were announced. Eight members were drawn from the world of management, leavened with trade union experience in one case, constituting both individually and collectively a wealth of industrial relations experience—but from the managerial perspective. The ninth member was a university professor of economics.

Not one of the twenty members of the Court is a woman. Leaving aside the issue of proportional representation, given that about 25 per cent of trade union members and 36 per cent of the national labour force are women, it would seem both equitable and sensible to have some women in membership of the Court.

The Industrial Court exercises original and appellate jurisdiction in relation to unfair industrial practices defined by the Act. In short, and to oversimplify: if a person is hurt or is likely to be hurt by an unfair collective bargaining practice he, the complainant, may eventually seek, but not automatically obtain, a remedy from the Court. Remedies are of three types "one or more" of which may be granted to the complainant (s101): an order determining the rights of the parties; "an award of compensation" to be paid to *A* by *B* where *B* has hurt *A*; and, in effect, a restraining order —an order to the "respondent" to stop doing what he is doing, or not to do what he is threatening to do, by way of an unfair industrial practice.

These simple statements conceal complex issues and formidable consequences—as the docks container dispute litigation in 1972 demonstrated (more will be said about the docks later). As a lawyer has well pointed out:

> . . . it is most important to note that these remedies are essentially discretionary remedies. . . . The Court will only grant them where *it considers that it would be just and equitable to do so* (s101(2)): so that it can withhold the remedy where it is of opinion that the complainant's own conduct has been unreasonable or provocative or too unbending or, in the case of compensation, it may award less than it would have done had the complainant's behaviour been more sensible [13, p84].

Such comments underline the need for a court which contains some individuals who have a deep and sympathetic understanding (particularly in the absence of trade unionists) of the machine operator's view of life, as distinct from a stockbroker's or company director's.

The Industrial Court is "briefed" not only to provide remedies for persons hurt by unfair behaviour but to promote the reform of industrial relations. In both processes elements of legal procedure are involved. Some of the more important elements and other technical features of the Court's activities are considered before turning to the reform aspects of the Court's work.

"Speed, informality and simplicity" [14] strike the keynotes of the Court's procedural style. Further: ". . . any person may appear before the Industrial Court in person or be represented by counsel or by a solicitor or by a representative of a trade union or an employers' association or by any other person whom he desires to represent him" (schedule 3 paragraph (21)).

Legal aid is available.

Consistent with its High Court/Scottish Court of Session status, the

Industrial Court can require the production of documents, the attendance and examination of witnesses. The Court may, at its discretion, award costs against a party held responsible for "unnecessary, improper or vexatious" proceedings or for unreasonably delayed proceedings. In plain English, such provisions are designed to deter the "trier-on" from trying and the excessively awkward cuss from being so awkward.

As mentioned earlier, the Court has both original and appellate jurisdiction. Those unfair industrial practices which are not the concern of the industrial tribunals (see Chapter 4) are the concern of the Court. The tribunals are charged with protecting the rights of individual workers. The Court is much more involved in the collective bargaining process and its associated problems. The Court's original jurisdiction therefore embraces the collective bargaining unfair industrial practices; complaints about an employer's failure to establish an agency shop or to provide a registered union with information required for collective bargaining; and applications, for example, by a registered union to be recognised by an employer as a sole bargaining agent.

Appeals on points of law (not on fact) lie to the Court from the industrial tribunals in any proceeding or decisions arising:

a Under the Contracts of Employment Act 1963
b Under the Redundancy Payments Act 1965
c Under the Equal Pay Act 1970
d On a complaint under this Act (s114)

and "in the exercise of any jurisdiction" about damages for breach of the contract of employment if the Lord Chancellor eventually decides, as he has power to do under section 113, to transfer this type of case from the long established civil courts to the industrial tribunals.

The Court also hears appeals from the Registrar's decision not to register a particular organisation and, from his decision to require an organisation to change its rules in a particular way as a condition of registration. Appeals against the Registrar's decisions on problems arising from the operation of a union's political fund or from the legal technicalities involved in trade union amalgamation, may also be made to the Court. From the Court appeals lie on questions of law, not of fact, to the Court of Appeal (England and Wales) or to the Court of Session (Scotland).

Section 136 leaves no doubt about the technical limitations of the Court's jurisdiction: "The Industrial Court shall not have any jurisdiction except that which is expressly conferred on it by or under this Act; and accordingly that Court (a) shall not entertain any proceedings in tort. . . ."

A tort is a civil wrong, such as libel or negligence, which gives rise to an action for damages. For example, men injured at work will continue to sue their employers for damages, on the grounds of the employer's negligence, in the County Court or Queen's Bench Division of the High Court but not in the Industrial Court.

Reference has already been made to the powers of the Court to make orders. Schedule 3 of the Act, which is much concerned with the technical and procedural functioning of the Court has empowered the Lord Chancellor to make rules (SI 1971 number 1777) for the Court which lend yet more muscle and sinew to the strength of the Court. The rules enable the Industrial Court, on the application of any party to any proceedings before the Court, to make "an interim order" for example, to require someone to "desist for the time being from an alleged unfair industrial practice" [9, p49]. Such an order is equivalent to an interim *ex parté* injunction—that is, a temporary injunction which can be of inestimable service to a keen gardener who sees his neighbour making energetic preparations for the destruction of the boundary hedge which the gardener considers to be his property. The temporary injunction stays the swing of the destructive axe under pain of penalty for non-compliance, until a full hearing on the problem can take place. Superficially (see below) the industrial relations parallel could well be that of an employer seeking "an interim order" to restrain the organisers of a projected unconstitutional strike from going ahead with their plans to disrupt production in breach of procedure. One such "interim order" which nearly resulted in a national dock strike was issued in June 1972, "restraining . . . three named persons from seeking to prevent lorries entering or leaving" a depot [15].

To seek is not necessarily to obtain, for the Act makes it clear that interim relief cannot be granted unless "all reasonable steps" have been taken to inform the alleged offending party of the application for an interim order and he has had an opportunity to state his case. (More will be said in Chapters 12 and 15 about the use of injunctions in industrial disputes.)

The Court has power to enforce its own orders—a simple enough statement but one replete with significant implications as the docks container dispute of June and July 1972 and the £50000 fine on the TGWU in April 1972 showed [16]. First let it be stressed that the Act is part of the civil, not criminal law. Except in a special and small class of cases concerning falsification of records, there is no question of offenders being prosecuted and fined for non-compliance with the law. But if orders of the Court are defied, the question of contempt of court (a criminal offence) arises as it would if defiance were shown to any other civil court of like jurisdiction. Contempt needs to be purged—sometimes in confined reflection. Ultimately, workers can be and have been sent to prison for *defying* the *Industrial Relations Act*. But it would seem that no one could be sent to prison for failing to pay over the money required by a compensation order of the Court, or for ignoring a declaration of rights order. Injunctions are a different matter and determined persistent defiance does land men in jail.

In June 1972, three dockers' leaders stood literally on the brink of imprisonment. At the last second, the three men were kept out of jail by an appeal to the Court of Appeal by the Official Solicitor, a law officer of whose existence until then most people were unaware. Among his duties is that of safeguarding the interests of those threatened with imprisonment for contempt. The Court of Appeal ruled that: "... the evidence was quite insufficient to prove breach of the order with all the strictness that was necessary when one was going to deprive people of their liberty" [17].

In other words, the Industrial Court had failed to do its homework. But its legal powers remained undiminished: "The Industrial Court ... had the like powers, rights, privileges and authority as the High Court had, with regard to proceedings for contempt of court ..." [17].

In the second round of the "dockers' defiance of the law" contest, the Industrial Court "won" and five men went to prison for not obeying anti-blacking orders. Their (unrequested) release from Pentonville where they spent but few days was secured by the Official Solicitor, whose application was successful essentially because the House of Lords had by this time ruled [52] that the T & GWU was responsible for the action of its stewards —which brought the union back to the "dock" rather than the men. These events were undoubtedly important in the decision to call the national dock strike which started in the same week.

The fact that five trade unionists were prepared to go to prison in July 1972 for defying the law (an order of a Court which they "did not recognise") contrary to the practice of obeying labour injunctions (sparsely used in pre-Act times in this country) is a measure of their intense hostility to the Act.

It can thus be maintained that the Act soon claimed its first "martyrs" but, in these days of overheated communications, the word "martyr" tends to be used somewhat loosely. It is worth recalling what one of the Tolpuddle Martyrs said in defending his attempt to form a farmworkers trade union: "We have injured no man's reputation, character, person or property; we were uniting together to preserve ourselves, our wives and our children from utter degradation and starvation" [18].

Not only in time but tone, this is a far cry from "You out, us in" as two groups of workers in Britain's largest and arguably most powerful union competed with one another and members of another union, in very unbrotherly ways for container work in a Welfare State.

It is entirely probable that during the first few months' operation of the Act, attempts were made to discredit the Court, the Act and thereby the Government—to create social, economic and political upheaval to the point of forcing a general election. This is not to pass judgement on such a strategy but simply to indicate its probable existence and its importance for the purpose of understanding industrial relations behaviour during 1972. In like context, the Act and the Court can be said to have succeeded or been brought into disrepute by the railway dispute in the spring of that year (see also Chapter 12).

Non-co-operation with the Court, a legitimate opposition stance from the TUC viewpoint, contained unforeseen complications. Apropos the TUC's suspension of the National Union of Seamen's membership from the TUC for that union's determination to remain registered, the Secretary of the Industrial Court reminded the General Secretary of the TUC that the TUC itself might be held in contempt of court for disciplining unions which apply to the Court for help. (The NUS sought the security of an approved closed-shop agreement.) While unions are free to oppose the Act "by lawful and constitutional means":

> The courts have always taken the view that the rule of law and the proper administration of justice requires that every man shall have free access to the courts without fear of the consequences. Furthermore, once an application is before the courts, no attempt must be made to dissuade anyone from giving evidence in those proceedings and still less must they be penalised for having done so [19].

From their subsequent behaviour, it is clear that the TUC saw the force of this reasoning and the threat to fundamental constitutional rights that outright non-co-operation might entail. Non-co-operation began to move if not to co-operation, then away from the inadvertent denial of the basic legal rights of others. This movement may partly explain why the TUC's decision to suspend thirty-two unions from membership (referred to in Chapter 2) did not prompt a re-opening of the "denial of rights" issues.

Courts are not impersonal—if only because judges have views. The President of the Industrial Court, Sir John Donaldson, is clearly a constitutionalist—in a double sense. The Court is constrained by the Act itself to apply a constitutional approach to industrial relations problems, for the Act is much concerned and is so framed to have power used in a constitutional—that is, authorised—way. But, in his obiter dicta, the President has implied his belief that management should seek the legal redress available to them [20] in order to promote more constitutional behaviour. Even if there is a cost in so doing, in terms of an immediate increase in unruly behaviour: "... short-term dangers ... must be faced in order that in the longer term we may have an orderly system of industrial relations ..." [21].

Running in parallel with this hard line approach to problems *where deemed appropriate or made inevitable* is the softly softly approach, designed to help people help themselves to find solutions to problems. It may well be that, in the long run, this latter approach may prove to be more important than the former, which inevitably provides the focus of attention for the mass media interested in spectacular dramatic confrontations.

The Court does not provide automatic penny-in-the-slot rulings and remedies. In the early stages of the Court's operation, the President took care to emphasise the importance attached by the Court to the conciliation process. (Paragraph 18(3) of schedule 3 introduces this conciliatory duty.)

"We shall measure our success not so much by the number of decisions we give as by the number of occasions upon which it becomes unnecessary to give a decision" [22] was the comment of the Court President on the occasion when Court-induced Department of Employment conciliation services had prompted a voluntary negotiation settlement between the parties.

When opening the Industrial Court on 1 December 1971, the President was clearly at pains to emphasise that the Court would not consist of red-robed, bewigged judges, laboriously scratching on parchment with quill pens but sober-suited men, conducting proceedings in the much more informal manner of a tribunal.

Substituting sober suits for red robes may eventually do something to allay understandable anxieties felt particularly by trade unionists and workers generally about High Court procedure, but it does not detract one whit from the ultimate powers of the Court to reform, by order, parts of the industrial relations system while allowing opportunity for settlement by the parties themselves, if this looks feasible. The principal parts identified for reform are: untidy, unruly bargaining structures—by way of the sole bargaining agent provisions; "unfair" closed-shop union security—by way of the agency-shop provisions; deficient procedure agreements—by way of the procedure improvement provisions; unfair use of power against the community—by way of the emergency procedures provisions. (All of these provisions are discussed in later chapters.)

In this immense task of potential reform, the Court needs assistance. Their assigned agent in the field is the Commission on Industrial Relations.

COMMISSION ON INDUSTRIAL RELATIONS

From having been the brainchild of Donovan and the actual creation of a Labour Government in 1969, the CIR has experienced, if not exactly a complete sea change, important alterations to its original role.

Donovan believed that the reform of industrial relations should proceed on the basis of consent but that this process could be quickened by an independent agency which could perhaps help employers and trade unions out of particular difficulties but which did not impose solutions. This philosophy was accepted by the Labour Government and the CIR was formed as a Royal Commission in March 1969. In its original composition the Commission reflected the traditional tripartite structure of independent, employer and trade union membership to which reference has already been made.

In essence, the CIR's purpose, as originally conceived and practised, was to try to do good by stealth, to bring about reform by inquiry, to investigate a problem, to persuade and nudge the parties involved towards a sensible solution. Sanctions were not sought by the CIR for the achievement of its reform objectives, whether they were improved industrial relations in a particular firm [23] or a particular industry [24]. Intelligent analysis and imaginative recommendations backed by diplomatic skills were thought to constitute the best way forward.

As the Labour Government had always accepted the Donovan doctrine that collective bargaining should not only be structurally reformed but fostered and enriched as a process, the CIR conducted their inquiries with those broader public policy objectives constantly in mind. Consistent with the attainment of those objectives was facilitating trade union recognition. A high proportion of the first references which Mrs Barbara Castle, then Secretary of State for Employment and Productivity, sent to the CIR for investigation, consisted of claims for recognition by trade unions which had been resisted by employers. The CIR had been given no criteria by which to test and judge union claims for recognition but a careful reading of the first reports on recognition references and of the *First General Report* [25] reveals a steady, pragmatic evolution of CIR recognition criteria. Bearing in mind the public policy of encouraging a spread of collective bargaining, it comes as no surprise to find that the CIR several times recommended that an employer should recognise a union even though the union's membership in the firm was by no means impressive.

The CIR's view was that on the evidence obtained, they were confident that if a union was recognised, it would grow because workers would then see the point and value of joining a recognised union. In short, the CIR applied liberal, flexible tests to recognition claims and not stringent or precise tests.

Under the Act, different criteria, different procedures and different approaches apply to the CIR's work. The CIR's composition has radically changed for (Royal College of Nursing Commissioner apart) it now contains no trade union element. It does not need to in order to function. The Secretary of State for Employment is simply empowered to "appoint persons to the Commission" section 120(3). Unlike lay membership of the Court, no reference is made to "special knowledge or experience of industrial relations" as a necessary qualification for appointment to the CIR.

Well before the Act received the Royal assent on 5 August 1971, the three trade union members of the original CIR had either resigned or expressed their intention to do so. All three were opposed to the then projected intervention of law of the kind envisaged into the voluntary industrial relations system. The Chairman of the CIR, Mr George Woodcock, former General Secretary of the TUC, gave an additional and telling reason that it was a waste of time for him to "soldier on" if the trade unions refused (and they had instructed their membership to this effect) to give information or to talk to CIR investigators. In short, if one of the major parties withdraws its consent to reform by consent (and to this policy Mr Woodcock was deeply committed) there was little point in his continuing as Chairman.

If these trade union resignations were predictable, the appointment of their successors was far less so. Mr Len Neal left his job as Industrial Relations Director of British Rail to become the new Chairman. From a trade union background to later experience of negotiating, as a manager, the Esso Fawley productivity agreements, Mr Neal has emerged in recent years as a leading national industrial relations practitioner. However, none of the members of the CIR (or the lay members of the Court for that matter) can be labelled as controversial figures but, whatever their calibre as individual managers or civil servants, they cannot draw upon the same kind of industrial relations knowledge or expertise which resided in Mr George Woodcock, Mr A Allen, General Secretary of USDAW, and Mr Will Paynter, the former national leader of the coalminers. Under the Act, the CIR, like the Court, was away to a limping start because of trade union opposition to the Act.

Inevitably, members of the CIR, and particularly its Chairman, are likely to be the figures on whom public attention is focused, as the visible and known part of that particular institutional iceberg. In terms of actual activity below the surface of public awareness, 200, initially, and perhaps up to 500, eventually, staff employed by the CIR will be working on the various references that come the CIR's way for investigation. No doubt a variety of individual beliefs exist among the staff about the value of the Act, but there is probably a much greater consensus among them about the value of the reform aspects of the CIR's work. Certainly there has been no shortage of applicants for CIR posts and numbers of senior ex-PIB staff transferred their abilities to the CIR. This was all to the good for, despite heavy political pressure to complete references quickly, the PIB was able to produce an appreciable number of sensible reports designed to improve industrial relations.

References to the CIR can be of two main kinds: investigating industrial relations problems in the manner begun in 1969 and investigating for the Court questions specifically provided for under the Act—such as a union's claim to become the sole bargaining agent in a particular set of circumstances.

Section 121 outlines the nature of the Commission's work on general references and would seem so widely drawn as to permit the inclusion of any conceivable industrial relations problem for investigation. References may be made by the Secretary of State for Employment alone or with another Minister on: "... any question relating to industrial relations generally or to industrial relations in any particular industry or in any particular undertaking" (s121).

The same section specifies particular features of our industrial relations system which, because they are so mentioned, imply a need for special attention. In essence these are: the organisational structure of the bargainers and their bargaining arrangements (presumably with a view to their rationalisation); procedure agreements; recognition and negotiating rights; disclosure of information by employers to employees or trade unions; facilities for training in industrial relations or in collective bargaining.

The first general reference made under the Act was a sensible one for it concerned one of the major problem areas in British industrial relations and could be conducted in such a way as to examine all the matters mentioned in the preceding paragraph. One has only to reflect on the labour troubles of some of the major motor manufacturers and their multi-plant suppliers to appreciate the significance of the "negotiating machinery for multi-plant undertakings" reference. Thus, the reform by consent process is to continue—but in a more hostile climate than was originally the case.

This is partly because of the nature of the second type of reference: the investigatory work (inquisitorial in some opinions) to be done by the CIR for the Court.

At the discretion of the Court, the CIR must set out to improve deficient procedures, to test union claims for recognition, for an agency shop or an approved closed shop. In defined circumstances and under prescribed arrangements, ballots must be conducted—for example, to determine the degree of support for a serious national-emergency-type strike as there was on the railways in 1972. Without going into the mechanics of such arrangements—later chapters will give some account of these—the essential, and to some, repugnant, point is that recommendations of the CIR may eventually become legally binding on the parties by order of the Court. A grievance procedure, for example, could eventually be imposed upon a reluctant party—admittedly after a lengthy and tortuous process, but the legal sanction is nonetheless there. Even on a technical matter such as the conducting of ballots, the Court is a near presence. In short, the CIR is caught up, as many trade unionists would see it, in the enforcement of the Act. That fact alone is sufficient to prompt a response of non-co-operation.

It is still too early to evaluate the effects both of the partly changed role of the CIR and of non-co-operation. There are grounds for believing that not all unions are equally un-co-operative when firms in which they have members are visited by CIR case study investigators. The Department of Employment has been used as a "post office" for unions anxious to have information forwarded to the CIR. Even so, it is certainly true that the CIR have been hampered in their work during much of the past two years because of the reluctance of trade union officers, shop-stewards and rank and file trade union members to talk to CIR men and women in the field or to provide information. The AUEW have even gone so far as to reject a CIR report (on a pre-Act reference) which found in the union's favour—that their claim for recognition by a firm was justified.

Provisions exist whereby the CIR can prise information from reluctant parties (see schedule 3) but except in carefully selected cases the use of such extraction powers would almost certainly militate seriously against the CIR's objective of achieving reform.

Other features of the changed role of the CIR require comment. While the CIR functioned as a Commission as distinct from a statutory body under the Act, it was free to develop its own investigation strategy, to evolve its own criteria—for example, to test union claims for recognition—always allowing that a major part of its purpose was to foster the spread and enrich the process of collective bargaining. Under the Act, constraints are placed upon some parts of the CIR's methods for certain inquiries

4

must be conducted in accordance with the fairly precise procedures set out under the Act. The investigation into a union's claim for an agency shop is a case in point. In brief, the CIR appears to have become much more the agent of the state and less able, therefore, to take an independent viewpoint than was previously the case. However, some offsetting factors must be mentioned.

From the wording of the Act and ministerial comments, it is apparent that although the CIR is now hedged about with more formal constraints, important elements of flexibility remain. Again, the fine print of the Act merits attention.

Paragraph 39 of schedule 3 carries the heading: "General power to take remedial action" and is followed by: "Where, on examining any question under this Act, the Commission are of the opinion that there is a defect in the existing arrangements out of which that question arose, the Commission may at any time, whether before or after making a report on that question, take such steps as they think fit for the purpose of securing the remedying of that defect."

In less generalised terms, this appears to mean that if the CIR see a chance of helping an employer and union to reach a solution to an associated as well as the main problem, they will do so, maybe by reforming the pay structure, the bargaining structure and so on. Self-government—assisted by free consultancy—is reaffirmed as a vital principle. Similar evidence on flexibility can be found in other sections of the Act, most notably perhaps in those sections concerned with "remedial action where procedure agreement is non-existent or defective" (ss37–43).

The CIR are formally greatly involved in the remedial action (see Chapter 9), but throughout the very intricate processes entailed, provision is maintained for a voluntary settlement and as the Department of Employment guide puts the position: ". . . the parties will always have a last opportunity to resolve their differences by entirely voluntary means through joint negotiation, conciliation or arbitration before the Industrial Court is involved" [9, p24].

For this and associated reasons conciliation forms an important part of the next chapter.

4

Change Agents—III

Of the imposing array of institutions with responsibilities under the Act, the institution whose work is likely to be of most direct relevance, both to employers and workpeople, is the industrial tribunal. This is not to argue that the Court, the CIR, the Registrar, are of little importance. On the contrary, the rulings and recommendations of these bodies may well modify people's behaviour. Concerning the Court's influence, the point has been well made by Innis Macbeath that:

> Even where employers and employees rub along together well enough, and never find themselves in the Courts, the Courts' decisions will determine the assumptions on which people have to work. They become incorporated in the information given people in training and they are taken into account by commentators and specialists who give advice to managements and unions [26, p105].

But for many people in employment, the Court, the CIR, the Registrar and all their works will remain in the background of their daily working lives. Much more in the literal foreground and much more accessible will be the industrial tribunals. It is to his local industrial tribunal that a worker will turn for help, and, possibly, to a local conciliation officer of the Department of Employment as well, if he runs into difficulties over redundancy pay or unfair dismissal.

INDUSTRIAL TRIBUNALS

For newcomers to the subject of industrial relations, it must be mentioned that industrial tribunals were established by the Industrial Training Act 1964, their function being to resolve problems arising from the operation of the training levy. From such modest beginnings the tribunals have burgeoned into what, in some other countries, might be described as labour courts. By 1972 their jurisdiction had been expanded to include claims, disputes, questions and little bits of bother arising from the operation of the Contracts of Employment Act 1963, Redundancy Payments Act 1965, Docks and Harbours Act 1966, Selective Employment Payments Act 1966, Equal Pay Act 1970 and the Industrial Relations Act 1971.

Most of the tribunals' work in the past few years has developed from the operation of the Redundancy Payments Act. Tribunal redundancy rulings, which are published, speak volumes both literally and metaphorically on the fascinating intricacies of employment situations. A large additional case load, of a very special character, presumably awaits the tribunals under the Equal Pay Act. From 29 December 1975, a woman who believes that she is not receiving the equivalent treatment to men, to which she considers she is entitled, may refer a claim to a tribunal for arrears of pay. Another major milestone in the life and times of the tribunals was 28 February 1972. From this date workers, with certain exceptions, have been able to seek from the tribunals redress against unfair dismissals and other injustices—this will be discussed later.

Until the unions began to become really cross in 1970–1 about the then projected "anti-union" legislation, it had been possible to maintain a tripartite structure for the tribunals. Lawyers were appointed as chairmen of tribunals and one of the two lay members of each tribunal was drawn from a panel of employers' representatives and the other from a panel of employed persons. Because the tribunals are empowered under the Act to award compensation against trade unions, the unions decided, through the medium of the TUC, to withdraw their membership from the workers representatives' panel. The scale of withdrawal of co-operation was sufficient to cause the Government to amend the law so that the tribunals could still function as non-tripartite bodies. Regulations SI 1971 number 1660 provide that the two lay members of each tribunal will be chosen from a single panel of persons who "have knowledge or experience of employment in industry or commerce." Appointments to and selection from the panel are the responsibility of the Secretary of State for Employment. The appointment criteria seem sufficiently catholic, at least on paper, to include chairmen of mammoth international companies—and barrow boys. In reality, a worker appearing before a tribunal would probably find himself talking to a local barrister (a lawyer must be the chairman), a practising manager with experience of employment problems in a nearby factory and another similar manager or even a retired trade union official.

As a result of the Act and particularly because of its "unfair dismissal" provisions, the number of tribunals has markedly increased. Compared with June 1971, the work of the tribunals, measured by number of sittings, had increased by nearly 50 per cent in June 1972.

Although unfair dismissal constitutes the major expansion of the tribunals' jurisdiction under the Act, the tribunals are also empowered to entertain complaints from workers who consider that other rights established for them under the Act (see Chapters 5 and 13) have been infringed by their employer or a trade union, be it registered or unregistered. A worker, for example, may believe that an employer is refusing to give him a job because he is not a union member (an unfair industrial practice). Another worker may complain because he considers that an unregistered union is unreasonably rejecting his application for membership (an unfair industrial practice). In certain conditions, the Registrar may complain to a tribunal, in effect seeking a remedy on behalf of a complainant.

Unlike the Court, tribunals are not empowered to make restraining orders. What they can do is to issue a declaratory order determining the rights of the people concerned and/or award compensation. Like the Court, the tribunals' powers to grant remedies are discretionary. Leaving aside, for a moment, the issue of unfair dismissal the tribunal *may*, provided "that it would be *just and equitable* to do so" grant one or both of the remedies mentioned above. In relation to unfair dismissal the tribunal may, if it considers the complaint well founded and that "it would be *practicable*, and in accordance with *equity*," recommend that the employer re-engage the unfairly dismissed worker—more will be said on this point in Chapter 6.

One further aspect of the tribunal's expanded jurisdiction under this Act may be mentioned here. Under section 57 major employers are required to disclose information to their employees (see Chapter 5). If an employee considers that his employer has failed to carry out this particular duty, he may complain to a tribunal. If the tribunal considers the complaint "well founded," it *may* "if it considers that it would be *just and equitable* to do so," make a determination of rights order. The employer can be given time to rectify the omission—that is, time to disclose the information required. If the employer persists in being dilatory, the employee can pursue his claim for information with the Industrial Court.

Some additional legal points may quickly be noted. Appeals from industrial tribunals on points of law on the Contracts of Employment Act, Redundancy Payments Act, Equal Pay Act and this Act are heard by the Industrial Court. (In the first few months' life of this Court, a number of Redundancy Payments Act appeals were heard.) No appeals on questions of fact are possible. Provisions exist under the Act which have enabled new regulations to be made [27] to govern the proceedings of the tribunals. These regulations (based on schedule 6) incorporate the previously established power to require the attendance of witnesses as well as new powers to award costs—to be used but rarely. "Applicants" and "respondents" may be represented by others—by a solicitor or trade union official, or anyone else. Other procedural rules are designed to ensure "fair play" and informality, bearing in mind that many applicants may be unskilled in their use of words and legal procedure. Legal aid, for the moment, is unavailable. Without discussing the need or otherwise for such aid, its non-availability reinforces the insurance policy value of union membership, for unions will represent applicants even if they will not help adjudicate their claims.

Tribunals have normally sat in public and will continue to do so but provision can be made for them to sit in private if issues of national security or confidential information are involved. If necessary, a compensation award granted by a tribunal may be enforced by a county court. (Similar provisions apply to Scottish cases.)

Such tangles of legal technicalities as those indicated, to say nothing of those unstated, may appear daunting to the man in the street, particularly if he wears overalls. Experience has shown, however, that no one, no matter how humble his status or how inarticulate his method of expression, should be deterred from approaching and appearing before a tribunal because of the "legal paraphernalia" which must inevitably provide the context and structure of the tribunals' work. Tribunal proceedings in themselves are informal and devoid of courtroom atmosphere. It is an important part of the legal chairman's function to put people at their ease, to tease out by humane and considerate probing, rather than by cross-examination, the facts that lie concealed within the often muddled thought processes and mode of expression of the applicants. The need for this particular judicial style was admirably expressed some years ago by the President in a letter to newly appointed chairmen of tribunals:

> To be a good chairman of an industrial tribunal, a man must be tolerant and patient with humble working people, who are usually unrepresented, incapable of expressing themselves adequately and overwhelmed by the occasion [28, p337].

Further legalistic and industrial relations points need to be made concerning the work of the tribunals.

Section 113 of the Act makes provision for a further possible extension of the tribunals' jurisdiction by empowering the Lord Chancellor to transfer claims for damages for alleged breaches of contract of employment from the civil courts to the tribunals. In short, to the claims of "unfair dismissal" within the tribunals' jurisdiction could be added cases of "wrongful dismissal." (Claims for damages "in respect of personal injuries" cannot be so transferred.)

Under regulations made in January 1972 [27] tribunals for the first time were empowered, in defined circumstances, to review their own decisions and to vary or revoke such decisions. For example, it may be that important new evidence comes to light which could not easily have been known or foreseen when the original decision was made.

While bound by High Court judgements (arising as they do on points of law) each tribunal remains very much in charge of its own factual cases. Each case is decided on its own merits and the tribunal is not bound by its own past rulings or by those of other tribunals. Obviously, individual members of tribunals are likely to be influenced by their own and other people's decisions but, more important, tribunal decisions can be read as signals particularly by employers. A personnel manager might well say to his works manager colleague: "Did you read that decision on unfair dismissal the other day? We had better do . . . as a consequence." Not every single decision is published but plenty are (by HMSO) and the national and local press often summarise cases of particular interest. A record of all decisions, with reasons (except where evidence is given in private) is kept in a register at the Central Office of the tribunals. The register is open to inspection.

A very important point remains—and what better to express it than the Department of Employment, for it is the Department's conciliation officers that are principally involved:

> No complaint of unfair dismissal or infringement of a worker's rights regarding trade union membership will be heard by an industrial tribunal until a conciliation officer has had an opportunity to consider whether he is likely to obtain a voluntary settlement of the complaint [9, p20].

Much of what has been said in this chapter about the exercise of the tribunal's jurisdiction and powers is, therefore, contingent upon the prior attempt to promote a settlement by conciliation, a process for which the Secretary of State for Employment is responsible.

SECRETARY OF STATE FOR EMPLOYMENT

It is usual for a major Act, often known as a parent Act, to bear many offspring. The Industrial Relations Act 1971, is no exception.

Parliament does not always have the time or the necessary expert knowledge to debate in detail the volume of intricate law that a complex society like ours is thought to require. Parliament therefore delegates some of its law-making authority to the Minister concerned for the administration and enforcement of a major Act of Parliament. By this process of delegated legislation various sets of regulations have been made by order of the Minister under the Factories Act 1961. Hazards arising from particular processes, machines or associated with particular industries are thus tackled in a highly specific way. Industrial relations "hazards" are of a much more elusive character and much given to subjective assessment. Nonetheless, Parliament has empowered the Secretary of State for Employment to make a variety of regulations under the Industrial Relations Act 1971. Some of the regulations may be seen as administrative in character, tidying up and rounding out certain provisions of the Act. For example, regulations can be made concerning:

1 Co-ordination of redundancy and unfair dismissal payment provisions—section 150
2 Conditions affecting registered unions and employers' associations audit proceedings—schedule 5
3 Industrial tribunals procedures—schedule 6

(Regulations made in January 1972 mentioned above.) Other regulations, of wider import, bear upon some of the core activities of industrial relations.

Section 57 empowers the Secretary of State to make "disclosure of information to employees by major employers"—regulations. (See also Chapter 5.) Under section 58, the Secretary of State may make regulations that enable him to build up information about procedures. Employers "of any description specified" or "any particular employer" may be required to provide the Ministry with details of "any procedure agreement" to which they are either a party or whose terms they observe. This information gathering process (a pre-condition of reform) was started on a voluntary basis in the immediate post-Donovan period, but it is a measure of the weight attached by the authors of the Act to the reform of procedures, in order to improve industrial relations, that what was once a voluntary obligation for the employer can become a statutory requirement. Further muscle and, therefore, significance is given to this process by section 59, one of the few sections of the Act which attaches criminal as distinct from civil sanctions to non-compliance. Any person who does not comply with the regulations made under section 58 may be fined up to £100 and any person who makes statements he knows to be false may be fined up to £400. As will be discussed later, other sections of the Act tie in with this "reform of procedures" strategy but it is appropriate to mention now that under section 37, the Secretary of State is one of the parties who can make application to the Court for remedial action to be taken where a procedure agreement is non-existent or defective.

Increased actual and potential intervention by the state into industrial relations is not restricted to the making of regulations which of themselves extend intervention. A number of sections empower the Minister to intervene in particular situations.

Among the more important initiatives permitted to the Secretary of State are:

1 Remedying deficient procedures—(referred to above)—section 37
2 Remedying deficient bargaining structures (associated with sole bargaining agent/unit provisions)—section 45
3 Furthering the general process of reform by referring problems to the CIR for examination—section 121
4 Seeking to protect the community from very damaging industrial action—sections 138–45

Before attempting some evaluation of this increased state intervention, a few other powers of the Secretary of State may be noted.

Sections 2 and 3 require, he has no choice here, the Secretary of State to prepare the Industrial Relations Code of Practice for approval by Parliament (see also Chapter 14); an order made by statutory instrument brought the Code into effect on 28 February 1972. Section 32 enables the Secretary of State to safeguard the interests of employees where it is thought that a dismissals procedure excluded by order of the Court from the provisions of the Act, is no longer working fairly (see also Chapter 6). Power is given to the Secretary of State (s118) to raise, at some unspecified time, the magic figure of £4160 fixed as the upper limit to compensation for unfair dismissal.

The Secretary of State appoints and has the power to dismiss or vary their numbers, the members of the CIR. He also appoints the lay members of the industrial tribunals and, with the Lord Chancellor, the lay members of the Court.

BIG BROTHER

What has so far been said under the heading of *Secretary of State for Employment* constitutes little more than an outline of what might be thought to be the major interventionist powers of the Secretary. But sufficient has been said for the question to be posed: does the sum of these powers, with the addition of the institutional apparatus, constitute the threat of State Big Brother control? Before attempting to answer that question a wry reflection is appropriate. The Conservative Party which historically and ideologically has been much more committed than the Labour Party to "let well alone" has set out to circumscribe *laissez faire* industrial relations in quite radical interventionist ways. This point will be developed in the last chapter but now to return to the Big Brother question.

Part of the answer to the question must be supplied by the reader through whatever political perspective he takes on life. Comment on some of the facts outlined earlier provides another part of the answer. Big Brother can have other connotations besides that of sinister oppression. An older, bigger brother can provide desirable protection for smaller fry. State provisions to help the unfairly dismissed worker would seem to fall in this category. State pressure, albeit not very great at this stage, on the big boss to release more information to the little man employee is also analogous to enlightened brotherly activity.

Another part of the answer can only be supplied by the ministerial style that develops and the degree to which this is influenced by government cabinet policy. Some Ministers of Labour have been non-interventionist and essentially conciliatory in their approach to problems. Sir Walter Monckton was a notable exemplar of this style in recent times. Other ministers have been much more spirited and interventionist, even rumbustious some might argue. Barbara Castle is held by some to fall into this latter category.

Under the Act, a Secretary of State could starve or create acute indigestion for the CIR dependent on the references with which he serves the Commission. A balanced diet is also possible. Lay members of the Commission and other institutions, being the people that they are, must also influence the outcome of proceedings. Without wishing to over stress the influence of personalities, it seems fairly obvious that the CIR, under the chairmanship of Len Neal, and no trade union Commissioners present, will be different from its Donovan predecessor with George Woodcock as its chairman and two other trade unionists among the Commissioners. A CIR headed up by someone such as Lord Watkinson of Cadbury

Schweppes or, supposing it were ever possible, Jimmy Reid of Upper Clyde Shipbuilding work-in fame, would be different again.

A large part of the answer to the Big Brother question must be supplied by employers, trade unions and individual employees, for it is they who essentially have to decide what to do about this complex and often baffling new law. An individual employer experiencing a series of unofficial strikes may well ask himself: "Shall I use section 96 and seek redress against the organisers of these disruptive wildcats?" A union's leadership may suffer anguish as it finds itself torn between using the sole bargaining agent opportunities provided by the Act and standing loyally by the TUC policy of non-co-operation. An individual may hesitate long or leap at the chance to disturb an "unlawful" closed-shop situation by complaining to the Court. Militants may set out to make the law look a decided ass. The range of examples could be extended and multiplied by an unknown, but almost certainly large, factor.

One essential point to be grasped, however, is that for the most part the law and its apparatus only swing into motion if appropriate levers are pulled. Even then, there is nothing automatic about the law's responses except its stated determination, in a number of circumstances, to encourage and help the contending parties to resolve their differences themselves if this seems at all possible.

PROCESS OF CONCILIATION

Even where the state, as represented by the Secretary of State for Employment, can take initiatives, the interested parties must be consulted, advised or assisted, as the case may be, to see whether there remains a possibility of a self-generated, as distinct from a legally imposed, solution emerging. Sections 37–43 provide perhaps the best example of this process. These sections are concerned with "remedial action where procedure agreement is non-existent or defective" (heading to this group of sections). The legal procedure to be followed in order to have collective bargaining procedures improved is lengthy and complex, meriting separate attention in Chapter 9. For present purposes, the pertinent point is that many stages of investigation, consultation, conciliation would need to be shown abortive before the Court imposed a legally binding procedure on an unwilling party at the request of the other. Even before the Court will entertain an application that a procedure requires attention, elaborate preliminaries must be observed. The Department of Employment guide explains the position as follows:

> Whoever decides to make the application must take certain other steps first. Before the Secretary of State applies to the Industrial Court, he must consult the parties concerned. Similarly before a firm or registered trade union applies, it must let the Secretary of State know it intends to do so. Either way it is left to his discretion whether to offer advice and help by the Department's Manpower and Productivity Service, or Conciliation Service, or a reference to the CIR, without application to the Industrial Court. Thus the parties will always have a last opportunity to resolve their differences by entirely voluntary means through joint negotiation, conciliation or arbitration before the Industrial Court is involved [9, pp24–5].

And those are only the preliminaries. Related sections where the CIR are much involved make it very apparent that a recalcitrant party would have to be very recalcitrant indeed before a procedure was finally imposed upon him by order of the Court. Without explicitly saying so, the Act in these and other sections appears to echo the recommendations of the Fourth Report of the Whitley Committee in 1918: "The advisability of a continuance, as far as possible, of the present system whereby industries make their own agreements and settle their differences themselves . . ." [29, p137].

Although this Whitley principle of self-government has been enshrined in public policy for many years, for example, through the voluntary arbitration legislation, the appearance of the Act seems to suggest that the "possible" in the "as far as possible" has not been working very effectively. (The 1964–70 Labour Government also inclined to this view.) Nonetheless, self-government, provided it is consistent with the Act's and Code's objectives, *a very significant proviso*, is still to be preferred to externally established and imposed arrangements.

To demonstrate that the conciliation, self-government strategy is not confined to procedures, two other examples of this strategy may be cited.

An employer caught in the cross-fire of inter-union rivalry may apply for help from the Court which could ask the CIR to investigate the bargaining structure problems and to recommend who was to be the sole bargaining agent (s45). Under the same section, a registered trade union may seek to become sole bargaining agent. The Secretary of State may also apply for an examination of bargaining structure problems and, presumably, this could happen where the disruption caused by inter-union warfare was seriously damaging the performance of a major exporter. Before making such application, the Secretary of State must consult with the parties concerned (s45(3)). An application made by an employer or registered union will not be entertained by the Court unless the Secretary of State has first been informed of the intention by the employer or union to apply to the Court and until the Secretary of State has had an opportunity to promote a voluntary settlement (s45(4)(a)). The use of the word "shall" in relation to this conciliatory activity indicates that the Secretary of State is under a duty to try to bring about a self-government solution. If his attempts prove unavailing and a claim passes to the CIR for examination, at any time thereafter and before the CIR reports: "The Commission may apply to the Industrial Court to withdraw the reference on the grounds that a satisfactory and lasting settlement of the questions in issue has already been reached" (s47(1)).

The third example of the self-government/conciliation strategy is taken from the area of individual rights. Without going into technical detail, section 146 makes it very clear that an industrial tribunal will not listen to a worker's complaint relating to his alleged unfair dismissal or an infringement of his trade union rights (as established by section 5) unless, and until, the local conciliation officer of the Department of Employment has had a chance to "promote a settlement of the complaint" (s146(2)).

From what has been said in the last few paragraphs, it comes as no surprise to learn that the conciliation resources of the Department of Employment have been very considerably expanded as a result of the Act.

Trying to look at the situation dispassionately, the Government and the Act's supporters do seem to have a case, and they have made the point repeatedly, that the complex procedures provided by this new law and particularly the operation of the Court, should be seen as measures not of first but last resort. (Anti-Act militants can, of course, create situations where the movement from first to last resort inevitably becomes fairly rapid because of obdurate opposition to attempts at conciliation.)

5

Rights of Individuals—I

A central, if unstated, purpose of the Act is to peg out anew the boundaries of rights—for the individual, for the group, for the community. Such a bald statement oversimplifies the position. Inevitably the three sets of rights are intricately interrelated not least because groups consist of individuals and the community consists of both groups and individuals. Through the Act, the community confers new rights on individuals, some of which it can be argued weaken the rights of those groups we happen to call trade unions. Section 5 perhaps best illustrates the clash between the competing claims of the rights of the individual and the rights of the group. Basically, section 5 establishes the right of the individual worker to be or not to be a member of a group of organised workers. But the numerous and commonly contentious implications of section 5 can best be discussed in Chapter 7 once the less and even non-controversial new rights of individual workers have been examined in this and the next chapter.

Many of the new rights of workers are established under Part II of the Act. Although Parliament has created these rights, they derive essentially from the contractual relationship existing between employer and employee. Without the contract of employment the rights would not exist. As will be seen, many of these individual contractual rights are elaborately interwoven with the social rights of collective bargaining, most notably as these affect union security as technically expressed by the agency shop and approved closed-shop sections of Part II. The new contractual rights which exist independently of collective bargaining are now considered.

RIGHT TO LONGER NOTICE

Until the enactment of the Contracts of Employment Act 1963, it would probably have been true to say that several millions of blue-collar workers were "only a week away from the gate," in the sense that their contracts of employment could be terminated by a week's notice—even though, as individuals, they might have had twenty, thirty, even forty years' service. The principle, long sanctified at common law, of "equal notice either side" was deeply entrenched in our employment practices. The 1963 Act changed this situation and in a very modest way introduced an element of job property rights into our social values. The 1963 Act recognised that while it might be irritating for an employer to lose the services of an employee at short notice, it could be devastating for an employee, particularly a long-service employee, to lose his job at a week's notice. "Equal notice either side" might be a neat and tidy formula, but it could operate unjustly. "Unequal notice either side" might be more complex but would certainly be more just if the employer were required to give longer notice than the employee, particularly to longer-service employees.

The 1963 Act, therefore, introduced a length of service-length of notice sliding scale whereby an employer was required to give, for example, not less than two weeks' notice for a person with two but less than five years' service and a month's notice for those employees with five or more years' service. The Act acknowledged that the more of his life a worker had invested with the firm, the greater his right to "compensation" if he was going to lose that "property." Section 19 of the Industrial Relations Act extends that sliding scale, its maximum requirement being eight weeks' notice for an employee who has fifteen or more years' service. Such an extension, given that the 1963 Act was the work of a Conservative Government, was fairly predictable. The principle of unequal notice to establish a better balance of rights is thus maintained and strengthened.

RIGHT TO MORE INFORMATION

"Knowing where you stand" is certainly one factor and often a very important one in establishing a sense of security for the individual employee. The 1963 Contracts of Employment Act (which as amended has become the Contracts of Employment Act 1972) acknowledged this point by requiring employers to give more information in writing, "written particulars," to their employees about their terms of employment. Section 20 of the Industrial Relations Act takes this process not one but several stages further, not so much in terms of the additional quantity of information that now becomes the employee's due, but more in terms of the *type* of information that must be given. To be better informed about his holiday pay and holiday entitlement (s20(1)(i)) is naturally important to an employee but the information duty placed on the employer by subsection (2) of section 20 carries much deeper and wider ranging implications.

In the written statement every employer must issue to every employee within thirteen weeks of his first being taken on, there must be included a note:

a Indicating the nature of the employee's section 5 rights and the effect on these of any relevant agency or approved closed shop agreement
b Informing the employee how and with whom he can take up a grievance relating to his employment
c Either explaining to the employee how he can process such a grievance or referring him to a document which is reasonably accessible and gives him this information

There is no lack of technical guidance to employers as to how these three information requirements may be met [55]. It is not difficult to find a form of words that is suitable. What may be challenging is the creation of grievance procedures where none have previously existed so that (b) and (c) above turn out to be substance and not shadow. In common usage we tend to think of "employees" as fitters, shop assistants, clerks but "employee" under the Act clearly includes foremen, supervisors—and managers of junior, middle, senior, even exalted status. For many, probably most, of the supervisors and managerial grades "grievance procedures" needed, may even still need, to be devised.

Grievance procedure agreements reached with trade unions will probably meet the requirements of (b) and (c) for most of the 41–42 per cent of Britain's labour force who are trade union members. But what of the remainder, the 50 plus per cent, the vast majority of whom are employees? Many firms have a mixture of union and non-union labour among the same categories of employees. Many more in retail distribution and catering, for example, have no union members at all. Given the guidance in the Code of Practice [30] the expertise available at the Department of Employment, from employers' associations and other bodies, it should not be hard for any firm in this latter category to establish a grievance procedure —at least in the form of words. Difficulties could arise, and in some cases have arisen, where hybrid situations exist of union and non-union membership among the same or similar grades of employees in a particular factory or firm. In most cases, the union members are likely to be covered by a joint employer/union grievance procedure. But a union, or the union members, may insist that such a procedure apply to only union members. There would appear to be nothing self-evidently wrong about such insistence, not even in agency or approved closed-shop situations. In fact, it would appear perfectly reasonable for a union to claim that the procedures it negotiates are designed to protect its own members and not those workers who do not wish to be members. Faced with such insistence, an employer would have to establish a separate grievance procedure for the "nonners" and to take particular care that sharp anomalies between the union and non-union procedures did not arise.

It will be some time before we can assess the effects of Section 20(2)(b) and (c) on our industrial relations system but there are at least two certain early results. An increasing number of managers have come to realise that there is more to a grievance procedure than saying: "My door is always open if a chap wants to complain." Section 20, with many others, has forced many more top managements than would otherwise have been the case, to look hard and seriously at what they have or have not been doing to allow their employees—*at all levels*—to seek redress for their individual grievances. Whatever frictional by-products develop out of this process, the process itself considered in the round, must mean greater justice between employer and employee and, therefore, improved industrial relations. These gains may, of course, be off-set or more than off-set by other losses particularly where *groups* now feel they have grievances—for example, the loss of the closed shop, a grievance they cannot redress within the existing law. Some commentators see section 20 as facilitating proof that procedures are incorporated in the contracts of employment and that such procedures if they include a "no strike until the procedure has been exhausted" clause, could further restrict the right to strike—the point being that even if due notice to strike is given before the procedure in the contract has been completed, a breach of the contract of employment would occur.

One other right to information remains to be mentioned. Section 57 requires major employers to provide written annual statements to their employees. Such statements "shall contain all such information as may be required in accordance with regulations made by the Secretary of State" (s57(3)). Taken out of context, such wording might suggest a range of information from the health of the office cleaner to the financial health of the company. Other parts of section 57 make it clear that it is the company's condition about which the employees are to be told. Section 57 has, therefore, provoked much speculation mixed with apprehension on the part of management about the exact amount and precise kind of essentially financial information that will have to be given about the firm to each employee "not later than six months after the end of the *financial year* to which it relates" (s57(2)).

"Major" employers are those who, discounting part-time workers (working less than twenty-one hours a week), short-service workers (employed for less than thirteen weeks) and employees who normally work abroad, employ more than 350 employees "on any date within a *financial year* of the undertaking" (s57(1)). Provision is made for subsequent alteration—up or down—to the figure of 350 (s57(7)). Section 57(4) establishes that the regulations may provide that the information to be disclosed shall also relate to associated and subsidiary companies of the "undertaking." The duty to disclose is placed on "the employer who is the owner of the undertaking." Given the spate of mergers, takeovers, rationalisation activities of recent years and the likelihood of their continuance, it is surely right that the individual employee should know for whom he is working and should have a better understanding of where the real financial power, and therefore presumably control, lies in the group of companies in which the factory where he works is only one of many taken over by a big group from the Midlands or some big American company or whatever the example may be.

Predictably perhaps the regulations may exempt certain "employers" and "matters" "of a prescribed description" (s57(6)) and various combinations of the two, from the duty to disclose information. The rationale for this exemption clause is not given in the Act. Neither are the detailed criteria against which exemptions shall be assessed. The Secretary of State may make exemptions he considers "necessary or expedient" (s57(5)). "Necessary" or "expedient" for whom? Obviously there is scope here in the consultations and discussions with interested parties that will precede the drafting of regulations for interested parties to plead special cases that they should not be required to reveal information of a certain kind for fear that, for example, it would damage in a very *specific* way their competitive position.

It is true that section 158 and subsection 1(e) in particular can be interpreted as protecting an employer's commercial position in a very *general* way:

> No employer shall, by virtue of . . . Section 57 . . . be required to disclose . . . any information the disclosure of which would be seriously prejudicial to the interests of the employer's undertaking for reasons other than its effect on collective bargaining. . . .

In any event, the contents of the section 57 written statement are "subject to section 158 of this Act" (s57(3)) which provides not only the presumed commercial protection cited above but immunity from disclosure of other categories of confidential information such as information about individuals.

In general and in outlined specific terms, therefore, adequate potential safeguards appear to be established in the Act for the protection of the employer's commercial interests. From the mound—it can hardly be described as a mountain—of law contained in sections 57, 158 and projected regulations, a mouse of a "written statement" may emerge. Many commentators have seen this statement as analogous to that issued to shareholders. However, as experience is gained of the operation of this part of the law, it may well come to assume greater significance. But more on this below.

It is one thing to give people information, it may be quite another for people to understand it. Section 57 imposes no duty on the employer to instruct, guide, educate his workforce concerning the information disclosed. This is not to argue that the employer should be placed under a statutory duty to instruct as well as supply. It *is* to argue the probable existence of a significant educational gap which the employer should do most to fill as the section 57 duty is presumably placed on him with a view to building up confidence and trust between employer and employee. Many of the educational deficiencies can only be made good in our society-wide educational and social processes whereby youngsters, even before entering employment, should achieve some understanding of the objective function of profit, of the purpose of investments, of the relationships between inputs and outputs, and so on.

The effect section 57 will have on our industrial relations in the short run is very difficult to predict. Among the influential variables bearing upon the operation of section 57 are: the levels of intelligence, education, sense of commitment to the firm among different groups of work-people in a firm; the size of the firm, its history of internal relationships; the character and extent of trade union organisation; the structure of the firm, its management ideology and style. On this last point, it may be that the Government intends to place the ruck of "major" employers under no greater obligation than the front runner employers have placed upon themselves for some time past by way of publishing company accounts with explanations—in house journals, to joint consultative committees, on noticeboards. For such employers, the new duty would appear to be largely one of increased printing costs for the written statement "shall be issued to every person" (s57(3)).

Another way in which section 57 may come to influence industrial relations arises from the Code of Practice's observation that: "Establishments with more than 250 employees should have systematic arrangements for management and employee representatives to meet regularly" [30, p16].

Given what is said under "Consultation" in the Code [30, pp16, 17] given the major *leit-motif* of the Code which can be read as a public policy instruction to management to "inform, discuss and consult with work-people on matters affecting their working lives," it seems more than likely that section 57 "written statements" will become a discussable item on the agendas of joint consultative bodies. Dramatic developments are not to be expected. Some consultative committees will be slow to emerge but over time, it is not outrageously optimistic to foresee regular and better informed discussion between management and workers on the firm's financial position becoming a standard feature of employment behaviour. Having said this, section 57 of itself will probably lead to only a modest improvement in the tone of management/labour relations but—taken in conjunction with the natural process of wanting to widen the range of items on the agenda once discussions have been initiated, and with the duty imposed on employers by section 56 to provide registered trade unions with collective bargaining information—the general level of dialogue between managers and managed may, in time, be appreciably improved.

RIGHT TO COMPLAIN

How are the rights so far outlined in this chapter to be enforced? Common sense, moral and diplomatic suasion from the Department of Employment, the widening and deepening influence of the Court and tribunals will supply a large part of the answer. But formal procedures also exist whereby a wronged worker can seek to have his rights enforced or, as the case may be, his wrongs redressed. To take the rights in the order indicated in this chapter.

A worker who claims he has not been given the period of notice or money in lieu to which he is entitled under his contract can sue his former employer for damages in a civil court. (The Act has not altered this position—that is, a remedy for "wrongful dismissal"—but only the period of notice that an employer may be required to give. The tribunals have as yet no jurisdiction over "wrongful" as distinct from "unfair" dismissal.)

An employee who receives no written particulars and believes himself entitled to them, or who receives allegedly inadequate or inaccurate information may complain to an industrial tribunal. In both cases the tribunal has the power to determine the particulars to be included in the written statement to be given by the employer to the employee. This power derives from the Contracts of Employment Act 1963 and not the Industrial

Relations Act, which, in this context, enriches the content of the "written particulars."

It can never be known whether the above and related rights—particularly those concerning unfair dismissal—will be used to the extent that they could be. Many people will doubtless remain only vaguely aware of how "individual rights" could be helpful to them. Yet other people will hesitate to press their rights for fear of how their employers might react. But the case load of the tribunals, the volume and nature of the work carried out by conciliation officers will provide some clues to the amount of injustice that without these features of the Act would have gone unchecked and unremedied.

An employee who is not given his annual section 57 financial statement may complain to an industrial tribunal. If the tribunal finds the complaint "well founded" and providing it would be "just and equitable" to do so, the tribunal may "make an order determining the rights" of the complaining employee and the employer. The tribunal may extend the period of time by which the employer is expected to supply the statement. If this time runs out and the employer has still failed to issue the required statement, the employee may complain to the Court. Again, the terms "well-founded" and "just and equitable" are employed as the touch-stones of judgement, if the Court is to issue, as it may, a binding order requiring the employer: "To issue to the complainant a statement containing such information as the Court considers appropriate, having regard to the rights determined by the order of the industrial tribunal" (s110).

Thus the Act contains formidable reserve powers to make the reluctant employer disclose section 57 information. However, it seems unlikely that such powers will be frequently deployed. Small firms, where the owner may also be managing the business, may be reluctant to disclose because of the strong sense of personal involvement the owner/manager commonly feels for *his* business. In such firms, "disclosure of financial information" like trade union activity can be seen as a threat to "property" and provoke deep, emotional and psychological reactions from the property owner. Realistically, such employers are unlikely to be found in large numbers among the "major" employers—that is, those employing more than 350 people which are the employers affected by sections 57 and 110.

Two other comments may be made. The major effect of the reserve powers, which may be seen as sanctions, is likely to result less from their use than their existence. "We should behave in such a way that we do not become entangled with the law" is likely to be the policy of very many firms, not only in relation to section 57, but many other sections of the Act as well. Proceedings before a tribunal but more particularly an order of the Court, under section 110, could attract a lot of unwelcome publicity for a firm. Image-conscious employers are well aware of this implicit sanction lurking in the express sanctions.

Under the Act the employee and, in specific situations, an ex-employee or even prospective employee, can complain about various types of employer "misbehaviour." Some of these rights are so important, particularly in relation to unfair dismissal, that they will be considered separately in the next two chapters. Certain of the new complaining rights concern the behaviour of trade unions. Other rights affect complicated employer/union/employee relations.

To take first the right of a worker to complain against fellow workers. As will be seen in Chapter 13, both registered and unregistered trade unions are required to conform to "guiding principles" of good behaviour in relation to their own members. A member of an unregistered organisation may complain to an industrial tribunal about an alleged contravention of the principles or of the organisation's rules. A former member (except one who has resigned voluntarily) or someone who has sought but not obtained membership may similarly complain (s107). If the tribunal finds that the action complained of constituted the "unfair industrial practice" of contravention of the guiding principles—or a breach of rules, it may "if it considers that it would be just and equitable to do so" grant to the complainant either or both remedies of a "rights order" or "compensation" to be paid to the complainant by the organisation which has behaved improperly (s109).

The member (former member qualified as above and prospective member) of a registered trade union enjoys similar rights to complain to a tribunal about "breach of principles" and "breach of rules"—*provided the action complained of was taken against him personally. Subject to the same proviso* he may alternatively complain to the Registrar (s81). The Registrar is placed under a statutory duty to try to promote a voluntary settlement of the complaint (s82(6)). If this attempt is unsuccessful the Registrar then refers the matter to the Court if it is of a "serious character" (s103(1))—or, in other cases, to the industrial tribunal (s108). Like the tribunal, the Court can determine rights and award compensation—but it can also make an order "directing the trade union . . . to refrain from continuing to take that action" (s103(3)(c)). Section 103(2) establishes that the Court can grant "one or more" of the remedies indicated above—quite formidable powers. Thus, it can be argued, although again there are off-setting factors as will be seen later, that the Act provides powerful safeguards for the individual against arbitrary action taken against him either by his employer or his own workers' organisation. Still more safeguards are provided where individual workers' rights mesh together in various intricate patterns with the relations established between employers and trade unions.

More will be said on this point in Chapter 7 but, briefly, a worker (which, under the Act, means a prospective as well as actual employee) who believes that his employer, or prospective employer has discriminated against him because he has chosen to exercise his section 5 rights, may complain to an industrial tribunal. Various forms of discrimination are cited in section 5(2) and predictably labelled as unfair industrial practices. If the discrimination is of a kind other than dismissal, the tribunal may, if the grounds of the complaint are "well founded" and provided that it would be "just and equitable to do so" (s106(2)(3)) make either a rights order or award compensation—or grant both remedies. If the complaint concerns dismissal and the grounds of the complaint are "well-founded" and it would be "practicable, and in accordance with equity" (s106(4)) to do so, the tribunal "*shall*" recommend that the dismissed worker be re-engaged. The alternative remedy is compensation. (Part of the conciliation officer's function is to facilitate re-engagement.)

One "catch-all" right for the individual may be mentioned here. Section 101 provides that "any person," which includes institutions and individuals, may complain to the Court about almost any action constituting an unfair industrial practice which has been taken against him. Infringement of trade union membership rights (s5) and unfair dismissal rights (s22) are excluded as these are separately dealt with in the Act.

Many publications give lists of "unfair industrial practices"—for example, the Department of Employment *Guide* in its Appendix 3 (given as Appendix 1 in this book).

INDIVIDUAL RIGHT TO CHALLENGE COLLECTIVE ACTION

It is under this heading that trade unions have seen some of the major threats developing to their established positions—particularly concerning union security within a firm.

A prospective employee who will not join a union and who considers he has not been taken on by an employer because of the employer's observance of what amounts to a pre-entry closed-shop agreement, may apply to the Court for an order. If the Court considers that the effect of the agreement, however worded, is to keep an applicant out of a job and, in so doing, substantially derogates from a worker's section 5 rights: "The Industrial Court shall make an order declaring that (closed shop) provision void" (s7).

While this threat to pre-entry closed-shop agreements is neatly consistent with the Government's case that no person's employment should be entirely conditional upon his holding a union card, this championing of the individual's rights may be at odds with other parts of the Act which are designed to promote order and stability. More will be said later about these issues.

As will be fairly widely known by this time, the provisions of the Act concerning sole bargaining agent/bargaining unit are designed to have trade union claims for recognition resolved by procedure rather than disputes, to reduce the amount of friction generated by inter-union competition for members and to establish more orderly bargaining structures. (The mechanics and implications of these arrangements will be examined in Chapter 8.) The present point is that the stable situation created either by recommendation of the CIR or by order of the Court, need only be of short duration. Any employee in a bargaining unit may apply to the Court claiming that the sole bargaining agent is no longer the adequate representative of the employees concerned (s51). If the applicant is supported in writing by a fifth of his fellow employees or two-fifths where a Court sole bargaining agent order is in operation, the Court must set in motion the investigation process whereby employees' opinions about their bargaining agent are sounded. This investigation could result in the Court's eventually making an order directing the employer not to recognise the sole bargaining agent as the sole agent for a period of two years (s53).

Very similar rights are given to the individual if he can find sufficient of his colleagues, a fifth, to act in concert with him to challenge the "secure" position of the union in an agency-shop situation. Leaving aside the mechanics of how the challenge is processed, the Court must, if the balloted workers vote against the continuance of the agency shop, make an order rescinding the agency-shop agreement and directing that no agency-shop agreement be reached with that union for a period of two years.

This right to challenge the "bargaining agent" and the "agency-shop union" has a certain democratic appeal. Only the affected workers can make the challenge and only then, if sufficient among them are disaffected. The sitting tenant union must do more than just sit if it is to maintain its tenancy. The status quo should be disturbed if it no longer reflects the wishes of the electorate—the basic arguments can be embroidered and elaborated in a number of ways. But this outward concern with democratic processes and principles conceals a number of complicating factors which are taken up later. It is sufficient for the moment to make the point that individual rights established under the act branch out in varying directions, some of which point fairly clearly towards "better" industrial relations—

the right to information, the right not to be unfairly dismissed—while others—the right to challenge and the right to join/not join a trade union—leave one much more uncertain about where they will take us. Cartograpy is both art and science—when applied to the Act soothsaying also comes into play.

6

Rights of Individuals—II

Of all the many sections of the Act, those on unfair dismissal probably do most to improve the lot of the individual employee. Two main reasons support such an assertion. The unfairly dismissed worker may seek redress against his former employer in ways that were not available to him before 28 February 1972. That redress is now available prompts circumspection on the part of employers in their use of dismissal powers. Safeguards against unfair dismissal come to be established not as a direct requirement but as a direct consequence of this intervention of statute law into the common law contractual relationship existing between employer and employee.

SAFEGUARDS AND REDRESS AGAINST UNFAIR DISMISSAL

Whatever the fate of the Act following a change of government, it is odds on that these safeguards and remedies will survive in some form because similar provisions were included in the Wilson Government's Industrial Relations Bill of 1970. We can therefore expect the concept of "no dismissal without good reason" to become a permanent and conventional feature of our employment law. In this respect we are just catching up with the established practices of, for example, West Germany.

It is assumed that by this time, most readers will have a reasonable understanding of the "mechanics" of the unfair dismissal sections of the Act. Explanatory material is widely and freely available [31]. Although "mechanics" will not be ignored in this chapter, greater emphasis will be placed on the major labour relations implications of the unfair dismissal provisions.

Why has it been thought necessary to introduce these new forms of statutory protection for the employee? The answer lies in the deficiencies of the common law and the use of power in an arbitrary way by employers. At common law (and common law principles still underpin the contract of employment) an employer could terminate, and still can, an employee's employment in any one of three main ways:

1 By giving the period of notice required by the contract
2 By paying money in lieu of notice—the money that would have been earned had the period of notice been worked
3 By dismissing the employee instantly where it was deemed that the employee had broken his contract by, for example, some gross act of misconduct

Except in this last case there was no general obligation on an employer to give clear, precise reasons for the dismissal, let alone justify them. His contractual obligation was fulfilled by his having given the period of notice or money in lieu of notice required by the contract.

Justification for instant dismissal rested upon breach of contract by the employee. This justification could be challenged by the dismissed worker in the civil courts where he would sue for and sometimes be awarded damages for *wrongful dismissal*. This process is unaltered by the Act except that, as already mentioned, provision is made for the possible future transfer of such cases to the jurisdiction of the industrial tribunals. Except in a relatively small number of cases, legal redress against wrongful dismissal has not been much help to the man in the blue boiler-suit or office dust-jacket. Shop-floor militancy, to have a wrongfully sacked shop-steward compensated by reinstatement, has been more common and effective.

Justification for dismissing a person by notice has not been required by common law. Employers have been indirectly encouraged by statute law—namely the Redundancy Payments Act 1965—to give reasons why they have dismissed work people, the Act presuming that dismissal is due to redundancy unless the contrary is proved. But such requirements fall well short of "justification" as generally understood by that term. Consequently, it has been argued that even when terminating employment by notice (a nominally fair arrangement) employers may have behaved *unfairly*: having sacked a manager not because he was incompetent or redundant but because "his eyes were the wrong colour," having dismissed a union activist attempting to recruit office staff into his union; having given his cards to a shop-steward who had admittedly transgressed but less so than other offenders who have been treated more leniently. Argument has been supported by evidence. An NJAC working party reported in relation to "disputes over dismissal" (excluding redundancies) for the three years 1964–6; "Stoppages arising from these dismissals . . . represented about 9 per cent of all stoppages and the time lost about 8 per cent of the total" (32, p3].

Workers unfairly dismissed before the Act had no means of redress except what their workmates or union could achieve by collective action. Now they have and because they have it is hoped by the Government that strikes over disciplinary and dismissal issues will be reduced.

Two things need to be made clear. The Act does *not directly* require the employer to give reasons for dismissal. His reasons may be sought and challenged only if a former employee considers himself unfairly dismissed and seeks redress. Unfair dismissal can arise even though contractual obligations regarding the period of notice have been met. This is a radical and very important innovation in our law.

Although the term "employee" is widely defined under the Act, not all employees are protected by the unfair dismissal provisions. Some excluded categories—registered dock workers and Scottish teachers—are protected by separate legislation. Without reciting the full catalogue, the major excluded categories are part-time employees who normally work less than twenty-one hours a week and full-time employees with less than two years' continuous service with their employer. It has been alleged that some employers will deliberately reduce the hours of their part-time workers who may be working more than twenty-one hours to less than twenty-one and dismiss full-time workers when they have worked one year and eleven months. Such a claim seems likely to have more substance as a debating point than as a reflection of employment reality.

Excluding part-time workers and short-service full-time workers reduces to a more tractable level the case load of the industrial tribunals. In the light of experience, the two-year qualifying period may be reduced and the exclusion of part-time workers modified. It should also be remembered that the excluded categories, particularly the short-service and part-time employees, parallel very closely the excluded categories under the Redundancy Payments Act 1965. Because of the linkages between these two Acts, it is sensible that many common exclusion criteria be maintained.

But there are some very important differences between the two Acts. "Unfair" dismissal connotes much more in the way of moral issues, subjective assessments, emotional human and industrial relations than redundancy dismissal usually does. Under the Industrial Relations Act, if a full-time employee considers he has been dismissed because he has used or tried to use his section 5 rights, the two-year qualifying period does not apply. In other words, a full-time worker sacked after only six months' service for wanting to join a registered trade union (he might be a manager) could complain to an industrial tribunal that he had been unfairly dismissed. This particular right is also enjoyed by full-time employees working in small firms (less than four employees) and by full-time employees over normal retiring age, both of these groups being excluded from unfair dismissal protection except in the section 5 circumstances indicated.

Concern for the protection of the individual in the exercise of his section 5 rights and in industrial conflict situations is manifested in sections 24–6. Sections 25–6 are designed to inhibit employer victimisation of individual workers in lock-outs or strike conditions.

Lock-outs, compared with strikes, have been few in number in conditions of widely prevailing full employment but may become more frequent if unemployment levels remain high. Section 25 provides that: "Dismissal of an employee by means of a lock-out is not unfair if he is offered re-engagement, either in his old job or in another job suitable to him, as from the date of resumption of work" [31, p6].

Leaving aside the varying interpretations that could be applied to "another job suitable to him" any employee who is not offered his job back can complain of unfair dismissal. (Unlike the strike situation, the *workers' choice* of industrial action—see below—this is not conditional upon the exercise of section 5 rights.) The position can be illustrated very simply. An employer may lock out 100 employees. Later, 95 of these are given back their old jobs. It so happens that the five who are not re-engaged are shop-stewards, militants, trouble makers, or whatever, in the opinion of the employer. At first sight, victimisation of this kind could engender not only injustice against individuals but greater industrial strife, and work counter to the claimed purposes of the Act. Conceivably, it would be open to the employer to argue that the chosen five in the above illustration were redundant, the industrial strife having led to a reduced order book. But although redundancy is a legitimate reason for fair dismissal, if a tribunal considers redundancy is a pretext to mask injustice, it may decide that such a redundancy dismissal is unfair (s24).

Similarly, if in a redundancy situation, say, two of thirty men doing like work were to be made redundant and the two happened to be those w ho wished to exercise their section 5(1) rights, their redundancy might well constitute unfair dismissal. Declaring redundant the two of thirty comparable cost clerks who wanted to join a registered union would seem to be unfair. Conversely declaring as redundant 2 of 30 comparable draughtsmen who would not join TASS (an unregistered union) would also be prima facie unfair. Here is another indication of the critical importance of section 5 in the structure and philosophy of the Act.

Further safeguards against unfair selection for redundancy are provided by section 24(5)(b). A redundancy agreement reached with a union or a redundancy procedure established by an employer may well, for example, place great weight on the application of the "last in, first out" principle to the selection of redundant employees. If an employer contravened such an arrangement and dismissed as redundant all the shop-stewards, or all the union activists or all employees who would not join a union—disregarding in all these examples the agreed length of service criterion—such dismissals would be unfair. The wording of section 24(5)(b) would cover a wider range of cases than those indicated but the examples serve to illustrate the anti-victimisation nature of this subsection. Such protection is not conditional upon the exercise of section 5 rights and so, for example, stewards of unregistered unions are protected against unfair redundancy dismissals.

In similar vein, discrimination against individual strikers can be unfair. The dismissal of a striker or of someone taking part in an "irregular industrial action short of a strike"—an overtime ban perhaps—is not, in itself, unfair. But, in the words of the Department of Employment: "Dismissal is unfair where an employee is selected for dismissal from among those taking part or is not offered re-engagement at the end of the strike either in his old job or another suitable to him while others are re-engaged" [31, p6] *because he exercised or sought to exercise his section 5 rights* (s26).

Although it can happen it is unusual for "nonners" to go on strike. Strikers are most likely to be members of unregistered unions. If their workplace leaders were not offered their jobs back, such action would not constitute unfair dismissal, protection in this context only being extended to membership of and participation in *registered* union activities. Here is yet another push, at least on the technical assessment level, in the direction of registration.

So much, if only in brief, for the victimisation type of unfair dismissals. What of the more run-of-the-mill cases, many of which will occur in non-unionised firms? What of the persons sacked, with or without notice, for incompetence, bad workmanship, persistent absenteeism, persistent lateness, fiddling the piecework system or swearing at the foreman? Section 24 establishes that reasons for justified dismissal may be related to the "capability or qualifications," "conduct" or "redundancy" of the employee. Capability is defined as "capability assessed by reference to skill, aptitude, health or any other physical or mental quality" (s24(7)(a)). On the face of it, such a definition seems broad enough to include a range of cases from the man who cannot sweep the factory floor adequately to a top management accountant who, though technically competent in every way, possesses such an irascible temperament that he constantly upsets his staff and lowers the performance of his department.

The fact bears repetition that the employer is not required to state or attempt to justify his dismissal reasons *unless challenged* to do so by an ex-employee who considers that he has lost his job unfairly. In this case, "*it shall be for the employer to show*" (s24(1)) to the satisfaction of an industrial tribunal that the dismissal was fair. *The burden of proof rests on the employer to establish fair dismissal not on the dismissed employee to establish unfair dismissal.* This is entirely just. It could be extremely difficult for a former employee to build up the evidence that he had been unfairly dismissed, to obtain copies of confidential memoranda, to have knowledge of confidential conversations especially from within the labyrinths that constitute many large organisations.

What the dismissed employee is now in a position to say is: "Where *is* the evidence that my work was poor, that my conduct was so much worse than other offenders who have kept their jobs?" And indeed, *where* is it? A major and beneficial consequence of the unfair dismissal provisions is the pressure generated on employers to improve disciplinary procedures, personnel records, employee appraisal arrangements. In this connection the Code of Practice offers sensible guidance particularly under "Disciplinary Procedures." Furthermore, an industrial tribunal is, in effect, required to measure the employer's disciplinary–dismissal practices against the procedural standards established in the Code. In the future the likelihood is increased that many more employers than in the past will be in a position to say, if challenged: "Yes, here is the evidence on the man's personnel record that we warned him, orally twelve months ago for persistent absenteeism. Six months later we warned him again for the same offence. Two months ago, as the man's record had not improved, we dismissed him, having observed the disciplinary procedure, modelled on the Code of Practice—copy of our procedure herewith." In short, an appreciable number of employers will have to think more carefully and behave more judiciously than in the past when they decide to dismiss employees. In the interests of consistency, particularly in multi-unit organisations, dismissal decisions will increasingly become a senior as distinct from junior management responsibility. On balance, these constraints on "management's right to manage" must engender improved industrial relations.

Much of this chapter has been concerned with safeguards against unfair dismissal created by the new need for employers to justify their dismissal behaviour. But what redress is available to the unfairly dismissed worker?

This is a matter for the industrial tribunals to determine but their jurisdiction is constrained in a number of important ways. A tribunal will not hear a complaint until a Department of Employment conciliation officer has had a chance to promote a voluntary settlement (schedule 6). As pointed out in Chapter 4, the tribunal under section 106 must observe the "just and equitable" criterion in relation to a declaration of rights, order and compensation—and the "equity" and "practicable" criteria if it is to recommend that an unfairly dismissed worker be re-engaged. Furthermore, under section 1, the tribunals are required to observe the guiding principles of the Act the purpose of which, it will be recalled, is to promote good industrial relations.

It would not be in accordance with equity to recommend that a former employee be re-engaged when he did not want to be. It might well be in accordance with equity and good industrial relations that a dismissed shop-steward be given his job back but *not* "practicable" to make this recommendation in the face of the employer's persistent refusal to take the blighter back. No wonder that the Act and its official Department of Employment explanatory literature place so much stress on the role of the local conciliation officer:

> Where employment has been terminated, the conciliation officer's primary aim under the . . . Act is to try, in appropriate cases, to promote a settlement by way of re-engagement [31, p15].
>
> Conciliation can continue right up to the date set down for hearing of the case by the industrial tribunal, so long as there is any prospect of a settlement [31, p15].

Where the employer still refuses to re-engage after diplomatic arm-twisting, compensation will be awarded to the person unfairly dismissed. In cases where the issue of re-engagement does not arise, compensation will be awarded. Unlike the redundancy pay formula which is mechanically related to the age, service and earnings of the redundant employee, compensation under the Act is more flexibly and more subtly assessed. The general principles set out in section 116 follow the compensation principles applied in the ordinary courts. The complainant is expected to mitigate his own loss—by looking for reasonable alternative work. His own behaviour prior to dismissal will be taken into account. It may be that his own provocative conduct was partly responsible for the unfair dismissal, in which case, the compensation would be reduced. "Expenses reasonably incurred"—for example, by looking for other work—and, "loss of any benefit" (s116(2)(b)) reasonably expected—for example, potential redundancy pay, unemployment benefit and pension rights—will be taken into account.

In appropriate cases where a former employee has refused re-engagement and the tribunal believes such refusal unreasonable, compensation can be reduced. The tribunal in making its re-engagement recommendation must state "the terms on which it considers that it would be reasonable for the complainant to be so re-engaged . . ." (s106(4)(b)). Conceivably, it would be unreasonable for a fitter in department *A* to turn down a fitter's job in the twin and adjacent department *B* but not in another plant in the same company twenty miles away. (Many decisions on "reasonable alternative employment" have been made under the Redundancy Payments Act.) An employer who unreasonably refused re-engagement might have to pay increased compensation.

Having taken the appropriate factors into account, the tribunal may award compensation of up to two years' pay, or £4160 (that is 104 weeks at £40 a week—the same weekly maximum as under the Redundancy Payments Act) "whichever is the less." Understandably, journalists tend to quote "£4000 for unfair dismissal" but the average figure is likely to be well below this sum. It is noteworthy that the maximum compensation for a fair redundancy under the Redundancy Payments Act is £1200, whereas an unfair redundancy under the Industrial Relations Act could theoretically bring £4160 to the complainant. But it is unquestionably right that an employer should have to pay more where he has behaved unfairly than where he has declared redundancies, sometimes through no fault of his own, as when a sharp increase in purchase tax or cancellation of a government contract has brought about a reduced demand for his products. That more liberal standards of compensation are to be applied in cases of unfair dismissal was made clear by the President of the Industrial Court in an appeal hearing in October 1972 [59].

Because an employer cannot be compelled to re-engage a worker unfairly dismissed, it can be argued that some dismissals will remain unfair even though the complainants have been compensated, perhaps to the magic tune of £4160. Some employers may reason to themselves: "It will only cost us a few thousand pounds to get rid of our handful of trouble-makers. Such an outlay will be cheap at the price. If the men strike to have the trouble-makers reinstated their strike will probably be an unfair industrial practice under section 96 being a strike called without due notice." (See Chapter 11.) To assert that £4000 is therefore the price on the head of every shop-steward, every union activist, is to be somewhat over-dramatic. But in some situations where union strength is tenuous but likely to grow, an anti-union employer may be tempted to dismiss workers for their union proclivities and accept the money cost of such action. (The Labour Government's Industrial Relations Bill, April 1970, empowered the tribunal to make an order for reinstatement, if the employee agreed to be reinstated and other conditions were met—clauses 37–9.)

Looking at the other side of the coin, it has certainly happened in the past and can certainly happen again that an employer dismisses a "nonner" when faced with the threat of a strike by the union workforce who refuse to work with the non-unionist. Under the Act, an employer would still have to pay compensation for unfair dismissal because only the employer can dismiss but he could seek redress against the "third party" which has brought unfair pressure to have the nonner dismissed. Unfair pressure could include go-slows and similar action because it embraces "irregular industrial action short of a strike" as well as strikes. The employer may "require the third party to be joined as a party to the proceedings" and the tribunal or the Court may order the third-party organisation, registered or unregistered, (or persons) to pay to the employer part or the whole of the compensation which the employer has had to pay to the unfairly dismissed employee (s119). Officials of *registered* trade unions are not required to make a "contribution" to the employer if their unfair pressure has been authorised by their union. Officials not so authorised and officials of unregistered unions, whether authorised or not, are technically at risk.

While both the logic and equity of the above arrangements are sound and consistent *if* the beliefs which inform section 5 are accepted, section 119's practicality and consequences are more dubious. The initiative to seek part compensation or "complete indemnity" rests with the employer, who is probably facing a threatened strike. Except in cases of ideological commitment to the Act, the employer's cost-benefit analysis is likely to suggest to him a course of action which mollifies rather than exacerbates an inflamed industrial relations troublespot. In other words, the likelihood is that section 119 will be used only in a minority of the cases where technically its use would be justified.

A different and authorised form of "contracting out" of the Act is contained in sections 31–2. Here, provision is made to encourage self-government. Parties to a procedure agreement, unregistered unions are not excluded, may apply to the Court for an order which exempts the employees covered by the agreement from the protection of the unfair dismissal provisions of the Act. Naturally criteria have to be met before such an exemption order will be made. Chief among these are:

1 That the remedies provided by the procedure agreement in respect of unfair dismissal are on the whole as beneficial as (but not necessarily identical with) those provided . . . by this Act" (s31(2)(d))

Clearly there is scope for flexibility here but we shall only know its extent when exemption orders are made.

2 Provision for the resolution of deadlock between the parties by arbitration or adjudication by an independent referee (s31(2)(e))

In the form of words employed there is no obvious safeguard against collusion between an employer and unions to avoid deadlock in order to have an "awkward" individual employee dismissed by unanimous agreement. No doubt the Court will be alive to this danger and to the need for a procedure's adherence to the recommendations on "Disciplinary Procedures" set out in the Code of Practice. (Section 31(2)(d) must also be kept in mind.) On the application of one of the parties an exemption order of the Court can subsequently be revoked but only if the Court is satisfied that one of the two following conditions is met:

1 That it is the wish of all parties to the procedure agreement that the order should be revoked, or
2 The agreement no longer meets the exemption criteria (s32(1)(2))

The Secretary of State may also apply for a revocation order and the use of such a discretionary power could be important where evidence existed of employees being cheated of their unfair dismissal rights. Collusion of the kind referred to above could be a case in point. In its revocation order the Court may prescribe that employees dismissed "during the period when the procedure was inadequate, even though it was covered by an exemption order" [31, p7] may still complain to an industrial tribunal that they were unfairly dismissed.

Some employers no doubt wish to apply for their voluntary joint procedures to be exempted from the statutory provisions. They see advantages flowing from resolving problems "on their own patch," speedily rather than subject to the "law's delay" and free of the possible publicity surrounding a tribunal's decision. Such employers might be prepared to give more generous compensation than that required by the Act, to be more ready to re-engage the unfairly dismissed—for example, on the ruling of some joint panel or independent chairman. Except possibly in the case of certain registered unions or where staff associations are "independent" within the meaning of the Act, employers' wishes for exempt voluntary procedures are likely to remain frustrated. On the evidence to date, unregistered unions are clearly not going to link hands with the employer in order to seek the exemption concession from the "union bashing" Court. Nevertheless, jointly agreed voluntary procedures may develop which provide more generous safeguards and remedies than those required by the Act and which therefore reduce the need, without removing the right, of a dismissed worker to seek redress from an industrial tribunal.

There is much to commend in the unfair dismissal provisions of the Act. Their weakness is common to social reforms generally. Trade unions can, for the most part, look after their own but who is to help the ignorant and badly informed, even hesitant, employees? Unions are not active in some trades or among the many small firms in this country. Employment Exchanges help workers to exercise their unfair dismissal rights.

While this is not the place to develop the case for the appointment of labour inspectors, such as exist in France, to help the underprivileged exercise their rights, the idea of such a function is worth mentioning. With the Act being a civil code, enforcement rests upon people's readiness to complain. While hard evidence is difficult to come by and to aggregate, it would be a rash person who felt confident, for example, that every employee entitled to "written particulars" under the *Contracts of Employment Act 1963*, let alone the fresh particulars required under this Act, had in fact been given them. How many employees know and how many do not know that they can complain and, if they do know, feel insufficiently secure to complain? Britain has various inspectors active in the employment field under—for example, the *Factories Act*, *the Offices, Shops and Railway Premises Act, and the Wages Councils Act*—who could be empowered to instruct, counsel and guide under the Act. There is surely much to be said for a factory inspector being authorised to say at his discretion to the managers he meets: "Oh, by the way, could you please let me have a copy of the written particulars you give to your employees?" In many cases, the educational process could start from there.

Having brought the issue of individual rights back to managers, two concluding points are made. Many managers are employed on fixed-term contracts and are therefore particularly affected by section 30 of the Act. If the contract was made before the commencement of the Act "for a fixed term of two years or more" and not renewed, then the expiry of the term does not constitute unfair dismissal. A similar contract made before *or after* the Act's commencement also falls outside the scope of the unfair dismissal provisions if it expires, is not renewed *and if* before it expires. "The employee has agreed in writing to exclude any claim in respect of rights under that section (22) in relation to *that* contract."

Some managers and professional workers are therefore likely to find waiver of unfair dismissal rights clauses in their fixed-term contracts.

Section 30 appears to create an expectation of renewal of contract and yet there would appear to be no bar to a "waiver of unfair dismissal rights" clauses being included in a succession of fixed-term contracts for the same person—with his consent. Presumably if a contract was not renewed and contained no waiver clause, dismissal at the end of the contract would be unfair. Here is one more reason to speculate whether an increased number of "insecure" managers will take out the "insurance policy" of membership with ASTMS or APEX.

Signals, to which earlier reference was made, are now being flashed to management in particular by the industrial tribunals with their decisions on unfair dismissal. It is impossible to summarise adequately at the end of this chapter what has so far been accomplished but the reader's attention is drawn to the following material for the particular signals it records:

> In October 1971, the applicant was given a written warning by his employer that his conduct had been unsatisfactory because he had not been co-operating with other members in his department. He was informed that further complaints would result in his dismissal. On 8 March 1972 the applicant assaulted another employee and as a result he was dismissed. . . . The tribunal *held* that his employers had been reasonable in dismissing him and that his dismissal was not unfair. The tribunal considered paragraphs 130–3 of the Code of Practice (Disciplinary procedures) [60].

> The applicant worked for the respondents as manager of the butchery department of their store . . . he was dismissed and given four weeks' wages in lieu of notice. Prior to his dismissal, the respondents had appointed another man manager of the butchery department so as to try to improve the turnover but he had refused to work with the applicant. The applicant claimed that he had been unfairly dismissed. The tribunal found that the respondents' reason for dismissing the applicant, namely that they had to choose between dismissing the applicant or losing another employee whom they wished to retain as manager, was a substantial reason but that, in the circumstances, the dismissal of the applicant was unfair. There were no grounds for complaint against the applicant and no grounds for dismissing him other than the other employee's refusal to work

> with him. The tribunal awarded the applicant £1900 compensation; he was sixty-three years of age and had been in receipt of a gross wage from the respondents of £25 a week [60].

According to a survey [61] carried out by Incomes Data Services Limited, during the first five months operation of the unfair dismissal provisions out of 2932 complaints processed by the Department of Employment's conciliation officers around 1100 were referred to industrial tribunals. On the cases examined this report suggests that ex-employees win their cases if the employer fails to identify the reason for dismissal or if the tribunal finds that the reason is not a "sufficient reason" for dismissal. Sufficient reasons for fair dismissal were commonly related to an "element of continuity or persistence" in the employee's behaviour—for example, "repeated failure to carry out work as instructed, unsatisfactory work after repeated warnings." Unfair dismissals often arose (as could be expected perhaps) from ill-considered managerial decisions—for example, "lack of warning of the employer's dissatisfaction, precipitateness, sudden change of attitude by employer, attempts to force change of duties without consent of employee."

Further IDS analyses will throw additional light on the operation of the valuable advance in our labour law that the unfair dismissal provisions represent.

7

Rights of Individuals—III

The Act contains 170 sections. Among these, two sections stand out with particularly sharp and controversial significance—not just because of their technical content and implications but because of the unstated philosophy which informs them. Section 96 is designed to inhibit wildcat strikes. Section 5 is designed to influence the level of trade union membership. Inherent in the operation of both sections is a subtle, contentious inter-play of individual and social rights. New legal rights of an individual and social character have been created to disturb well-established, conventional "custom and practice" rights which, although they carried no legal force, were none the less very powerful in their influence. Section 96, as it affects the social right to strike, will be discussed in Chapter 11. Section 5 in establishing new *individual* rights in the social context of collective bargaining is examined now.

HAMLET'S RIGHT AND THE ISSUE OF EQUALITY

To be or not to be a member of a trade union can be an important question for an individual worker to resolve, not least because his decision affects other people and may materially alter the state of labour relations in a given situation. Before the Act, "Hamlet" made his choice for one or a number of reasons—the pressure of his individual conscience or convictions, the pressure from his workmates, shop-stewards, a trade union, his employer. The law did not interfere with this social process. Now it does. It is therefore important to try to understand why, because the Act does not tell us.

The Consultative Document [5] which gave the underlying rationale of the legislation is helpful on this point, but only to a limited extent. The first of the four General Principles which the Government regarded as fundamental to its policy was:

> That every individual should have a right to join a trade union and participate in trade union activities, and an equal right not to do so [5, p2]

Just why there should be this right or why the right to join or not join should be considered as "equal" was not explained. A principle regarded as fundamental assumes the nature of a belief. It has been clear for some years that, broadly speaking, the Conservative Party has been consistent in its belief that the closed shop is a bad thing. Strikes to enforce the closed shop are therefore also bad. Bad for whom? In the Government's view apparently, bad not only for the employer and the community but for individual workers as well. If two basic premises are accepted, at least for analysis purposes, the rationale of section 5 and related sections on the agency shop becomes much clearer. These premises, beliefs might be a better term, are:

1 That no person's employment should be conditional upon holding a union card; employment should be conditional only upon ability to do the job
2 No one should be forced into an organisation against his will

In 1958 Conservative lawyers expressed the position as follows: "We consider that a workman should not be prevented from taking up or continuing the work of his choice merely by reason of his failure to belong to a particular union" [1, p41].

If the above propositions are believed to be just and the will and power exist among the proposers, statutory changes to the "voluntary" closed-shop conventions and practices, must come about. Whether these statutory changes engender real substantive change or a better situation are separate, if related, matters.

Thus, at the heart of section 5, we find established the right to join balanced by the right not to join. Section 5 is silent on the issue of whether the two rights are considered "equal." Whether it was good law or good sense or both to drop the word "equal" that appeared in the Consultative Document (see above) is an interesting point of discussion. Including the word "equal" would not seem feasible for, as expressed in section 5(1)(a)(b) the right to join and the right not to join are self-evidently not equal. If the rights were equal the individual worker would surely have the statutory right to join a registered *or an unregistered union* as well as the statutory right not to join a registered or unregistered union. As is by now widely realised, the positive right to join attaches only to a registered union. To be consistent with and to sustain the registration principle (central to the Act's purpose as we have seen) unequal rights for individual workers have been created.

Other parts of section 5 reinforce the importance of the registration principle. Only the member of a registered union has the statutory right to take part in union activities at "any appropriate time" which may include with the employer's agreement or consent, time within "working hours" (s5(1)(c)(5)). Only the member of a registered union can seek legal redress against an employer who has committed any of the unfair industrial practices listed in section 5(2) namely—and to give only the main illustrations:

1 Trying to stop the worker from joining a registered union of his own choice
2 Sacking him for joining such a union
3 Refusing to take him on because he is a member of a registered union

The member, or would-be member, of an unregistered union is not so protected. For example, it would not be an unfair industrial practice for an employer to say to a member of the unregistered AUEW: "We are not taking you on because you are a member of the AUEW." Dependent on the circumstances such a practice might not be very wise—but it would be lawful.

The converse of the rights outlined above apply to the individual that does not want to join either a registered or unregistered union. Two illustrations make the point clear. If an employer put pressure on an employee, which went well beyond encouragement, to join a registered or unregistered union when the employee did not want to, such unfair pressure would constitute an unfair industrial practice on the part of the employer. If an employer dismissed an employee who would not join either a registered or unregistered union, this would be an unfair industrial practice. (In agency-shop conditions, this position is modified as will be seen later.)

SECTION 5 AND THE LEVEL OF UNION MEMBERSHIP

Although there can be many and often conflicting views about the means employed, there can be a broad measure of agreement that a major objective of the Act is the reform of collective bargaining procedures. It is far less clear whether another objective of the Act is the extension as distinct from reform of collective bargaining. Is section 5 a "nonner's" charter or will it enable unions to recruit members more readily? Will section 5, surrounded by its cluster of agency-shop provisions, weaken union security and therefore both debilitate collective bargaining and reduce its area of operation? It is still too early to attempt to evaluate the practical effects of section 5 on our industrial relations system, assuming that these can be successfully unravelled from the effects of the many variables that influence employment behaviour. Even so, the collective bargaining implications of section 5 require discussion.

Every worker now has a right to join a registered union and must be so informed in writing by his employer. "Worker" is so broadly defined in section 167 that the "right to join" is obviously available, at least in law, to supervisors, foremen, technicians, engineers, chemists, managers at all levels of status, responsibility, salary—even probably to many directors. An employer who deters (a word not defined by the Act) the office manager or the office boy from exercising this right commits an unfair industrial practice. The extent to which this right will remove fears and inhibitions among, for example, many white-collar workers in the private sector and prompt them to join registered unions, is as yet largely an unknown factor. There can be many reasons, quite unrelated to the law, which influence a person in his decision to join or to stay out of a trade union. But as was mentioned in Chapter 2, a registered union is now provided with recruitment opportunities which it did not previously have. Given that the growth area of employment is white-collar employment and that only a modest proportion of white-collar workers in the private sector are union members, the temptation to a thrustful ambitious union to register to win section 5 members must be a strong one.

Supporters of the Act have repeatedly and accurately claimed that "for the first time in our history workers have a statutory right to join a trade union." Reference to the registration qualification receives less emphasis and the fact that unions have not pressed for such a right is rarely mentioned. Historically, unions have preferred to rely on their own organic strength and the non-intervention of the law in the social processes of recruiting and retaining membership. "What the state can give the state can take away" summarises a large part of their thinking on this issue.

Another largely unknown factor is the extent to which section 5 will encourage workers to use their "right not to join" to keep out or to drop out of unions. The latter point finds its acutest focus in the closed-shop situation. Unions have always regarded the non-union member, the "nonner," as an actual or potential threat to employment standards won by trade union exertions. Hostility is often shown to the individual worker who accepts the results, most typically a pay award, of the collective efforts and strength of his workmates but who remains a "free-rider" not being a union member. The workgroup, workforce, the union may therefore often attach far more importance to the solidarity of the group, to social rights, to collective rights than to individual rights. Many people, estimates would be hazardous, must be union members not out of a strong personal conviction of the rightness of being a union member but because they acknowledge the need for organised collective countervailing power in relation to the employer.

Reasons for dropping out of a union can be mixed. Some people begrudge paying even the low level of subscription required by some unions. Other workers may be dissatisfied with the union's lack of achievement for them and allow their membership to lapse. Apathetic members where union organisation is not strong may be encouraged by section 5 to fall into arrears, and eventually out of membership. Whatever the full catalogue of motives for using the negative right might be, there can be little doubt that the "right not to join" represents a blow to union security. This is true even in the modified form of post-entry closed shop, the so-called agency shop that the Act permits.

True to its philosophy that no one shall be forced into an organisation against his will, the Act, at least technically, permits a "nonner" to retain his job if he is prepared to pay the general subscription to the agency union or an equivalent contribution to a charity if his conscience is of the kind to justify the use of this option. While the arguments are not conclusive, it can be claimed that the "right not to join" in the context of the agency shop, may prompt the emergence of dissident groups within, be it remembered, a registered union. If this looked like happening a union might have to become more militant in its relationship with the employer in order to prevent potential from becoming actual dissidents. Not the least important of the counter arguments runs to the effect that "there is little point in being a 'nonner' if you have to pay a sub. It's better to pay, be a member and enjoy the security of union membership and peace and quiet with your union mates."

SECTION 5 AND UNION SECURITY

Where an agency shop is not possible because the union is unregistered and the closed shop in all but name persists, many managements and unions concerned will no doubt co-operate in a variety of ways best known to themselves, to try to ensure that the rugged individualist who will not join a union is kept out of the firm. Oblique advice on how to try to preserve a stable situation (short of committing an unfair industrial practice) finds tactful expression in the Code of Practice. Where an employer recognises a union—registered or unregistered—he should make clear to employees that he "welcomes" their membership of one of the recognised unions (para 4 iii). Applicants for jobs should be given "any relevant information about trade union arrangements before an applicant is engaged" (para 31 v). (What a wonderfully euphemistic way of hinting to managers that they should leave prospective employees under no illusions about the strength of values and practices in the particular workplace culture, the intense opposition to the free-rider and so on.) Paragraph 117 i of the Code recommends that shop-stewards should be given "lists of new employees" —obviously so that "the strength of things" can be explained to the newcomers.

The assurance of a job applicant who says he will join the appropriate union has still to be taken on trust. As an employee he may refuse to join and, assuming there is no agency shop, his dismissal as the result of workforce pressure would be unfair. An employer might be prepared to pay compensation to a "nonner" rather than take a strike. Such an employer might also prefer not to seek indemnity against those responsible for bringing about the dismissal by unfair pressure, although technically he is entitled, as we saw in the last chapter, to seek such redress. His usual top priority is to maintain a stable situation in order to produce goods and services.

Another potential threat to stability comes from the job applicant who claims before a tribunal that (in a non-agency shop situation) he has been kept out of a job because he will not join a union. The tribunal could award compensation—this time for the loss of a potential job. Again, an employer might think it worth while to pay compensation to such an individual to maintain stable labour relations with his union security conscious workforce. Yet another challenge to such security lies in section 7 of the Act. Someone who considers he has been kept out of a job because of his refusal to join a union, which is party to a pre-entry closed-shop agreement, may apply to the Industrial Court to have such an agreement declared void.

Experience, observation and comments indicate that employers who have become accustomed to closed-shop (pre- or post-entry) conditions will only exceptionally seek to disturb them. The body of evidence suggests that where a workforce is highly unionised, an employer prefers to have one class of citizens (union members) rather than two (union and non-union) for friction between union members and "nonners" can be highly disruptive of orderly labour relations. Such employers, therefore, are likely to be very careful when interviewing job applicants to ensure that more than one applicant is interviewed for one post. Such a procedure should increase the probability of the post being filled by a worker willing to join the appropriate union. The unsuccessful applicants would no doubt be told that they were insufficiently well qualified or not quite suitable, which might, indeed, be true, but not that they were showing unwillingness to conform to a union membership arrangement. Such selection/appointment practices may be contrary to the spirit of section 5 but are they really contrary to one of the major purposes of the Act—the promotion and maintenance of orderly labour relations? I shall return to this question in a moment.

In addition to, or quite apart from, what an individual employer may decide to do or not do in relation to section 5, unionised work groups can exert formidable social sanctions against the nonconformist—the "nonner" employee. Some of these sanctions may constitute unfair industrial practices, where, for example, a trade union, registered or unregistered, or "any person" puts pressure on an employer in order that the employer infringes the section 5 rights of the individual. What is meant by pressure? Well, it is clear (s33) that a strike (official or unofficial) to enforce a closed-shop agreement by bringing about the dismissal of the "nonner" would be unfair. Less-dramatic pressure is deemed to be "irregular industrial action short of a strike" and is defined as:

> Any concerted course of conduct (other than a strike) which, in contemplation or furtherance of an industrial dispute:
>
> *a* Is carried on by a group of workers with the intention of preventing, reducing or otherwise interfering with the production of goods or the provision of services, and
>
> *b* In the case of some or all of them, is carried on in breach of their contracts of employment (or where they are not employees) in breach of their terms and conditions of service (s33(4))

In plain terms, this appears to mean that if a group of pieceworkers refused to work at piecework rate because one of their number was refusing to join their unregistered union, this would be unfair. Their concerted action would certainly cause production losses and would probably be a breach of their individual employment contracts. The position of an overtime ban in the same context is less certain because it is not always apparent whether overtime working is a condition of employment. Since the Court of Appeal's decision on the railway working to rule in May 1972 [33] some uncertainty has arisen about the contractual nature of working rules and whether "working to rule" is unfair within the meaning of the Act.

Set against the above background, it must be stressed that the *economic* sanction of "irregular industrial action short of a strike" against an employer is only unfair if its purpose, for example, is to force the employer to force an employee into a union against his will or have him dismissed if he will not join. Although some forms of workplace sanctions against the nonconformist are now technically at legal risk, there are many other forms of sanction, particularly of a social character, which are not proscribed by section 33—or anywhere else in the Act for that matter.

Any group of people can make life miserable for an individual if they are brought together in regular contact—be it in the school classroom, a barrackroom, a tennis club, the factory or office. After all, the term "blackball" originated not in an engineering workshop but in gentlemen's clubs. Both upper-class ostracism of "caddish" behaviour and working class "sending to Coventry" spring from the desire of the group to protect itself from the person who threatens its values. Realistically, the law can only go a limited way to protect individuals from the expressions of disapproval, even sense of outrage felt by the group when its conventions, norms of behaviour, have been seriously affronted.

Given the premises from which sections 5, 7 (outlawing of pre-entry closed shop) and 33 appear to be developed (see above) the logic of these sections appears impeccable. Their wisdom is another matter. Put bluntly, these sections appear to subordinate the rights of the group to the right of the individual. Except in the case of the "conscience" escape routes of the agency shop and the approved closed shop (see Chapter 8) the motives of the person who does not wish to conform to group standards cannot formally be called into question. It seems to be implied that the group must be wrong if the individual wants to opt out, for it is the right of the individual to opt out that must be protected and given paramount consideration over the group's right to keep individuals in membership. As organisations grow larger in our increasingly complex society, there is something attractive about strengthening the rights of the individual but so much depends on the specific context in which this general issue is set. Given the increase in concentration of economic power into fewer firms and the growth of multi-national companies, the individual's interest might be served better by laws which deliberately facilitated union growth so as to promote effective countervailing power, than by section 5 which appears to champion the individual's right at the expense of workgroup and union solidarity.

Section 5 and its associated sections form a meeting ground where the clash of political ideologies over the merits/inequities of the Act can, perhaps, most readily occur. To some people section 5 represents a triumph, striking as it does a firm blow for the freedom of the individual; for other people, this same section constitutes a serious threat to group cohesion and effectiveness which remain the real source of strength for individuals who, if they are unorganised, will be comparatively powerless in their relations with employers and governments. This ideological conflict was well brought out by Mr Brian Walden MP, in the committee stage of the debate on the Bill:

> It is very difficult for people with a certain basically individualistic background, a certain view of patriotism and the courts, of responsibility and duty, to grasp how much so many in the Labour Party were shaped by a different set of values—no better, no worse, just different. These were collective values. The whole reason why the Labour Party exists is that we were able to stand together as a group when we were anonymous [34].

"Different set of values . . . no better, no worse, just different"—a refreshing view for a politician to take, particularly after the tendentious, often acrimonious contributions which marked many of the debates in Parliament. Nevertheless, the "individualistic values" prevailed as section 5 demonstrates. In this sense section 5 is essentially political in character for it appears to say: "True to our individualistic values system we must first protect the individual and then consider the implications for the industrial relations system." A different approach would have been: "Let us devise means for promoting collective organisations, collective bargaining and then consider the implications for the individual."

As other parts of the Act—for example, the sole bargaining agent, disclosure of information provisions—and particularly the Code of Practice—for example, shop-steward facilities—appear designed to promote (and to reform) collective bargaining, section 5 appears something of a paradox. Because of the weight placed upon individualistic values, section 5 is unlikely, except where established unions with white-collar interests register, to promote significantly collective organisation or collective bargaining. Because it weakens the closed-shop position, section 5 may prove divisive, setting brother against ex-brother, registered brother against unregistered brother—and disruptive of hitherto orderly labour relations. Other provisions of the Act and Code which are designed to bring about order may offset some of the potentially disruptive repercussions of section 5 but it is unlikely that new statutory procedures and sanctions will be of much use to promote an accepted and durable, as distinct from botched-up, solution to problems where emotions run high as they commonly do where union members are in conflict with "nonners."

Because Conservative politicians have "a certain basically individualistic background" they take a particular view of industrial relations, which as expressed in sections 5, 7 and 33 and elsewhere in the Act, is seen by trade unionists imbued with "collective values" as an attack on trade unionism. Whether the Conservative Government intended such an attack on trade union strength is a matter for the individual reader to judge but the collective belief of trade unionists remains that such sections were basically designed to weaken their organisation.

After all, if any massive demonstrations of workers have besieged Tory central office clamouring for the "statutory right not to join a trade union" the fact has gone unrecorded.

On the whole, working-class people accept the need for collective action, for solidarity and an element of rough justice that "one out, all out" may sometimes entail. One, not necessarily definitive, conclusion must be that section 5 and its associated sections accord more with the reality of a particular political philosophy, with the values of a Surbiton housewife and a public school lawyer than with the realities of workplace bargaining and the values of coalface workers from the Rhondda. The need to promote, in Mr Walden's terms, "meaningful dialogues" between the disparate sections of our community remains as pressing as ever.

8

New Rules for Collective Bargaining—I

As Allan Flanders has pointed out [35] effective organisation and mutual recognition by employers and unions are prerequisites of collective bargaining. Some of the implications, particularly of section 5, which the Act carries for organisations have been considered. Now recognition and further issues of union security will be dealt with.

RECOGNITION

Before the Act, our industrial relations system contained no general orderly or systematic procedure whereby a union claim for recognition could be evaluated. Donovan recommended the development of such a procedure not least because recognition disputes were thought to be an avoidable form of industrial conflict. The 1964–70 Labour Government agreed with this view and, as mentioned earlier, through carefully chosen references to the CIR recognition claims, particularly by white-collar unions, were investigated by the CIR. Recognition assessment criteria were not set by the Government for the CIR. The CIR was left free to evolve its own, always allowing that part of the CIR's basic remit was not only to reform but to *extend* collective bargaining. It followed from this that union recognition should be facilitated. In specific sets of circumstances, therefore, the CIR recommended that employers recognise unions even though unions were in a relatively weak position. In short, the recognition evaluation criteria were evolving flexibly and in ways sympathetic to union growth [25]. On the other hand, CIR recommendations carried no legal force and some employers refused to recognise unions in "defiance" of CIR counselling that they should.

Both Act and Code have significantly altered the above situation. Recognition criteria are incorporated in the Act and appear more onerous for the unions than the original CIR criteria. In some circumstances an employer can be "made" to recognise a union and a union "made" to stop badgering an employer for negotiating rights. Sanctions can be invoked if recommendations fail in their purpose.

Act and Code cater for various types of recognition claim. A union may be seeking recognition for the first time. A typical case would be of a white-collar union seeking negotiating rights on behalf of its foremen and technician membership in a particular firm. If the union is *not* making a claim to be the "sole bargaining agent" for particular grades of employees, then the reference document for the employer is not the Act but the Code (paras 82–6). These paragraphs contain sound, if very general, advice about: bargaining structure; the interests and negotiating rights of other unions which may be present; the hinted desirability of different unions for supervisors and the supervised; management's right to know the membership strength of the union but not the identities of the members. "Where the extent of support cannot be agreed, it should be determined by arrangements agreed between the parties, for example, a secret ballot" (para 83). If claims for recognition cannot be settled on a voluntary basis "the procedures set out in paragraphs 79–81 may be used" (para 86).

Paragraph 79 outlines three, presumably sequential, procedures:

1 Self government—refer the problem to the employers' association where appropriate and higher trade union levels
2 Seek "advice and conciliation from the Department of Employment"
3 Ask the Department of Employment to refer the matter to the CIR "for examination and advice"

Section 121 of the Act provides the Secretary of State with wide discretionary powers to refer almost any conceivable industrial relations problem to the CIR for examination but subsection (2)(d) specifically refers to "recognition and negotiating rights for purposes of collective bargaining." In its examination of the recognition claim the CIR will presumably be more influenced by the recognition criteria contained in section 48 (which relates to a claim to be sole bargaining agent) than by the generously disposed to the union criteria in the pre-Act CIR reports on recognition. It will be interesting to observe the course which the CIR steers in relation to recognition criteria in cases which *do not* involve sole bargaining agent issues, bearing in mind that the CIR must also try to provide a durable settlement. But it may be that the majority of recognition references will only reach the CIR in "sole bargaining agent" form. [82]

BARGAINING STRUCTURE

"Sole bargaining agent" and "bargaining unit" are fundamental concepts. They are integral to a basic purpose which is both simple and sensible—to tidy up bargaining structures and to reduce inter-union rivalry for membership, which is too often attended by industrial conflict. The basic purpose is to be realised by a process which is far from simple. This fact of itself raises doubts about the sensible nature of the process. Section 44(c) reads:

> "Sole bargaining agent," in relation to a bargaining unit, means the organisation of workers or joint negotiating panel having negotiating rights in relation to that unit *to the exclusion of* all other organisations of workers and joint negotiating panels, except in respect of matters which are dealt with under more extensive bargaining arrangements.

Several points require comment. "Bargaining unit," "negotiating rights," "joint negotiating panel," "more extensive bargaining arrangements" are all defined in section 44. Briefly, "bargaining unit" means a specified group of employees. "Negotiating rights" are collective bargaining rights recognised by the employer in relation to the agent representing employees in the unit. "Joint negotiating panel" may consist of a mixture of registered and unregistered unions. "More extensive bargaining arrangements" is really a reference to industry-wide, JIC type bargaining arrangements. For these "sole bargaining agent" agreements cannot be achieved, the provisions of sections 44–55 applying only to individual employers, or to employers who are "associated"—where one employer has control of another.

A union already recognised by an employer may claim to be sole bargaining agent—so may a union not yet recognised by an employer. If arguments arise, if a dispute develops, a union may apply to the Court for the problem to be referred to the CIR for investigation. Such an application can only be made by a *registered* union—either unilaterally or jointly with the employer concerned. An employer may also apply "to have this recognition/bargaining structure problem sorted out" whether the unions involved are registered *or* unregistered. The Secretary of State can take the initiative and clearly may chose to do so if attempts at conciliation by his officials have failed and inter-union warfare is continuing to damage the firm concerned and, perhaps, its export performance. Once application has been made, the tortuous "due process" begins. The mechanics alone of this process are so complicated as to warrant separate attention in Appendix 2.

To avoid confusion let us consolidate. Sole bargaining agent/unit agreements may be reached in three ways:

1 Voluntarily between the parties concerned; whether the unions are registered or unregistered is immaterial
2 In dispute or challenge situations by accepting voluntarily the recommendations of a third party, the CIR. The CIR may recommend either a registered or unregistered union to be the sole bargaining agent or a combination of both
3 As a development out of 2 the Court may make an order directing that an employer recognise a particular union as sole bargaining agent, *providing the union is registered*

In the words of the Department of Employment Guide: "The employer then has a legal obligation to negotiate seriously with the sole bargaining agent, and will be committing an unfair industrial practice if he does not do so" [9, p30].

Again the sanctity of the law stands firmly behind the registration principle. Only a registered union can have its position as sole bargaining agent made secure by law.

System 2 is complex and system 3 even more so. Hence a further need for Appendix 2.

Three important aspects of these bewildering provisions are selected for discussion here: the sole bargaining agent recognition criteria to be observed by the CIR; some general considerations affecting the rationalisation of bargaining structures; the right of the workforce to challenge a union's established position.

In preparing its recommendations on whether a union or group of unions (joint negotiating panel) should or should not be the sole bargaining agent, the CIR is required under section 48 to consider a number of factors.

The "interests in common" shared by the "different descriptions of employees" concerned (s48(3)) must be studied by reference to "the nature of the work" and "training, experience and professional or other qualifications." Homogeneity of interest was a factor to which the CIR paid a great deal of attention in its first, immediate post-Donovan, recognition reports. Even junior technical staff with humble professional qualifications may well prefer to be represented by a union distinctly different from the general labour union which bargains for the process workers in the plant.

The CIR shall *not* recommend a union as the agent unless it is satisfied that the union is "independent" of the employer (staff associations may cause some problems) [50]; recognition of the agent for the particular unit "would be in accordance with the general wishes of the employees" in the unit (procedures for taking soundings of opinions and ballots can be devised); and "would promote a satisfactory and lasting settlement of the questions in issue" (a much more subtle matter of judgement) (s48(4)); "without prejudice" to the foregoing, the CIR must ascertain whether union or panel has or "*would have* the support of a *substantial proportion* of the employees comprised in the bargaining unit" and "has or *would have* such resources, and is or *would be* so organised, as to enable it effectively to represent those employees" (s48(5)).

The "would haves" and "would be" are particularly interesting for the affinities they suggest with earlier CIR thinking. Briefly, this ran as follows: "Our investigations show that relatively few employees have joined the union because they think it pointless to join as the firm will not recognise the union. Our evidence strongly suggests that if the firm recognises the union, many more employees would then become union members. We therefore recommend that the firm recognises the union even from a low level of union membership, thus giving the union a chance to grow" [25]. We await with interest the interpretation under the Act by the CIR of "substantial proportions" actual or potential of employees who support the union. [82]

The "would have" in relation to resources and "would be so organised" in relation to effective representation are also important. Staff associations which have converted themselves into white-collar trade unions partly with a view to achieving exclusive bargaining rights at the expense of traditional unions, may find it difficult to convince the CIR that they have or are likely to have sufficient industrial relations and bargaining expertise to justify their sole bargaining agent claims. Some unions such as NUBE and ASTMS are prepared through the institutions of the Act to contest such claims. It may well be that the registered Royal College of Nursing, in deciding to develop a shop-stewards system (a radical decision unaccompanied by convulsions of horror that would have occurred had the decision been taken ten years ago) did so in order to protect its bargaining position ("resources," "effective representation") given that other more experienced unions (registered and unregistered) in the health service have interests and ambitions in representing nurses.

Section 48(7) enables the CIR to attach conditions to its recommendations. Under section 48(7)(a) the CIR may require the agent or member of a joint negotiating panel "to make sufficient trained officials available for purposes of collective bargaining." The definition of "official" under section 167 clearly includes shop-steward, or equivalent, and the inclusion of "trained" lends added point to the training of stewards which is regarded in the Code of Practice as a joint management/union responsibility. Under section 48(7)(b) the CIR may require the agent to undertake not to claim sole bargaining rights for another bargaining unit in a named undertaking. Presumably the intention is to avert inter-union conflict over organising and bargaining rights and so reduce inter-union jurisdictional disputes.

In effect, section 48(8) enables the CIR to say: "We recommend union *A* to be the agent for these groups of employees in this particular firm but only in relation to matters of, for example, bonus negotiations, shift arrangements, but not in relation to basic rates of pay and shift premia as these are determined nationally by industry-wide agreements to which the firm in question is a party."

Whatever experience of the above criteria eventually proves, there is much to be said in favour of reforming untidy and friction-provoking bargaining structures at plant and company level and of enabling an independent agency to recommend who should bargain on behalf of whom. (There may even be merit after the involved processes indicated in Appendix 2 in having such recommendations made legally binding.) Too often in the past, managements have prompted, by default, jurisdictional disputes between unions. An AUEW member, for example, a setter, may be promoted to inspector—a management decision. The AUEW, in this particular firm, has not paid much attention to the employment conditions of their few inspector members. Neither has the management. An enterprising white-collar union, such as ASTMS, seizes the opportunity created by others' neglect, recruits most of the "staff" inspectors and seeks recognition from the firm. The sitting tenant "worker" union, AUEW, is stung into militant retaliatory action and the employer is caught between the cross-fire of battling unions. In this situation—and a fair number have arisen in the past—the employer may be glad to pass his problem to the CIR.

Additionally, now that there is recognition criteria and apparatus for resolving recognition problems in a systematic fashion, as distinct from *ad hoc*, management are not only given opportunities but a stimulus to develop more orderly bargaining structures. A focus of attention is created and increasingly refined recognition "case law" is emerging. As a result of these influences management are now much more likely to pay attention to the type of bargaining structure and particular unions with whom they wish to bargain than in the past when all too often a firm has been overtaken by events similar to the one illustrated above. Typical management reasoning might be: "If we allow that our supervisors are likely to join unions in increasing numbers, shall we offer to give sole bargaining agent rights to union *A* for the supervisors rather than union *B* which caters for production workers but which has a supervisory section?" Only a little imagination is needed to extend this illustration to technicians, chemists, junior managers—and other unions. There is much to be said for averting disruptive inter-union competiton for membership—not least because such competition tends to embitter not only relations between unions, when brother will sometimes not sit at the same table with brother, but to sour relations between management and workers.

This is not to claim that the sole bargaining agent/unit provisions of the Act will resolve all recognition problems or that they are appropriate to all circumstances. An employer could make mischief by encouraging a registered union to compete for membership with an unregistered one. (It is significant that the CIR can recommend that an unregistered as well as a registered union should be the sole bargaining agent, particularly when the criterion of "a satisfactory and lasting settlement" is borne in mind.) It would be ludicrous to formalise, via the CIR even, let alone the Court, or even disturb, by the same means, the informal flexible arrangements that exist in many companies whereby an AUEW steward often speaks on behalf of a small maintenance force which, though it consists principally of maintenance fitters, also includes a handful of electricians, perhaps a couple of pipe-fitters and two or three building tradesmen all of whom belong to different unions. Such arrangements have grown organically in advance of the Act. Again, it is a question of "horses for courses" rather than universal rigid application of generalised rules.

Curiously while engendering order, the sole bargaining agent/unit sections contain provisions for the promotion of disorder. This is in deference to the democratic principle that if the representative agent no longer appears to be representative, his credentials should be withdrawn. Any employee (he does not have to be a union member) in the bargaining unit may set this form of protest in motion provided he has the written support of one-fifth of his colleagues, in the case of a voluntary sole bargaining agent agreement, or two-fifths where the Court has previously issued a recognition order (which has a guaranteed life of two years). At this point we enter the convolutions of "due process," similar to that in Appendix 2. The upshot can be—it does not automatically follow from the "protest"—that the Court eventually orders the employer to cease recognising the union as sole bargaining agent for a period of two years.

One important implication, for the union, of these provisions appears to be: "If we wish to keep satisfied those whom we represent, we must win adequate concessions from management"—a factor encouraging increased militancy and disorder? Conversely, a management by its own obduracy could weaken an agent's position—perhaps where management nursed a hope of encouraging a rival union agent, whose character it preferred, to emerge. Ramifications are endless but there is one certainty: the creation by the Act of a potential challenge to the established *recognition rights* of a union. A similar potential challenge exists in relation to union *security rights* as evidenced in the agency-shop provisions.

UNION SECURITY

A brief restatement of the nature of an agency-shop agreement may be useful. An agency-shop agreement can only be reached with a *registered* union. The agreement is to the effect that as a condition of continuing employment (not entry to the firm) a worker:

1. Becomes a member of the union, or
2. Becomes a paying non-member (the general subscription only, not the trimmings or political levy), or
3. On grounds of conscience pays an equivalent contribution to a charity

If the employee concerned is unwilling to exercise any of these options he can be fairly dismissed. "Conscience" may be tested before an industrial tribunal.

Agency-shop agreements may be concluded on a voluntary basis between an employer and a registered union recognised by the employer or established by order of the Court, after "due process." The process may be initiated by the employer concerned or by a registered union (recognised by the employer) whose claim for an agency-shop agreement has not been conceded. Either party may apply to the Court for a CIR investigation. In other words, the merits of the claim and counterclaim concerning union security can be tested under the supervision of a third party (any bargaining agent—recognition problems must first be resolved) [9, p13].

The critical test is a ballot of the affected workforce: "If the result of a ballot . . . is that either a majority of the workers eligible to vote in the ballot or not less than two-thirds of those who voted in it have voted in favour of an agency-shop agreement . . ." (s13(1)), then it becomes the statutory duty of the employer to enter into an agency-shop agreement—enforceable if need be, by way of complaint to the Court [9, p54].

The "or not less than two-thirds" marks a Government concession during the debate on the Bill, being a far less stringent test than a "majority of the workers eligible to vote." This latter form of majority is a much more onerous test than the conventional democratic practice followed in national and local government elections: "majority of those voting." Given the Government's anti-pre-entry closed-shop philosophy, their desire to prevent an agency shop being achieved by default, by abstensions or by apathy is understandable, if questionable, as to its wisdom and fairness. Ironically, the concession referred to now makes it *theoretically* very easy for an agency shop to be achieved. If, for example, the electoral roll numbers 100 then to pass the "majority eligible" test more than fifty people would need to vote and fifty-one of those vote in favour of the agency shop. On the two-thirds test, perhaps only thirty of the 100 might vote but, if twenty voted (out of 100) in favour of the agency shop, then an agency shop there would have to be. This would appear to be true, *reductio ad absurdum*, if only three people out of the 100 voted and two were in favour of the union. In reality such a situation seems hardly likely to arise.

If the necessary majority is not obtained by the union, the Court *must*, not may, make an order barring the introduction of an agency-shop agreement for a two-year period. After this time an agency-shop agreement may be reached voluntarily—or through the ritual indicated. Attempts to thwart the effectiveness of the order may well constitute unfair industrial practices (see Appendix 1).

If the necessary majority is obtained the security of the agency shop is secured for two years—by order of the Court. After this period *or at any time* in the case of a *voluntary* agency-shop agreement, the continuance of the agency shop may be challenged by the workforce affected. "Any worker to whom the agreement applies" section 14(1) may apply to the Court for a ballot to determine whether or not the agency-shop agreement should continue. If his application is supported in writing by one-fifth of the affected workforce, the Court will order a ballot with the same tests as those already indicated. Dependent on the results, the agency shop could survive for a further two years, protected, from formal challenge, by the Court. Alternatively, the Court would have to make an order rescinding the agency-shop agreement and debarring application for another ballot, to establish the agency shop, for a period of two years. Attempts by voluntary methods to form an agency shop during the two-year quarantine period would run up against "unfair industrial practices" barriers.

Two main constructions can be placed upon these challenge aspects of the agency shop. Industrial life is dynamic and union security should be assured only if the union continues to reflect the wishes of the workers. It is only democratic that if a significant number of workers feel dissatisfied with their agent, they should be free and enjoy the procedural means to challenge the agent's position. The opposing construction runs to the effect that this apparent concern for workers' wishes, democratic standards and procedures is a plausible device to conceal the real intention of these sections which is to weaken trade unions; to destroy the traditional form of union security, the closed shop, the preservation of which is essential in many firms if a reasonable power balance, decent conditions of employment and orderly procedures are to be maintained [36] [2].

In practice, because most unions have stood firmly by the policy of non-registration, few agency-shop agreements may be reached. Ironically, given the Act's concern for order, the agency-shop provisions, as mentioned earlier, arguably contain elements of potential disorder. Warring factions within the union membership and/or between union and non-union groups in the workforce could create havoc. A group of union members dissatisfied with a particular union-negotiated settlement could express their dissatisfaction with their union by dropping out of membership, while contributing to the union as non-members, force a ballot, partly with a view to joining and having established in the firm, a rival union. Hypothetical illustrations of potential disorder are only too easy to conceive but here, as elsewhere, we are pushed to the "proof of the pudding . . ." position.

Compared with its original intentions, the Government made one further concession to union security in the form of the "approved closed shop" to which a separate schedule (1) of the Act is intricately devoted—in addition to sections 17 and 18. The approved closed shop is another form of post-entry closed shop. Approved-closed-shop union security is appreciably greater than agency-shop union security in that under an approved-closed-shop agreement a worker must either be or become a member of the union as a condition of continuing employment or claim (as in the agency shop) exemption on conscientious grounds and pay a contribution to a charity. The escape route of the contributing non-member, available under an agency-shop agreement, does not exist. As union security is appreciably greater under the approved closed shop than under the agency shop, the hurdles to be cleared before the goal can be attained are higher, more numerous and decidedly bristlier. It must be remembered too that the approved closed shop represents a rent in the philosophical fabric of "no person to be pushed into a union against his will; no person's employment to be dependent on holding a union card." (An approved closed shop permits a worker to be kept in union membership against his will if not against his conscience.) The rent must not be allowed to grow bigger and tear asunder that precious fabric.

It is widely held that few unions will be able to clear all the hurdles successfully. Predictably only a registered union can be party to an approved-closed-shop agreement. Such an agreement cannot be reached voluntarily. Application has to be made to the Court by the registered union and employer together. The application is tested by the CIR against stringent criteria. If, in the opinion of the CIR, an agency-shop-agreement would meet the needs of the parties, the CIR is required to say so. Paragraph 5 of schedule 1 sets out the stringent criteria and these are neatly summarised in the Department of Employment *Guide*. An approved closed shop must be seen as necessary:

1 To secure orderly and effective industrial relations
2 To maintain reasonable terms and conditions of employment and continuity of employment
3 To ensure that collective agreements are honoured
4 To enable union organisation to be effective [9, p14]

Assuming the CIR is satisfied these criteria are met, it so reports to the Court. Time is then allowed for the workers concerned to seek a ballot, if one-fifth of them consider it necessary to establish whether the proposed agreement enjoys adequate support. (The votes test is the same as for the agency shop.) If no ballot is sought or the vote is favourable, the Court then makes an order enabling the employer to operate an approved-closed-shop agreement. If the ballot is unsuccessful no further application may be made for two years. Once an approved-closed-shop agreement has been operating for two years, it can be challenged in the same way as an agency-shop agreement. Formally assured security has only a short life span. The various procedures are protected against unfair pressure by the creation of a customary cluster of unfair industrial practices against which redress can be sought.

The above sketch is sufficient to indicate the complex and demanding nature of the approved-closed-shop provisions which were designed to meet the special needs of a very few unions, notably Equity and the National Union of Seamen which lobbied hard for concessions. Acting and seafaring are precarious forms of employment—the former because there are far more actors than jobs which, by their nature, are usually of short duration; the latter because the union's membership is scattered over the high seas, thus weakening the union influence both over its members and their day-to-day employment conditions. (It is worth referring back to the criteria at this point.) As mentioned in Chapter 2, both Equity and the National Union of Seamen felt the need for security so strongly that they chose to remain registered unions, in defiance of TUC instructions, in order to seek approved-closed-shop agreements. Evidence that the seamen are a "special case" was provided by the CIR in July 1972 when the Commission reported that "it appears to us that it is necessary for these seafarers to be comprised in an approved-closed-shop agreement . . ." [62, p23].

From this tangled skein of union security issues, one prediction seems safe: there will be far fewer approved-closed-shop and agency-shop agreements than "unapproved" closed-shop agreements. Unions will defend, perhaps less openly than in the past, the closed-shop securities they have won and most employers, one suspects, involved in such situations, are going to co-operate, almost certainly less openly than in the past, in the defence of the established union position. Managements are usually more concerned to produce goods and services in conditions of fairly stabilised labour relations than to promote the anti-closed-shop views of any particular government.

9

New Rules for Collective Bargaining—II

COLLECTIVE AGREEMENTS

The Act's main provisions on organisation, recognition and certain aspects of the bargaining process have now been considered. It is therefore logical to examine next what the Act has to say about the product of collective bargaining—namely the collective agreement. Light is thrown on the purpose of section 34 "presumptions relating to collective agreements" by the Consultative Document issued in October 1970 [5]. The essential presumption created by section 34 is that a collective agreement reached in writing is legally binding unless the parties concerned state the contrary, in writing, in relation to a part or the whole of the agreement. Paragraphs 112 and 113 of the Consultative Document read:

> 112: At the present time collective agreements between employers and unions have a doubtful status in law. In principle there is no reason why a collective agreement, like any other valid contract, cannot be made legally binding; but in practice the attitude of the parties to collective agreements, the lack of any clear indication that they are to be legally bound, and the form and language of agreements have encouraged the view (which has been accepted by the courts in some cases) that most collective agreements are not intended to have the force of legally binding contracts.
>
> 113: In the Government's view this is an unsatisfactory state of affairs. First, it is essential that the legal status of collective agreements should be clear and unambiguous. Secondly, it is highly desirable that agreements should be expressed in language which makes quite clear what it is the parties have agreed to. Thirdly, the parties should regard—or come to regard—the signing of agreements as a responsible act which binds them in law to honour their commitments [5, p16].

Paragraph 112 is not markedly dissimilar from the Donovan findings on the same subject. Paragraph 113 contains more debatable material. Throughout our industrial relations history, the intention of employers and unions—and the legal presumption—was that collective agreements were *not* legally binding unless the parties said they were.

"Hear, hear!" would probably summarise most people's reaction, including employers and trade unions, to the "Secondly . . ." sentence of paragraph 113. The "Thirdly . . ." sentence contains the heart and mind of the issue. If the words "in law" had been omitted we should presumably have been left with an oft-repeated pious resolution and no section 34 with its supporting sections. Is there then a good case for section 34?

Historically employers and unions have, by and large, honoured their commitments and behaved as gentlemen in sustaining their gentlemen's agreements. But the past twenty years have witnessed the disturbing phenomenon of substantive agreements repudiated and procedural agreements frequently flouted—not by the union signatories to the agreements but by the disaffected (wildcat) workforces covered by the agreements. In evidence to Donovan the Department of Employment estimated that around 95 per cent of our strikes were unconstitutional—in breach of collectively agreed avoidance of disputes procedures. In that case, can there be any reason why our voluntary collective agreements should not be made binding in law? If voluntary agreements were given contractual force redress would become available to the injured party from the party breaking the contract. Collective agreements in some other countries take a contractual form, notably in the USA—why not here? Why should trade unions be above the law? People who enter into commercial contracts are required to abide by them or pay penalties if they do not.

To the manager harassed by wildcat strikes and by irate customers whose orders are not completed on time, to the many and particularly middle-class people who have never experienced the frustrations of factory-floor employment conditions and to the many Conservative lawyer MPs who are much given to contractual values there is understandable appeal in the idea of having collective agreements made binding in law. The desirability of legal enforceability was argued before Donovan by numbers of employers groupings including the CBI. Donovan remained unconvinced about the wisdom of such reform. Donovan's reasons are best read in Donovan but various Donovan-style points may be made here.

In the past there was no legal impediment to an employer reaching a legally binding collective agreement with a union if both parties desired such an agreement. The fact that very few contractual agreements were made suggests that the voluntary system was the one that most closely accorded to the bargainers' wishes. Legal enforceability might suppress the symptoms rather than probe to the causes and so frustrate the cure of the British industrial relations wildcat malaise. *In Place of Strife* recorded: "95 per cent of all strikes are unofficial (and of these the vast majority are unconstitutional); they are responsible for three-quarters of the working days lost because of strikes" [3, p27]. Investigations suggest that some substantive agreements have been repudiated because official union negotiators have misjudged the rising expectations of workpeople. Other inquiries indicate that some procedure agreements are frequently broken because the procedures themselves are out of date and ill-suited to handle the pressures emanating from workplace negotiations. Much harm could result from an attempt to prop up, by legal sanctions, a decayed regulatory system. Attempts at voluntary reform, even if induced by legislation and an Industrial Relations Commission should precede sanctions.

In the event the Government has not made voluntary collective agreements legally binding by statute. To have done so would have been a radical departure in law, the common law of contract having been evolved to give legal force to the *wishes of the parties involved* reflecting *their intentions* to create legally binding rights and obligations. Furthermore, "it takes two to tango." Had the Government transformed voluntary agreements into contracts, collective bargaining, in the long practised conventional sense, would almost certainly have disappeared, the unions withdrawing from the process and maintaining relationships with employers in a bizarre cloak and dagger world of unwritten understanding.

Section 34 constitutes a push in the direction of "legally binding" but not at the moment a very powerful push because of trade union resistance. "Tina Lea" has become the union's doughty resistance fighter. "*T*his *i*s *n*ot *a* *l*egally *e*nforceable *a*greement," or many other phrases to the same effect are automatic additions to written collective agreements, memoranda, minutes of meetings, anything that might be construed as an agreement as a result of TUC instructions to affiliated unions. Employers have been quite prepared to accept these disclaimer clauses when concluding agreements. TUC opposition derives not just from a dislike of sanctions (it is an unfair industrial practice to break a legally enforceable agreement) but from fear that legalism will "impose a rigidity and inflexibility" on a very adaptable, rich in custom and practice, collective bargaining system. Parts of many of our collective agreements are renegotiated daily, by work study engineers, line managers and shop-stewards as allowed times, rates, and so on, are adjusted under payment-by-results schemes. If these local negotiators had constantly to be thinking about what the law might say, inhibitions, excessive caution and rigidity of response would almost certainly follow accompanied by a deterioration in workplace relations.

Nonetheless, section 34 must be seen in more than one timescale. While allowing for initial trade union opposition some managements may decide that any future agreements they negotiate should be more firmly structured, worded with greater care and precision with a view to their possible eventual transformation into contracts. Contracts may become a negotiable issue. Unionists are pragmatists.

A union, particularly if it is registered and therefore less directly constrained by TUC policy, may well reason: "If the price and conditions are right we are prepared to enter into a legally binding agreement, which includes a 'no strike' clause, for a period of two to three years." Some managements would doubtless pay quite a generous price for a period of peace and certainty of this length, if they were confident that the union could adequately enforce its undertaking. Three, even two years' stability, on the American pattern, could be an attractive proposition. A clean, open fight, if a fight came at all, at the end of the contract (again after the American pattern) would be much better than the constant, guerilla strikes which can so debilitate a company's performance.

The Act embraces two enforcement aspects both of which apply to employers as well as to unions. As mentioned above, it is an unfair industrial practice for any party to a legally binding agreement to break it or to break that part of an agreement, possibly a procedure agreement, which is legally binding. If, to put the position at its simplest, such an agreement or part of it *is* broken, then it becomes an unfair industrial practice for any party "not to take all such steps as are reasonably practicable" section 36 (2) "not to do its best,"—in the Department of Employment's terms, "to prevent or end any action by its members or agents (or anyone purporting to act on its behalf) which a legally enforceable term of the agreement binds it not to take" [9, p24]. Presumably, if workers struck in defiance of a legally binding "no strike" clause, union officials would put their organisation at legal risk if they did not "do their best" to achieve a return to work—whether by persuasion, exhortation, threats of fines or expulsion from membership remains to be determined on the circumstances of the case by the Court.

Registered and unregistered unions could be at risk, the achievement of legally binding agreements not being restricted to registered unions, a plain signal of the Government's hope that legal commitment will catch on whatever unions decide to do about registration.

Despite the probable initial rarity of legally enforceable collective agreements, the chances are that more firms (particularly the bigger ones) than in the past, will pay more attention to: clarifying who in the organisation has the authority to bargain about what; taking greater care to record arguments employed in negotiations; giving better form and greater precision to the agreements reached. Donovan strongly advocated such professionalism and greater codification. Informality can be contracted and formality expanded without damage to the flexibility of plant or company bargaining arrangements. Excessive informality drifts into chaos, excessive formality into absurd rigidity. But the point of balance does need to be moved in the direction of formality so that people do know in increasing measure where they stand, particularly in larger companies. Some worthy attempts are being made to that end [37].

Sections 34 and 35 of the Act may quicken the process, urged by Donovan and furthered by some of the early work of the CIR [23, 38] of clarification, codification and commitment as distinct from ambiguity, fractionalism and friction.

PROCEDURE AGREEMENTS

The absence of "satisfactory procedure agreements" may "in some cases . . . be an important contributory factor to poor industrial relations" [5, p16]. This quotation could well have come from the Donovan Report but is in fact taken from the Consultative Document, which on this point bears witness to the influence of the Donovan doctrine that "reform procedures whereby employers and unions regulate their joint relationships, and procedures will be better observed." "Satisfactory" and "poor" beg many questions but there is widespread agreement, not least between the major political parties, that some industrial strife is avoidable and could be avoided if procedures were improved. How is this desirable objective to be achieved?

Part of the improvement process entails information gathering. The 1964–70 Labour Government initiated the arrangements, approved by the CBI and TUC whereby employers were requested to supply copies of and answer questions about their procedure agreements. This information was collected by the Department of Employment, presumably for the purposes of analysis and eventual identification of inadequate procedures. Presumably the Department of Employment had ideas about the nature of "good" procedures. The Donovan Report certainly expressed its mind on the principles if not the detail of the "good" procedure and commissioned a number of valuable research papers on the procedural theme [39].

Information gathering about procedures is continued under the Act but the definition of "procedure agreement" under section 166 is so all-embracing as to warrant its quotation in full:

a Machinery for consultation with regard to, or for the settlement by negotiation or arbitration of, terms and conditions of employment
b Machinery for consultation with regard to, or for the settlement by negotiation or arbitration of, *other questions arising* between an employer or group of employers and one or more workers or organisations of workers
c Negotiating rights
d Facilities for officials of trade unions or other organisations of workers
Procedures relating to dismissal
f Procedures relating to matters of discipline other than dismissal
g Procedures relating to grievances of individual workers

It is difficult to think of any conventional feature of industrial relations omitted from the above list. Items (a) and (b) are particularly significant as they would seem to cover the machinery of *substantive* negotiations and might include, for example, JIC or Whitley Council machinery as well as company or plant bargaining arrangements. It would seem sensible to include "bargaining procedures on pay" with "procedures for avoidance of disputes" as the two are often closely interrelated and influence one another [37].

Information about these widely defined procedure agreements may be required as distinct from requested by the Secretary of State for Employment if he decides to make regulations under section 58. This enabling section itself is widely and flexibly drawn. Regulations may require:

"Every employer of any description specified" or "any particular employer":
1*a* To inform the Secretary of State whether he is a party to any procedure agreement or has agreed to observe such an agreement even if he is not party to it (a non-federated employer for example).
1*b* To provide a copy of any written procedure agreement (or particulars of any unwritten agreement) to which he is party.
1*c* To provide a copy of any written agreement (or particulars of an unwritten agreement) "to which he is not a party" but "whose terms he has agreed to observe as mentioned in paragraph (a)." If a copy of the written agreement has already been lodged (for example, by the federated employers) with the Secretary of State it

will be sufficient for the (non-federated) employer to identify the agreement he observes. If the agreement is unwritten "the prescribed particulars of it" must be "furnished."

1*d* To inform the Secretary of State *which descriptions of his employees fall within the terms of each procedure agreement* of which the employer is required by the regulations to furnish a copy or particulars, and *which (if any) descriptions of his employees do not fall within the terms of any such procedure agreement* and, in the case of each such description, to inform the Secretary of State how many employees of his fell within that description on the date by reference to which the information is given.

The core of section 58 has been presented in somewhat tedious detail in order to demonstrate the potential power of the Department of Employment to draw a pretty accurate and detailed map of the extent and nature of Britain's procedure agreements, of the workers who are covered by such agreements and those that are not. By workers is meant, potentially, the whole of Britain's employed labour force. Provision is made to keep the map continuously up to date by requiring employers to report what may be construed from the wording of the Act as objective technical changes in procedure and subjective assessment of the procedure's operation. Subsection (3) allows for the inclusion in the regulations of a requirement that every employer (covered above) furnish the Secretary of State "on the occurrence of any act or event of a prescribed description" with "such further information, or such copies of, or particulars of, procedure agreements, as may be prescribed."

As suggested above, such wording could reasonably be taken to include the duty to report a straightforward technical change to a procedure and the duty to report, for example, the number of times in a given period a procedure had been broken by unconstitutional action on the part of the workers. Instant reporting is not required of the employer. The regulations must allow a period of at least six months grace both in relation to the reporting of existing procedural arrangements and of "the occurrence of any act or event of a prescribed description" (s58(2)(4)). Flexibility is permitted the Secretary of State in that he can exempt from the regulations employers who have voluntarily furnished him with information of the kind required by subsection (1). Interestingly nothing is said of subsection (3). It is not clear whether this means that an employer who has a good record of voluntary notification, from the days when the 1964–70 Wilson Government initiated this process, can be exempted from the procedure notification but not from the "changes to and operation of" these arrangements notification. Notification loopholes seem unlikely as the self-evident need, whether by voluntary or statutory required arrangements, is for the up-dating of information about procedures and progress reports on their operation.

Section 58 permits and may even encourage *voluntary* notification. Section 59 is designed to deter non-compliance with the statutory duties imposed by regulations made under section 58. Section 59 provides one of the few instances in the Act where non-compliance can attract prosecution, conviction and a fine. Non-compliance with the regulations is a criminal offence for which "any person" is liable to a fine of up to £100. Presumably the "any person" would be from the management side of the table as it is the employer's duty to comply with the regulations. If false or inaccurate information is *knowingly* supplied by "any person" the maximum fine may be £400.

By a mix of pressures, therefore, it seems that the Government's intention is to have lodged with the Department of Employment a swelling volume of information of improved quality about procedural arrangements. Quality is important as the belief persists that some procedure agreements notified under the Department of Employment's original arrangements were more a product of the employer's imagination than a reflection of reality. An improved information bank should make it easier to identify procedures that are inadequate when checked against some model standards. Other procedures may at first sight be deemed inadequate because they are failing to cope with the tensions—the unruly industrial relations in a particular firm or industry. Such procedures, therefore, merit investigation with a view to their reform. Donovan, too, had this objective seeing in such reform the essential key to the resolution of many of Britain's industrial relations problems. But whereas Donovan strongly urged that reform should be based upon consent and saw the CIR as the main instrument of persuasion, the Act develops a different approach. The major difference from the Donovan reform by consent philosophy is the Act's provision for the imposition of reform if circumstances seem to warrant such a course. To represent the clash between the two approaches as reform by consent *v* reform by imposition would be misleadingly simple as will be shown.

There is now a clear and firm public policy expression of "model standards" for procedure agreements. Without going into fine detail the Code of Practice establishes some sound guiding principles for the creation of negotiating, consultation, grievance and disciplinary procedures. Adequacy of a procedure agreement, at least in the form of words it employs (and section 59 may encourage accuracy) can therefore be checked against a national code. Presumably it becomes part of the Department of Employment's educational function to help an employer reform a procedure that falls short of the Code's requirements. More serious procedural problems would be encompassed, at least technically, by sections 37–43 of the Act. The heading above these sections reads: "Remedial action where procedure agreement non-existent or defective" and should alert one to the complicated nature of the "due process" procedure for procedures which follows.

To start off in simple fashion—help is available to people who have procedural problems of one, or possibly more of the following kinds:

1 The absence of a procedure agreement (s37(1)(a))
2 A procedure agreement which is unsuitable for "settling disputes or grievances promptly and fairly" (s37(1)(a)). [How prompt is prompt and how fair is fair?]
3 A procedure in a condition of breakdown as manifested by "lock-outs, strikes or irregular industrial action short of a strike contrary to the terms or *intentions* of that agreement" (s37(1)(b))

Application to the Court for help may be made by the Secretary of State, the employer or *registered* trade union involved. Here is another instance of the state's powers under the Act to initiate proceedings with reform objectives in mind. If engineering employers and unions, who have been trying for years in an ill-tempered manner to replace the 1922 Avoidance of Disputes (York) Agreement with an improved procedure, failed to do so, there is something to be said in favour of the state referring the problem to independent investigation. The application could only be made in respect of a firm—or possibly two or more factories in the same group of companies—but not in relation to an industry (ss37, 43). But it is not difficult to think of key individual engineering employers who might qualify for such a reference on the section 37 (1)(b) criterion and where the results of the inquiry would be of wider significance for the engineering industry.

An employer *or* registered union may apply unilaterally to the Court. Presumably, as with the sole bargaining agent provisions, an employer could apply even though the procedure agreement to which he is party has been reached with an unregistered union. There is no obvious prohibition on such an employer making application and it would seem short-sighted if there were, given that the most vehemently anti-registration unions are not uncommonly involved in dispute-prone disputes procedures.

As many other provisions of the Act demonstrate, the issue is not simply one of putting an application/complaint into a smoothly running machine with the confident expectation that a remedy will be automatically delivered. Conciliation is to be given not one but several chances to promote a solution. The manner in which this is to be done has already been described.

The same flexible conciliatory approach persists through most of the subsequent stages of the "due process." The Court does not automatically refer an application for investigation to the CIR but checks whether section 37(1) conditions are present in "the unit of employment." If they are and as a consequence:

a The development or maintenance of orderly industrial relations in that unit has been seriously impeded, or

b There have been substantial and repeated losses of working time in that unit (s37(5))

—the problem is referred to the CIR. If the CIR considers the reference it receives needs to be widened in scope, in terms of the "unit of employment" to be examined, then after consulting the employer and trade union concerned, the CIR submits appropriate proposals to the Court. Such proposals are published and *any person* affected by them has two weeks in which, in effect, to challenge the boundary lines around the constituency to be investigated—clearly of importance in a multi-plant situation. Once the boundaries are defined the CIR can go ahead with its prime tasks of establishing the causes of the procedural problem, devising new procedures and attempting to *persuade* the parties concerned to accept their proposals. But even at the persuasive stage the CIR is charged with devising "new or revised provisions . . . *so formulated as to be capable of having effect as a legally enforceable contract*" (s39(3)).

Section 39(3) may spur the parties to reach a voluntary procedural agreement before the CIR has completed its reference. Whatever the stimulus, if the CIR (before its own work is finished) considers sufficient progress towards such a solution has been made by the parties themselves, the CIR may so report to the Court. ". . . where such a report has been made, the Industrial Court, on the application of any of the parties to the reference, may withdraw the reference" (s39(4)). Up to this stage it will be clear that ample provision is made for the traditional principle of self-government to prevail.

If a reference is not withdrawn the CIR soldiers on and produces its procedural reform report to the Court—"a report setting out such new or revised provisions as in their opinion are required and would be capable of having effect as a legally enforceable contract" (s40(1)). The report is to indicate the extent to which the parties agree to any of the recommended provisions. At this point the report's recommendations have only a persuasive not a legally binding force. Presumably if the parties accepted and implemented the provisions they would still be free to add a "Tina Lea" disclaimer so that the provisions did not become legally enforceable. It is this legally enforceable aspect of the CIR's work, not least in relation to section 41, that partly explains the TUC's policy of non-co-operation with the CIR.

Section 41 is undoubtedly controversial. Within six months of the CIR's report, on *unilateral* application a procedural solution may be imposed on the parties by the Court. "Any employer or trade union included among the parties to the reference may apply . . ." to the Court for an imposition order. Clearly the Secretary of State may not apply. Unregistered unions although they may not apply may be involved for the procedure provisions may obviously affect both registered and unregistered unions. Unless the Court "is satisfied that an order . . . is not necessary for . . . securing acceptance and observance of the provisions recommended . . ." by the CIR, "the Court shall make an order." The effect of such an order would be to translate the provisions into "a legally enforceable contract" as if it had been made between the parties.

It can, of course, be argued that if disputing parties know an application for an order may be made and granted, they may feel encouraged to accept recommended provisions more readily. It can be counter-argued that the threat of legal sanctions can prompt some people to greater intransigence. What remains fact, as distinct from speculation, is that never before have we sought in such a way to impose, on the application of one party, procedural arrangements, as distinct from substantive standards, on another.

It can be claimed that the complex "due process" contained in sections 37–43 bends over backwards to facilitate voluntary accommodation before the law is invoked let alone applied against what must obviously be a mulishly stubborn party. Even at one minute to high noon the stubborn party could see sense, thus allowing the Court to be convinced that an "order . . . is not necessary." If an order is made, provision exists for self-government to reassert itself for the parties may apply jointly to the Court for the order to be varied or revoked. The Court has no discretion for it must carry out the wishes of the parties (s42(2)).

On unilateral application by one of the parties the Court may revoke the order if it "is satisfied that the order is no longer necessary for the purpose of securing observance of the provisions." Before making up its mind on this point the Court may seek the CIR's help. (Unilateral application for variation of the order is not possible.) Unlike the sole-bargaining-agent or agency-shop orders there is no minimum period for which an imposed procedure agreement order is to run. Application for such an order to be revoked can be made at any time. Revocation on joint application is made immediately as indicated. Revocation on unilateral application is likely to be harder to come by as it does not rest on joint consent.

These highly involved procedures may appeal to some because of their neat, lawyer's logic and their legally enforceable content. Major misgivings, for exactly the same reasons, may be felt by others. It is one thing for the Industrial Arbitration Board to impose a new contractual wage rate or overtime premium on an employer but quite another for the Court to make legally binding a procedural arrangement which attempts to regulate relationships between dozens, hundreds, possibly thousands of people and varied organised sectional interests as these all bump into one another in the course of daily working life.

But again it has to be conceded that because the law is there people's behaviour may begin to change in ways Donovan advocated. Keeping out of the clutches of the law may be one spur to procedural reform. Let us hope so.

10

Pressures to Improve Collective Bargaining

DEVELOPING THE UNDERDEVELOPED: ENRICHING THE PROCESS

As our industrial relations system begins to change its character under the impact of the Act, it is understandable that the interest of the public and commentators should be concentrated on the dramatic changes—the cooling-off order applied to the railway dispute of April 1972—the £55000 fine imposed by the Court against the T & GWU for contempt of court—also in April 1972 ("April is the cruellest month . . ."[40])—a decision upheld by the House of Lords in July 1972.

Such spectacular events including the committal to prison of five dockers in July 1972 and the attention that such events attract make all the more important an adequate examination of what the Act may do to those sectors of employment which by definition have been underdeveloped and underprivileged because legal minimum rates of pay and conditions have been established for them by wage councils.

WAGES COUNCILS

In recent times some 3½ million "underprivileged" workers have worked in wages council trades—a far greater number than the estimated 100000 workers engaged in the incipient General Strike in July 1972. This is not to argue that miners and railwaymen are particularly privileged. Who could possibly maintain that the lowest paid miners and railwaymen are anything but poorly paid? But the railway unions and the NUM are sufficiently powerful to wrest a better deal from their employers, and at one remove from the Government, and at two removes from the tax-payer, than is for example USDAW from Britain's myriad small shopkeepers, where both USDAW and the shopkeepers are affected by wages councils. Without the wages councils prop, too many shop assistants would probably be less well-paid than at present. What then does the Act do to the wages council situation?

Inevitably the technical nature of the law obscures the underlying purpose of the changes made to the Wages Councils Act 1959, by the Industrial Relations Act 1971. The underlying purpose is revealed, if not fully, in paragraph 157 of the Consultative Document:

> The Government believes that greater progress can now be made in promoting the growth of voluntary arrangements for collective bargaining in Wages Councils industries, and accelerating the abolition of councils which have outlived their usefulness, by amending the Wages Councils Act, 1959, and the Terms and Conditions of Employment Act, 1959, broadly on the lines recommended by the Donovan Commission [5, p21].

We are not told of the evidence which brought the Government to the belief that the accelerated abolition of wages councils is desirable. It seems to be implied that the belief should not be construed as illiberal for the liberal Donovan Commission held a similar belief. Motives having less congruence with Donovan philosophy may be guessed at if not established: the desire to reduce state expenditure in running the wages council system, particularly the salary bill for enforcement by wages inspectors; the desire to reduce the amount of Government intervention; the desire to encourage people to stand on their own feet and fend for themselves. Consistent with occasional flurries of public policy concern, expressed during the past twenty-five years, that abolition should proceed at a brisker pace, the Government may desire that JICs should rise Phoenix-like from the ashes of incinerated "lame-duck" wages councils. Some reservations on this last point are expressed below.

Trade unions have been divided in their views on the speed-up of abolition issue. The major pro-abolitionist has been the T & GWU this union believing that wages councils get in the way of the development of more generous voluntary wages settlements, particularly in road transport. USDAW, on the other hand, the union with the biggest investment in the wages councils system, has been much more cautious—an understandable stance given the immense difficulties of attracting and retaining in membership sufficient numbers of a retail trade's labour force, characterised by high turnover, a high incidence of part-time employment, a high proportion of women employees and dispersion through many small units of employment. Another major wages council union, the NUTGW (garment workers) has been criticised for using the garment trades' wages councils as crutches instead of springboards [41]. In the light of this PIB criticism (much oversimplified by my crutch/springboard analogy) it came as no surprise that in January 1972, the CIR received a batch of abolition variation references for ten garment wages councils.

What the Act does is to facilitate the initiation of an abolition challenge and to change the criteria against which the abolition claim is to be tested. The criteria are so altered as to facilitate abolition. First, a consideration of the new challenge set in a brief historical context.

When the wages councils system was massively expanded by the Wages Councils Act 1945, provision was made for a council to be abolished on the joint application to the Minister of the employers and unions concerned. If adequate voluntary bargaining machinery had been constructed, the statutory prop could be withdrawn on joint request. Despite continuous and widely prevailing full employment, an important safeguard if not complete guarantee against low wages, few wage councils were abolished between 1945 and 1959. With the enactment of the Wages Councils Act 1959 the opportunity was taken to quicken the abolition process, public policy remaining the promotion of JICs in substitution for wages councils.

The 1959 Act enabled the Minister to initiate the abolition preliminaries of investigation and assessment. Judicious use of "ministerial initiative" powers, it was thought, might spur employers and unions into livelier activity concerning the creation of JICs. Measured against that objective, the strengthened abolition procedure achieved but a very moderate success between 1959 and 1971. As a result of the Industrial Relations Act, while the pace of wages council abolition may well increase, the pace of the hitherto corollary of abolition—JIC creation—may well be slowed down even to the point of stagnation. The reasons for saying so will shortly be made clear.

To the "joint application" and "ministerial initiative," the Act adds a third means of accelerating abolition. Schedule 8, which amends the Wages Councils Act 1959, provides that an abolition inquiry can be applied for "by any organisation of workers which represents a substantial proportion of the workers with respect to whom that wages council operates." The right to make such application to the Secretary of State for Employment is not restricted to registered trade unions. It is ironic that the union which in other circumstances would be most likely to apply unilaterally for the abolition of a wages council will probably not do so because of its opposition to the Act. The unregistered T & GWU has for years been keen to see the Road Haulage Wages Council abolished, believing this council to be a shelter for many road haulage firms content to pay low basic wages to drivers.

While "a substantial proportion of the workers" is an elastic rather than rigid standard, it will doubtless be carefully applied. Most workers' sides of wages councils are multi-union in character. It would be wrong and possibly mischievous for a union with minority representation on a council and therefore in the industry, when compared to other unions, to set in motion the abolition procedure.

Interesting is the exclusion of an employer and employers' associations from the right of making unilateral application for abolition. One possible inference is that our legislators incline to the view that on the whole employers, rather than trade unions, are concerned to maintain the status quo of our wages councils system. Providing unions with the potential to disturb that status quo may be good not just for the union and its members but for the industry in which the disturbance is created. More dynamic and progressive bargaining relationships might result from abolition or even potential abolition but that prediction is a matter for the applicant union, rather than the employers, to assess. Some union confident of its ability to shake up sluggish wages council employers, may *eventually* make unilateral application for a council's abolition.

Whether "unilateral" or "joint" the Secretary of State screens abolition applications. Screening joint applications would seem to be a formality. Screening union unilateral applications will presumably command greater attention, both because the process is new and because a party is involved whose consent to prospective abolition has not been forthcoming. It will be possible to form some assessment of the latter form of screening only in the light of experience. The screening ("considering" is the Act's term) is with a view to the making of an abolition order.

Technically, the Secretary of State could abolish a wages council on joint or unilaterial application, if he considered the grounds of the application sufficient for such action (1959 Act s6(1)(a)). Most probably the application, particularly if unilateral, will be referred to independent investigation. If the Secretary of State decides to set the abolition ball rolling, he refers the matter to such an agency. For many years the independent investigation which preceded the establishment, abolition or variation in scope of operation, of a wages council, was carried out by tripartite, *ad hoc* commissions of inquiry. All this work has now become the responsibility of the CIR, an institutional change which should strengthen consistency of investigation and recommendations.

Applications for abolition orders, as distinct from ministerial initiatives to that end, must be made on the grounds that:

> The existence of a wages council is no longer necessary for the purpose of maintaining a reasonable standard of remuneration for the workers with respect to whom that wages council operates (s5(2)) of Wages Councils Act as modified by the Industrial Relations Act).

This joint and unilateral application criterion constitutes a radical change to the past criterion which applied to joint application when the grounds were:

> That the organisations jointly provide, machinery which is, and is likely to remain, adequate for the effective regulation of remuneration and conditions of employment . . . (s5(2) 1959 Act).

In practical terms application for abolition is not now conditional upon the claim that a JIC is ready to take on and improve the work done by a wages council. Admittedly a joint application would seem to suggest the existence of some form of joint representative body. Admittedly a union can now seek to prise reluctant employers away from the defences of a moribund wages council and have them engage in livelier company and plant bargaining. But complete substitution of "a reasonable standard of remuneration" assertion for the "adequate JIC" assertion is disturbing and becomes increasingly so as the argument is advanced.

When an abolition issue was referred to a commission of inquiry, the commission was required to consider:

> The extent to which there is, and is likely to remain, adequate machinery (joint and voluntary) for the effective regulation of remuneration and conditions of employment . . . (of the workers concerned) (1959 Act s6(2)(*a*)).

This provision is deleted by the Industrial Relations Act. No alternative abolition criterion is provided. The CIR is simply required to report. The nature of the report's recommendation to is be no different from before: abolition, variation or retention of the wages council/s in question. The central question remains: against what criteria is the CIR to assess the abolition case in the absence of express criteria? It may well be that the CIR will pay close attention to "a reasonable standard of remuneration" which is part of the *application* criterion. The Consultative Document maintained that: "The only condition to be satisfied before a wages council can be abolished should be that the council is no longer necessary to maintain reasonable standards of remuneration . . ." [5, p22]. "Reasonable standard" by its very nature eludes precise definition. Is a reasonable standard to be calculated only for the lowest paid grade in the industry or for higher grades as well, as is standard wages council practice? Shall we be working towards some concept of a notional minimum entitlement to pay for each industry, a group of industries, the whole of industry? How is a "reasonable standard of remuneration to be maintained"—by collective bargaining, by a JIC? Doubtless the CIR will take into account an industry's institutional arrangements for wage determination but as pointed out above, the existence of a JIC is *not now a prerequisite* of abolition.

Conventional economic wisdom of the past has claimed that full employment ensures a reasonable standard. Research has shown that such thinking needs to be seriously qualified [42]. In any event there seems no immediate or even short-term prospect of a return to full employment.

It is a major purpose of a union's existence to have views about reasonable standards of pay. But there are no trade union CIR commissioners. While CIR staff will carry out the necessary researches, commissioners must take responsibility for the recommendations that are finally framed. Managerial commissioners may well take a different view of a reasonable standard from the workers themselves, the unions, or union commisioners on a tripartite CIR.

CIR investigators assigned to abolition inquiries have no easy task given the sensitive state of industrial relations and the probes to be made into the underdeveloped areas of collective bargaining. A large part of the investigators' work must be data, information and opinion gathering. Officially the unions are boycotting the CIR and so the bizarre unofficial position is reached where the Department of Employment is used as a post box by the unions so that their evidence may be unofficially forwarded for examination by the CIR.

A few other points merit a mention. "Effective regulation of remuneration and conditions of employment" (1959 Act) would seem to be significantly different from "a reasonable standard of remuneration" (1971 Act). Why have conditions of employment been omitted from the abolition test? The Consultative Document is silent about the omission. Theoretically it might be argued: "Even though the standard hours are long and holidays poor under this wages council, the pay is reasonable and therefore the council should be abolished." Such a recommendation would hardly seem likely to improve the lot of the weakest wages council workers whose weekly hours might well have been longer and their holidays poorer but for the wages council.

On the other hand, the "effective" in "effective regulation" seemed sometimes to place more stress on maintaining bargaining relationships than determining a reasonable level of pay. Some wages councils have "effectively regulated" at a low level of basic rates. Nonetheless, collective bargaining machinery of a kind existed. Now the stress seems to be on level of pay rather than adequacy of bargaining machinery. The reasons for this change of emphasis, for this break with the long-established public policy of fostering effective self-government through the creation of JICs, have not been made clear. It can be said that other parts of the Act such as the new statutory right to join a (registered) union should help union organisation and the development of voluntary bargaining machinery in the wages council trades. Such optimism is questionable. Misgivings remain that the new abolition criteria suggest more of the cost-saving exercise and reflection of market forces philosophy than a promotion of collective bargaining commitment. While retaining unilateral application (by the union) it would have been possible to combine both the old and the new abolition criteria: "adequate voluntary machinery" (which can take forms other than the JIC) and "effective regulation of a reasonable standard of pay *and* conditions."

Without seeking to pre-judge the CIR's work and recommendations it would not be reckless to wager that if the Laundry Wages Council were abolished on the criterion of "reasonable standard of remuneration," the gap between the rich and the poor laundry worker would grow wider. Whatever its deficiencies a wages council does establish a floor of graded rates on which varieties of wage superstructures can be built by unilateral management action or voluntary collective bargaining. If that floor were taken away because laundry pay, at all work grade levels, seemed reasonable and likely to remain so, then with no wages inspectors for the trade, scant union organisation, outside the Co-op and the National Health Service, the pay of the lower paid laundry workers in small laundries under fierce commercial competition would seem almost certain to decline relative to the better paid. The risk of substituting the vagaries of labour market forces for a bargaining institution is one that the CIR will need to weigh very carefully. The following statement reinforces the point:

> The present [wages council] legislation specifies in detail the criteria, concerning the extent and adequacy of existing negotiating machinery to be applied by ad hoc commissions of inquiry. With the change in the grounds for abolition and the substitution of the CIR for ad hoc commissions of inquiry, these provisions would *no longer be relevant* and it is proposed to remove them from the Act [5, p22].

How neat! If *B* is substituted for *A*, *A* is no longer relevant. What is not given are reasons for the lack of relevance of the "fostering collective bargaining" criteria. Such reticence justifies the relevance of the length and character of the wages council discussion in this chapter.

ISSUES OF QUALITY: DISCLOSURE OF INFORMATION

After features of the Act which clearly affect the *quantity* of collective bargaining carried out come sections which concern the *quality* of collective bargaining. Section 56 has aroused particular interest in managerial circles. This section places a statutory duty on the employer to disclose information to trade union representatives "for the purposes of *all the stages* of collective bargaining." Such information is to be all that relating to the undertaking which is both:

a Information without which the trade union representatives would be to a material extent impeded in carrying on collective bargaining with him, and

b Information which it would be in accordance with good industrial relations practice that the employer should disclose to them for purposes of collective bargaining

These requirements are so general, so question-begging that management's anxiety to know what section 56 means in practice is hardly surprising. Before examining practical issues some procedural points may be mentioned. Only the representatives of *registered* trade unions have a statutory right to section 56 information. But no prohibition is placed on the employer to give such information to representatives of unregistered unions. (A trade union representative is defined by section 56(5) as an official—which includes shop-stewards, or other authorised representatives.) No employer shall be required to disclose confidential information as defined in section 158(1). Protected information includes the conventional categories of "in the interests of national security, of the individual, of information obtained in confidence."

A registered union may complain to the Court that an employer has failed to fulfil his section 56 duty (s102). If the Court considers the claim well founded, it may (providing "it would be just and equitable to do so") issue an order authorising the union to present its claim to the Industrial Arbitration Board. The procedure which then follows has been outlined in Chapter 2. Additionally, or alternatively, the Court may determine the rights of the parties by order and direct the employer by order to fulfil his statutory duty to disclose information.

Employers must, if so requested by (registered) trade union representatives, provide "the relevant" information in writing (s56(3)) but further safeguards for confidential information and against excessive work and expense in preparing information are contained in section 56(4). In short an employer cannot be required to provide copies of or allow access to *all* his files, records and data. His duty is to select and furnish that information deemed, by the Court if necessary, to be desirable for unimpeded collective bargaining and "good industrial relations practice." Ample scope for argument appears to exist in "to a material extent impeded"—section 56(1)(a) above, "an amount of work or expenditure out of reasonable proportion to the value of the information"—section 56(4)(b) and other terms in the section.

Section 56(2) provides that the Code of Practice shall give guidance on how the "good industrial relations practice" information requirement of section 56(1)(b) shall be met. While the three paragraphs (96, 97, 98) under the heading "Disclosure of information" in the code are fairly innocuous in themselves, it must be remembered that many parts of the code "require," by implication, disclosure of information. Paragraph 97 does make the specific point that management "should make available (to trade unions) in the most convenient form, the information which is supplied to shareholders or published in annual reports."

More significant is the footnote to this page (22) of the code which refers to the anticipated CIR report on "disclosure of information" which is to form the basis of the eventual revision of the sections of the code concerned with disclosure. The CIR received its disclosure of information reference in May 1970 and at one time was under intense pressure to produce its report by the late summer of 1971. The report [63] eventually appeared in September 1972. This period of labour produced twenty-nine pages of text and twenty-eight pages of appendices, a somewhat modest contribution perhaps, at least in quantity terms, to the disclosure debate. But—"soon after we began our inquiries, the trade unions, acting in line with TUC policy, withdrew co-operation from the Commission" [63, p3]. Such withdrawal must have hampered the effectiveness of the case study investigations carried out in ninety-seven establishments. Some trade union views on disclosure were, of course, available in various publications [43] including written evidence to the Donovan Commission.

The CIR did not restrict its inquiries to Britain but studied and reported upon disclosure practices in Sweden, France, West Germany, the Netherlands and the USA. In Britain "the trade union case for more extensive disclosure of information rests on two main arguments" . . . the need to bargain more effectively for their members and the "wish to extend their sphere of influence and involvement into matters previously determined unilaterally by management . . . policies and decisions which affect the working lives of their members" [63, p13]. Management reactions to increased disclosure varied but a particularly sensitive area for protection, as management see it, is a "detailed breakdown of cost and pricing information" which could damage a firm's competitive position.

The CIR identified two main views concerning the value of information for negotiations. To oversimplify for the purpose of contraction, the "power school" believes that what matters is the strength at their command, the skills and aptitudes of the negotiators in striving for their objectives, with information serving more a propaganda than objective purpose. The opposing "idealist" school believes that information can be used as an "objective reference point" which can mean more rational bargaining, diminishing "both the area of conflict and aggressive attitudes" [63, p16].

The CIR identify their own central dilemma of "reconciling general principles with particular local circumstances . . ." and properly see as inadequate a general shopping list of requirements which might be inappropriate for many individual situations. Inevitably, therefore, the report ends somewhat lamely with two sets of guidelines and the cautious preface that:

> All the items mentioned are suitable in principle for disclosure and have been disclosed in actual practice. Whether and in what degree any particular item should be disclosed depends on the bargaining circumstances and the considerations set out in the later guidelines on conditions and methods" [63, p27].

The first set of guidelines is concerned with "types of information" under the following headings: organisation and activities of the employing unit, manpower, pay, conditions, financial information, prospects and plans. The second set refers to "conditions and methods" comprising: need and relevance, availability, timing, "seriously prejudicial" information, confidential information, multi-plant firms, productivity bargaining, industry-wide bargaining, training.

This CIR report, if unexciting, could provide a sensible base for expansion providing as it does a well-reasoned *method of approach* to the issues involved in disclosure as distinct from drawing up detailed lists of information "goodies." It will, for example, be interesting to see what develops out of the CIR's guideline on "seriously prejudicial" information which reads:

> The reasons why information is seriously prejudicial should be explained, if possible, *and be capable of standing up to independent investigation if challenged.* Ways of providing information in a form which meets the need but avoids disclosing seriously prejudicial information should be sought, e.g. by use of charts, indices or percentages.

"Seriously prejudicial" is a phrase that appears in section 158(1)(e) of the Act, a section that, among other things, is designed to protect the competitive position of the employer in relation to the disclosure of information. E J Robertson has well illustrated some of the thorny snags jutting from section 158(1)(e):

> . . . the legislation clearly envisages that, while the release of certain sorts of information (for example, we might surmise, stock levels, cash flow situations, forward orders) may be prejudicial to the commercial interests of the employer, it may also be prejudicial to his collective bargaining strength and is not to be exempted from disclosure only for that latter reason. Thus, an employer would have to be certain that his stock levels of a given product on the eve of a strike was information of a type vital to his competitors to defend himself against giving this crucial information to his trade union representatives. The example is a crude one, but it does not take much wit to see that certain sorts of information are of immense importance to the trade unions in deciding not only whether or not to pursue a claim to the point of striking, but how long to keep the strike going" [37, p107].

Indeed, it needs little imagination, let alone wit, to envisage how "protection of competitive position" considerations may be intricately interwoven with "duty to disclose information for collective bargaining" considerations.

Information is one dimension of power. Mr Robertson rightly points out in the same article that unions will be concerned to obtain information which will shift the balance of power in their favour. In this connection, a few notable attempts to raise the level of sophistication of bargaining have been made in the last few years, particularly the T & GWU case to Fords [44] and the Chemical Workers Union case to ICI. But Ruskin

College, Oxford (Trade Union Research Unit), inspired swallows do not make a summer. Conceivably section 56, and its cluster of associated sections, may help to increase the number of swallows. Whatever the risks and ambiguities entailed these sections appear to be aimed at raising the level of expertise employed in collective bargaining and thereby hopefully improving the tone of industrial relations.

A vital concomitant of the disclosure of information provisions is the training of a greater number of people, particularly on the trade union side, in order that the enlarged information market be used in knowledgeable, imaginative and constructive ways. The Act is not very vocal on industrial relations training. The Code at several points recommends the value of industrial relations training and clearly indicates (para 118) that shop-steward training should be accepted as a joint management/union responsibility. The CIR produced an industrial relations training report in November 1972 [84]. But in their disclosure report devote only one short paragraph to "training in the use of information." It may still be wondered whether this body of activities is sufficient to the needs of the situation, not least because of the cultural and time-lag that could develop between information supplied and information adequately understood and handled. (The Labour Government's Industrial Relations Bill revealed awareness of this issue by making provision for public money to be spent on industrial relations training for trade unionists.)

While it is one thing to establish, under the Act, the broad contours of disclosure, and even some of these are understandably fuzzy, it is quite another to undertake detailed cartography. The $2\frac{1}{2}$ inches to the mile scale may well have to be established by case law. And yet, for too many employers section 56 will remain a non-event as such employers have no representatives of either registered or unregistered unions to whom collective bargaining information can be given.

11

Handling (Mishandling) Industrial Conflict—I

Organisation, recognition, bargaining, agreement and the Act's involvement with these matters have been considered. Disagreement now comes under scrutiny. Supporters would claim that many of the Act's procedural provisions should avert a significant number of disagreements which in the past have erupted into overt conflict. A union need no longer strike to win recognition from an employer because orderly procedures have been devised to handle recognition claims. A walk-out is no longer so necessary to ensure that justice is done to an unfairly dismissed worker. Pressure can be applied to the parties concerned to reform out-of-date procedures and thereby materially reduce the causes and incidence of industrial conflict. In this procedural reform approach the Act bears affinities with the major recommendations of the Donovan Commission and part of *In Place of Strife*. Where the Act differs radically from Donovan but less so from *In Place of Strife* is on the issue of sanctions against strikes.

Sanctions can, technically, be applied against micro and macro strikes—against the action of a handful of men in the firm just down the road, against the action of several hundred thousand railwaymen nationally, and against all groups in between. But, and this but is a big but, certain conditions have to be met before sanctions can be sought and obtained. Sanctions is a misnomer, if a convenient term, for the remedies which may be claimed by the injured party against the party allegedly committing the defined unfair industrial practice or nationally damaging dispute. Injured parties could include the smallest of employers and the community on whose behalf the Secretary of State for Employment would intercede.

SECTION 96

Section 96 which is concerned with the generality of "unfair industrial practice" strikes is so important as to warrant its almost complete quotation:

96(1) It shall be an unfair industrial practice for any person, in contemplation or furtherance of an industrial dispute, knowingly to induce or threaten to induce another person to break a contract to which that other person is a party, unless the person so inducing or threatening to induce the breach of contract—

a Is a trade union or an employers' association, or

b Does so within the scope of his authority on behalf of a trade union or an employers' association . . .

(3) In this section "contract"—

a Does not include a collective agreement or any part of a collective agreement, but

b Notwithstanding anything in the preceding paragraph, includes so much of any contract of employment as is implied or incorporated in that contract by reference to a collective agreement

Without beating about or even into the many bushes of legalistic interpretation that have sprung up around section 96, it can be said without fear of contradiction that the intention of this section is to put at legal risk the organisers of the wildcat strike. Justification for such a policy is said to lie in the need to check the misuse of power, expressed in unconstitutional strikes—the British disease, which has so harmed our reputation in export markets. How is this legal risk created and what effect is it likely to have on industrial relations? Although the creation process is somewhat complicated it remains far easier to answer the first than the second part of that question.

It is apparent from subsection (3) that any legal proceedings are to be rooted in and routed through individual contracts of employment rather than collective agreements. A collective agreement may well provide that "there shall be no strike or lock-out until the above (avoidance of disputes) procedure has been exhausted." Such a provision might be deemed to be "implied or incorporated" in the individual contracts of employment of the workers concerned but a "Tina Lea" (this is not a legally enforceable agreement) disclaimer clause would seem to weaken seriously that possibility. Nonetheless, if workers go on strike in breach of procedure some among them *may* fall foul of the law under subsection (1). The "some" of some workers is critically important because it is the intention to put at legal risk *not* the mass of unconstitutional strikers but their *organisers* if certain constitutional conditions are not met. Technically the problem of potential *mass* defiance of the law has been averted.

Many inducers of unconstitutional action are potentially at risk. Unregistered organisations, in reality this means unregistered trade unions, fall automatically into this group and so do their strike leaders even though such leaders may have been authorised by their union to take inducing action in relation to an official—backed by the union—strike. So much is clear by the restriction of protection to registered unions and their *authorised* organisers by 1 (a) and (b). In short a registered union may safely induce a breach of contract 1(a) "in contemplation or furtherance of an industrial dispute" and so may members who are duly authorised by the registered union 1(b). If such members are not so authorised they will be at risk.

In plain terms, a major practical implication of "within the scope of his authority" is that registered unions need to authorise their stewards to "induce" if stewards given to inducing are to be protected. Few registered unions are likely to authorise their stewards to call strikes. The fact that stewards (equating them with the inducers for the convenience of argument) of registered unions are likely to remain unprotected may prompt them to behave more cautiously, to observe the constitution of the disputes procedure rather than organise a walk-out. This, of course, is the hope of the legislators and the logic of their optimistic case applies equally to stewards of unregistered unions.

Stewards may think two or three times before resorting to unconstitutional action—in breach of a procedure agreement—whereas previously a wildcat had become an almost automatic reflex to "provocative" managerial action or inactivity in a strike-happy plant. (A further check to stewards calling strikes has been created by the important House of Lords ruling [52] which held the union concerned ". . . responsible for the acts of its shop stewards," an issue discussed in the next chapter.) Such reasoning is persuasive, neat and consistent with the Act's concern to have power identified, authorised and used in a constitutional manner—as defined by the Act. It is this very neatness and the consistency that arouse unease because such qualities of tidiness may be ill-suited to the search for the flexible accommodations that are often needed where a strong sense of injustice is felt by workers and emotions are running high. Much will depend on the extent to which section 96 is invoked, a point to which later reference will be made.

We now approach, with caution, the critical word in section 96: induce. Caution is needed because although lawyers may enjoy the intellectual exercise induced by attempts to define "induce," the word seems to elude precise definition. One lawyer has put the position very cogently in terms from which the following are *only excerpts:*

> It does not mean that if three or four workmen spontaneously walk off the job together that each has induced the other to break his contract . . . .
>
> Again, if the conditions of work in a factory are intolerable as, for example, where the premises are overheated or very badly ventilated . . . and one worker induces the others to walk out, there will be no inducement of a breach of contract because the employer in these circumstances would be in breach of contract himself . . . .
>
> The term "to induce" imports in law an element of deliberation: it must be shown that the person who does something which may result in someone else breaking his contract intended that what he did should have that consequence . . . the [TV] commentator will not be guilty of inducing that strike unless it can be shown that it was his intention to cause it.
>
> A person cannot be charged with inducing a breach of contract the existence of which he did not know [bear in mind the use of the word "knowingly" in section 96].
>
> Lastly, the breach of contract must be shown to have resulted in damage to the other party to it.
>
> Idle threats would not be sufficient (it is suggested) to constitute an unfair industrial practice; the threat must have some kind of reality: there must be the likelihood that the person making it could achieve the result he was threatening [13, pp73–5].

Despite these reservations and subtleties, it would seem much more likely than not that most of our pre-Act lightning strikes would be unfair industrial practices within the meaning of section 96. So what may happen in the case of post-Act lightning strikes? Nothing *need* happen, at least in terms of litigation, unless someone complains of an unfair industrial practice to the Court. The someone is most likely to be, but is not restricted to, the "struck" employer. As indicated above, the contract alleged to have been broken is not restricted to the contract of employment. (Five types of contract were identified in the 1972 docks container dispute.) As pointed out on page 28, section 101 provides that the Court may issue one or more of the following remedies—a rights order, compensation, an injunction.

As the "struck" employer is the most likely complainant (and plenty of complaints in the non-legalistic sense were made by employers in the years of lobbying that preceded this law) we will look at his position. Two main issues seem to arise for his consideration: the feasibility and the desirability of his complaining to the Court. If proceedings are to be undertaken against individuals rather than an organisation then clearly the "inducers" have to be identified. Can the employer be certain he has identified all of them? If he cannot or has not, he is open to the charge of victimisation and may unwittingly create martyrs.

How is the employer to obtain his evidence? He may be trapped into a situation where with or without justification he can be accused, in very emotional terms, of sending managerial spies among the workers. Given the ingenuity of human nature, it is easy to imagine that some workforces would ensure that the inducing was carried out not just by the stewards but by a much larger number of workers, so that the organisation of the unconstitutional strike was frequently passed from one small group to another. Such tactics could make it very difficult to establish who at any particular point in time were the inducers.

Whereas shop-stewards have often justifiably claimed that they are trying to keep the men at work, or get them back, not take or keep them out, such a claim could become a "front" behind which other inducers organised the industrial action. Relatively little imagination is required to devise guerilla tactics. However, the desire to take part in such manoeuvres is likely to be held by relatively few workers. It is to be hoped that management do not fan that desire, which could easily be done, if section 96 were used on *every* occasion when its use was technically justified.

Assuming the employer can identify the inducers would he be wise to take legal action against them? If asked this question the issue uppermost in most managements minds would almost certainly be: "Will using section 96 improve or worsen our labour relations? They could hardly remain the same if we initiated legal proceedings." It might be argued that if the lance was judiciously applied, a little blood-letting could usefully reduce the temperature of a feverish industrial relations patient.

Other thoughts might run as follows: "If the grounds of action were carefully chosen, would the eventual legal ruling (assumed favourable to us) establish a useful precedent and curb the incidence of wildcat strikes in our other plants? Should we rather wait and see what case law emerges and take our cues from this? There are sure to be some employers more ready than us to put their heads on the block. An American owned firm, given that the Americans are used to operating in a complicated framework of labour law, may chance its arm on section 96. After all it was Fords of Britain that sought to establish in a High Court action [45] that their collective agreement with the unions was legally binding. [This view should be set against the claim that 'the strategy was developed by the English labor relations staff' [57, p119]. If we seek an injunction against the inducers will it be obeyed? If it is not will the six men, if persistently defiant, be sent to jail for contempt of court? Shall we then have a massive official 'due notice' strike on our hands which we would not otherwise have had? If we seek compensation there will inevitably be some delay between filing the complaint and the hearing taking place. The three-day strike, as it might well prove to be, might have been over several weeks, several months before the claim for compensation is heard. Old wounds could be reopened. Will the men refuse to pay—even on the 'never never' system? If they do pay shall we be faced by the shop-stewards, the Works Council, with a request to hold a disco or a bingo session in the canteen, the purpose of which we know is to raise money to reimburse the 'victimised' inducers? Shop-floor raffles to the same end would be likely to increase. If the Court ruling is unfavourable to the inducers on Monday we may well get a very dusty response from the rest of the workforce when we tell them we want them to work overtime for the rest of the week." So one could multiply the conjectures—which are far from unrealistic.

Although some employers and employer groupings pressed clamorously for sanctions against wildcat strikers and irresponsible unions in the pre-Donovan era, few people are really surprised that once given such sanctions employers are wary of invoking them. This is not to say that section 96 is without effect. Taken with other sections of the Act and features in the code of practice, section 96 adds to the pressures on management to overhaul and reform the industrial relations system in which they operate —to reform grievance and disciplinary procedures, to improve facilities for shop-stewards, to engage in more industrial relations training—thereby ameliorating some of the probable causes of wildcat action. If such reform programmes are reasonably successful, the need, assuming there is one, for the direct use of section 96 correspondingly declines.

It remains a point of nice moral interest whether those who pressed hardest for section 96 type sanctions are under an obligation to use them. In reality the point is unlikely to bother many managers for very long because managers will relate the use or non-use of section 96 to their immediate working contexts rather than their external political commitments or sympathies. Their central thought is likely to be: "Let us so try and shape events that we do not feel impelled to use section 96." No legal compulsion, we must remember, is placed on an injured party to seek the remedy that is technically available to him.

The real potential dangers to the quiet, unspectacular management overhaul of industrial relations policies and practices lurk on the extreme right and left of our political and industrial systems—among those employers that would enjoy "bashing the stewards" and those workers that would joyfully defy the law in order to secure martyrdom and historical importance. These dangers relate not only to the use of section 96 but to all parts of the Act which enable *A* to achieve an injunction remedy against *B*, thereby opening up the redress/defiance dilemma. Section 96 happens to be a significant illustration of the dilemma because of its wildcat strike focus.

Section 96 may change our strike patterns. The TUC has been very conscious that the policy of non-registration has left union negotiators, particularly unregistered unions now held responsible for the acts of their stewards [52], vulnerable under the law. Unregistered inducers are at risk—therefore stewards should not induce other workers to break their contracts of employment. If strike action against an employer is contemplated, due notice of the intended action should be given to the employer [12]. Due notice is equivalent to the longest period of notice that any of the intending strikers would need to give if terminating their contracts of employment. In other words, a group of would-be strikers might consist of some workers who could terminate their employment at a week's notice, others at two weeks' and yet others at a month's notice. In this illustration (not typical of shop-floor situations) a month's notice of the strike would be needed to avoid giving grounds for a complaint to be made under section 96. If due notice is given in this way the strike leaders are protected—section 147 (2)(d)—*subject* to the qualification given below. Strike leaders *and* the led are additionally protected in that due notice shall not be construed by the employer as notice by the employees to terminate or repudiate their contracts of employment (s147(1)).

The important condition to be met if the due notice is to protect workers from section 96 attack is as follows. The intended strike must not be in breach of any no-strike undertaking the employees may have given *in their individual contracts of employment, either as individuals or because a no-strike clause in a collective agreement is implied or incorporated in the terms of the individual contracts of employment (s 147(3))*. Given trade union hostility to the Act, the ubiquity of "Tina Lea" and the legal restrictions now placed upon the organically developed as distinct from legally established right to strike—contractually enforceable no-strike clauses are likely to be something of a rarity.

It is still too early to say whether the Act is causing a substitution of due notice strikes for lightning strikes, as is the obvious intention of this law. Due notice *may* encourage more constitutional behaviour. As a concept, it certainly draws the sting and effectiveness from the lightning or short-notice strike which management are unable to predict but to which concessions have frequently had to be made. Due notice entails predictability of labour withdrawal for which management can prepare off-setting savings—for example, by stock piling—against projected production losses. Counter strategies can be devised to replace the "caught on the hop" responses to the "downer," walkout activities of the past. Section 96 and the due-notice provision therefore represent a determined effort by the legislators to shift the balance of power by easing the wildcat pressures on management. If the strike pattern does not begin to change in the way intimated, we shall no doubt hear a great deal more about wildcats—particularly when General Election time approaches.

Section 96 either separately or in combination with other sections of the Act is unlikely to stop all unconstitutional strikes. If a group of workers feel sufficiently incensed about a particular injustice, no power in a free society can prevent them from walking off the job to demonstrate against the injustice. Even the Act acknowledges that no one shall be "bludgeoned" to work at his bench against his will (s128).

Causes of strikes are often complex. Frustration may be a justifiable cause or it may be a pretext. How do we know? If workers' frustration with a work situation is genuine and its expression is inhibited by section 96, the frustration may find its release in other ways—by absenteeism, bad time-keeping, high labour turnover, even acts of sabotage. If a group of workers wish to hamper production in an attempt to harass management into concessions, they can readily devise means for doing so wthout falling foul of the law. If everyone on the assembly lin eexpressed the "need" to go to the lavatory at much the same time, who could maintain that such an overloading of the sanitation system constituted an unfair industrial practice or breach of the contract of employment? It is highly unlikely that many people would play "games" of this kind for very long. The illustration is made simply to suggest that whatever the law may do or not do to redirect the channels of discontent, the law's operation needs to be accompanied by continuous, sensitive social analysis in order to try to establish the true causes of unruly behaviour.

Within the very intangible cost/benefit evaluation of section 96 there undoubtedly resides a very tangible cost for some strikers and/or their union. As mentioned above, the Court can award compensation to the injured party. For probably the first time in our industrial history we are approaching a more realistic assessment of strike costs to the employer than the wild assertions so frequently made.

RIGHTS OF THIRD PARTIES

The subject of the rights of non-combatants—employers or workers—who are hurt by the industrial quarrels of others, has occupied an increasingly important part in public discussion in recent years. Such concern is understandable given the growing and complex interdependency of production processes and services. It is against this background that the Act's provisions on sympathy strikes and strikes against the public interest must be set.

Section 97 is introduced here to build a bridge of consistency between the preceding and next paragraphs. In effect, section 97 states that industrial action—that is, strike, "irregular industrial action short of a strike," and a lock-out—in support of an unfair industrial practice, is itself an unfair industrial practice. An illustration from the "naughty behaviour" practices of employers, for a change, makes the point. An anti-union employer runs a garment factory. Of his 100 workers ten decide they want to join a registered union. The employer threatens the ten with the sack—the unfair industrial practice of deterring a worker from the exercise of his section 5 rights. The ten do join and in a fit of pique the employer, to break the union support, locks out his entire labour-force—industrial action in support of an unfair industrial practice and therefore in itself unfair. It would clearly make nonsense of much of the Act if pressure in support of an unfair practice were not itself made unfair. To remove ambiguity and to give the unions another incentive to register, section 97(3) establishes that it is not unfair for a registered union to support or to make official a strike which under section 96 started life as unfair and unofficial. The protection given to a registed union under section 96 (1)(a) will be recalled.

Section 98 is designed to deter "blacking" or, in the American term, "secondary boycotts." The simplicity of the deterrent concept vastly exceeds that of its operation—as events in the docks in July 1972 demonstrated. Persistent defiance of the Industrial Court's anti-blacking orders by five dockers led to their imprisonment, an action which helped spark off a national dock strike. Further reference to these matters, to picketing and to the relationship between a trade union and its stewards will be made in Chapter 12. For the moment it is more appropriate to clarify the intention of section 98 than its possible consequences.

Firm *C* has a commercial contract to supply goods to firm *A*. Firm *A* is in dispute with its workforce represented by union *B*. If *any person* takes industrial action by way of strike, "irregular action" or lock-out to stop firm *C* from delivering goods to firm *A*, this constitutes an unfair industrial practice. Basically, therefore, section 98 sets a higher value on protecting the party not directly involved in the dispute, on strengthening the position of the employer in dispute, than furthering or protecting the interests of the workers involved in the original dispute (union *B* in the above example).

Section 98 constitutes a deliberate weakening of the strikers' position in this type of circumstance. Unions have argued and will continue to argue that they need to enlist support from and/or apply pressure to parties not directly involved in their dispute, as a necessary means of achieving a reasonable balance of power with the strong but reluctant employer with whom they have been negotiating. If fellow unionists come out in sympathy or are laid off as a consequence of their employers' goods being "blacked," the reasons for such a sacrifice are usually well understood by working-class people. Labour history abounds with illustrations of such sacrifice.

However, section 98 remains committed to the protection of the "innocent" third party rather than the achievement of a fair balance of power. Some, including the Conservative Government, would argue that the former objective ensures the latter objective, which is another reason why the Government and union viewpoints diverge widely.

To return to technicalities. "Any person" in the above illustration can clearly include other unions than the one directly engaged in the dispute. Any person is at risk if he takes the cited industrial action if "he knows *or has reasonable grounds for believing*" that a commercial contract exists between *A* and *C* (s98(1)(a)). Pre-Act court rulings sometimes made it difficult for a third party to seek redress against a "blacking" union, it being held that a union did not necessarily know of the existence of a commercial contract and that the union's prime intent was to further the dispute not to have the contract broken.

The innocent third party can only be protected under section 98 if his innocence equates with "extraneous party" to the original dispute—"extraneous party" being defined broadly in subsection (2) and in more detail in subsection (3). An extraneous party is one that is "not a party to that dispute" section 98(2)(a) and (*not* or) has not "taken any action in material support of a party" in dispute (s98(2)(b)). Scope would seem to exist for controversy about the material nature of material support and the point at which moral support edges into material support. Section 98(3) adds further potential complications. A party is not considered to be a party to the dispute or to have taken (2)(b) action simply because:

a He is "an associated employer" in relation to the employer in dispute. Plenty of grist here for the lawyers' mill of interpretation concerning "associated employer" despite the definition of "associated employer" in (s167(8))

b He is a member of an employers' organisation another of whose members is in dispute

c He has contributed to an employers' association strike indemnity fund as a general activity and not just to help a fellow employer in a particular dispute

d He had entered into a commercial contract with the party in dispute —before the dispute began

"Extraneous party" is thus sufficiently widely drawn to afford potential protection against "blacking" and sympathy strikes to employers who on past experience could have been drawn into or materially affected by the original dispute. Section 98 constitutes a significant potential check to the use of union power to involve other employers and workers to further the unions' claims or protests against the employer directly concerned.

12

Handling (Mishandling) Industrial Conflict—II

EMERGENCY PROCEDURES

Community interest can become a special case of "extraneous (third) party" interest in need of protection as seen and provided for in Part VIII —Emergency Procedures. Within a few weeks of their coming into operation sections 138–45 were hitting the newspaper headlines because of the railway dispute of April–May 1972. Although other motives were undoubtedly present, it may be that the railway unions were not averse to testing the strength or weakness of the emergency procedures contained within "an anti-union" act. Be that as it may, the emergency procedures are succinctly summarised in the Department of Employment's *Guide* as follows:

> This part of the Act enables the Secretary of State in an emergency situation to apply to the Industrial Court for orders:
>
> (i) Restraining named organisations or individuals from calling, organising, procuring or financing industrial action, or threatening to do so, for a maximum of sixty days where its discontinuance or deferment is likely to help promote a settlement
>
> (ii) Directing a ballot to be held where there is doubt whether the workers concerned support the industrial action and have had an opportunity to express their wishes
>
> If no settlement is achieved during the sixty-day period there is nothing then to prevent the industrial action from going ahead. The result of any ballot under this part of the Act is not binding [9, p61]

The "cooling-off" period principle expressed in (i) and balloting "presumed reluctant worker" principle in (ii) bear familiar resemblance to the conciliation pause and balloting provisions in the 1964–70 Labour Government's *In Place of Strife* [3]—but that is another story.

Certain key points need to be kept in mind in relation to the emergency procedures. The Secretary of State must make a case to the Court that a national emergency exists or is likely if the industrial action is not stopped or averted. The substance of the case is that the industrial action is of such a scale or nature:

> . . . as to be likely—
>
> *a* To be gravely injurious to the national economy, to imperil national security or to create a serious risk of public disorder, or
>
> *b* To endanger the lives of a substantial number of persons, or expose a substantial number of persons to serious risk of disease or personal injury (s138(2))

The Secretary of State made such a case in relation to the railwaymen's work-to-rule industrial action and much clearly hinges upon "gravely injurious to the national economy." But it is not enough to persuade the Court that an emergency exists or is threatened. A cooling-off order (a discontinuance or deferment of the action) will then only be made if the Secretary of State can further persuade the Court that such an order "*would be conducive to a settlement* of it [the dispute] by negotiation, conciliation or arbitration" (s138(1)(c)). If one party to the dispute so deeply entrenches itself into a position of hostility against the other that no constructive dialogue, even with a conciliator present, is possible, then an order will not be made. It is unlikely to be sought in such circumstances.

Several bites at the cooling-off period cherry may be made—if justified by the circumstances. In the railway dispute a period of twenty-eight days was applied for and one for fourteen days granted. Further orders could extend such a period by one or several instalments up to a maximum period of sixty days in relation to any one dispute.

The purpose of the cooling-off provisions is clear: to restore or maintain normal working so that wider sectors of the community are not hurt by a quarrel that is not directly theirs—and to enable strenuous efforts to be made to reach a settlement in an atmosphere of peace, albeit enforced, rather than war. Whether cooling-off periods will become hotting-up periods as is sometimes conjectured, remains to be seen. Generalisations from a sample of one—the railway dispute of 1972 which contained special features—would be unwise. American experience of similar provisions under the Taft-Hartley Act is somewhat inconclusive, unless one starts off with a particular point of view in which case it becomes easy to praise or condemn the cooling-off concept.

Unions tended to deride the value of the Industrial Court's rulings on the railway dispute. Union criticism, if understandable politically, was somewhat unfair to the Court whose freedom to chose between making or not making orders (cooling-off or compulsory ballot) is very severely constrained by the wording of the Act itself. In fact, it might be said that if the Secretary of State has done his homework the Court has almost no alternative but to make the order sought. The following paragraphs help to explain this point.

The second arm of the emergency provisions enables the workers involved to express a point of view through a ballot to be held by order of the Court. Again it is up to the Secretary of State to initiate the process. He must be persuaded and in turn must persuade the Court that a ballot should be held because:

a An emergency exists or is threatened as defined in section 138(2) above and/*or*

b The effects of the industrial action in question on a particular industry are, or are likely to be, such as to be seriously injurious to the livelihood of a substantial number of workers employed in that industry (s141(2)(b)) and because

c There are reasons for doubting whether the workers who are taking part or are expected to take part in the strike or other industrial action are or would be taking part in it in accordance with their wishes, and whether they have had an adequate opportunity of indicating their wishes in this respect (s141(1)(c))

Condition (c) is the nub of the issue. From the first experience of its operation (the railway dispute) it is enough for the Secretary of State to assert in good faith that he has his "reasons for doubting" for the Court to make the ballot order if the other conditions are met. The Secretary of State does not have to explain his reasons for doubting [33].

Justification for the doubting provision is put forward in the argument that the community should not suffer because the leaders of industrial action are misleading the led. Militants should not be allowed to exploit the response of loyalty from the rank and file union members who may well have serious misgivings, but inadequate opportunity to give them expression, about the justice and merits both of the case and tactics pursued by the union leadership. Objective empirical evidence in support of these lines of reasoning is somewhat slender.

Some unions—the NUR is a notable example—do not provide for a balloting of their members before calling a strike. The leaders are held by the led to be competent to judge the state of industrial play and the tactics required to achieve objectives. It is conceivable, but not very likely, that some unions might change their strike-calling rules because of section 141. A more probable union reaction would seem to be: "If the legislators are so keen on ballots, let the state foot the bill for conducting them." And the state will do the footing if a ballot order is made.

A ballot order made by the Court requires the industrial action to be stopped or the threat of such action withdrawn until such time as the result of the ballot is known (s143). A digression is necessary here. Cooling-off and ballot orders are required to be drawn with great care. Before persons or organisations can be bound by the Court they must be named by the Secretary of State (ss138(3), 141(3)) and be given the opportunity to state their case to the Court if they choose to do so. Orders can only bind people or organisations who "call, organise, procure or finance" the industrial action or who threaten to do so. In short, those to be bound are the leaders not the led. As under section 96 the problem of mass-defiance of an order is averted, at least technically. Putting the leaders at risk can obviously create tensions between the leaders and the led. Events on the railways again come to mind. Between the granting of the cooling-off order and its commencement date several days' grace were allowed in which railway union leaders worked strenuously to persuade men to work normally instead of "to rule." Sharp protests resulted in the form of continued industrial action by Southern Region drivers in particular but by the time the cooling-off order began almost complete normal working had been resumed.

Orders may not name the officials of registered unions (ss139(3)(b), 143(6)) provided that the organising of industrial action or would-be action by such officials is authorised by their unions. In such circumstances the bound party is the registered union. It follows that unregistered union organisers do not enjoy the same legal protection—another registration pressure point.

Are ballots likely to weaken or strengthen rank and file support for the action? There are arguments both ways [2]. On balance, given union hostility to the Act, an enforced ballot might be seen by union members as a Government gauntlet to be picked up and slapped back with a resounding "Yes, we strike." On the other hand, a Secretary of State might consider that union hostility to the Act and support for the strike is strongest among the vocal leaders at all levels in the union. A different story, in his view, might be heard from the rank and file. If union members vote against industrial action they do, of course, incur the risk of discrediting their own leadership, a danger of which union members are likely to be well aware. Clearly any Secretary of State himself takes a risk in seeking a ballot order. He may think this justified in his attempts to influence public opinion and in buying an interval of peace while the ballot is conducted.

Some ballot technicalities require explanation and comment. The Court determines "the question on which the ballot is to be taken" (s142(2)(b))—a critical question indeed as the railway dispute showed. On this and other technical matters, such as determining voting constituencies, the Court may seek the help of the CIR (s142(5)). Constituencies are called "areas of employment" under section 142(2)(*a*) and the wording of 2(*a*) and (3) is such that the electoral roll is clearly not restricted to members of registered or unregistered unions. *Employees concerned* in the dispute are to be balloted. (In the railway dispute, non-unionists voted three to one in favour of resumed industrial action.) In a monolithic industry, such as coal mining, with a very high level of union membership, constituencies would be easy to define and ballots relatively easy to organise. But the imagination balks at the prospect of thinking through the arrangements for a ballot in the event of a national engineering strike. What with thousands of federated and unfederated firms, a variety of unions and varying mixtures of union and non-union labour forces involved, the task of establishing the electoral roll would bristle with difficulties.

Returning to the question on the ballot form, unlike the American Taft-Hartley procedure the Industrial Relations Act does not require a ballot on the employer's latest offer. Such an arrangement places a premium on rejection of the offer in the expectation that a solid "no" will lead to a better offer once the cooling-off period is over. The Industrial Relations Act leaves the options open.

Conventional safeguards are established to ensure the secrecy of the ballot the organisation of which is the responsibility of the CIR. If a registered union is involved the CIR may invite that union to conduct the ballot under CIR supervision (s144).

Once the CIR has declared, to the Court, the result of the ballot, the "restraining of industrial action" ballot order lapses. Those previously restrained by the order become free to organise industrial action *whatever the result of the ballot*. If the dispute is resumed, no further ballot order can be made (s143(7)). But there would seem to be no obvious legal bar to the Secretary of State eventually applying for a cooling-off order under section 138 in the circumstances and manner already outlined. Conversely, although a section 138 prompted cooling-off order has been issued, in one or several instalments, and has expired, the Secretary of State could apply for a section 141 prompted compulsory ballot order, as in fact happened in the 1972 railway dispute. Ways, therefore, exist whereby the cooling-off and compulsory ballot orders, if technically separate, can still be interlaced in relation to the same dispute. But limits are set (the two procedures can be involved only once in one dispute) to the extent of the interlacing.

As intimated earlier, one not unreasonable interpretation of events in the national emergency dispute on the railways is that the unions deliberately manoeuvred to prompt the Secretary of State to seek orders in order to prove that although Court orders might be obeyed, they would not promote a settlement or good industrial relations. In this way the Court, the Act, the Government would be discredited. If this explanation is sound, then with such a special sample of one experience, any generalisation about the worth of the emergency procedures would be very rash.

BLACKING, PICKETING, SHOP-STEWARDS

Within the general strategy of industrial action various tactics may be pursued. Blacking is one and picketing another. In both activities shop-stewards are likely to be much involved. It is useful, therefore, to consider these three topics together.

Although dock employment and the dockland culture are "special" (the docks have been the subject of more official labour relations inquiries than any other British industry) the container dispute of 1972 provided an arena where blacking, picketing and union responsibility for its stewards could do battle with the Act—the outcome carrying significance for industrial relations generally. Whether the Act exacerbated the container dispute or served as a catalyst, albeit a painful one, to achieve a more durable settlement of the dispute we cannot yet say with assurance.

With insufficient imaginative leadership by unions, employers, shipowners and governments (both past and present) to safeguard dockers against the worst effects of the "container revolution," the dockers turned once more to reliance on their own intrinsic strength and traditions of solidarity to protect their jobs. With the development of inland container ports and the creation of new warehouse facilities near to but just outside physical areas of registered dock work:

> . . . men saw their jobs drifting away just when, after years of struggle, they had achieved considerable improvements in their standards of living, with the post-war de-casualisation of dock labour and the scheme of fall-back pay [46].

Jobs were drifting to workers paid less than dockers, an additional threat to the standards mentioned above. To the dockers blacking was the obvious means of self-defence. In defending themselves dockers hurt others—other workers, drivers in the same union, members of other unions and the employers of these latter groups of workers. As a general proposition it must surely be right that other workers besides dockers have a right to work and other people a right to engage in business necessary to the operation of the ports and road haulage industry. We are, therefore, confronted with competing rights. The fundamental question then arises whether recourse to the Industrial Relations Act—by a "hurt" employer or "hurt" fellow workers—is the best means of resolving this problem of competing rights. It would seem not because relief (and that of a dubious kind) is granted only to *one* of the competing interests and the symptom of the problem rather than the problem itself (the container revolution) is tackled. The way forward out of the resultant mess can only be a reasoned examination of and reasoned recommendations about the whole container issue which was precisely the purpose of the Aldington-Jones inquiry and report [47].

A central weakness of the anti-blacking provisions would seem to be the implicit assumption that those carrying out the blacking must always be wrong and those blacked always right, because the third (extraneous) party—just because he is a third party—must be innocent. Such an assumption is neat but over simplified. Given the immense variety of industrial activity in this country, a more sensible starting point for anti-blacking legislation, if this is thought to be necessary, might well be: can some tripartite body identify situations where on some agreed scale of values blacking appears wrong in some cases and right in others? The inevitable problem of grey areas would arise.

To the dockers, certain warehouse and haulage enterprises seemed anything but innocent extraneous third parties. They claimed that the activities of such firms constituted unfair competition and they reacted accordingly to defeat this threat. In moral, social and economic terms, as distinct from narrow legal terms, history may judge the dockers to have been right. The defiance of the Court order by the five men sent to prison is quite another matter. History will decide whether the five were martyrs, misguided or downright mischievous. Section 98 expresses more of an anti-blacking ideology *per se* than a serious attempt to get to grips with this particular part of the more general issue of what should be the legitimate pressures one party can apply to another in an increasingly complicated society.

Blacking often entails preventing goods from reaching their destination

—fuel to an electricity generating station or containers to the docks. Picketing is therefore frequently an integral feature of blacking. Somewhat surprisingly the Act has little to say about picketing. But the changed nature of some recent forms of picketing may bring about changes to the Act. More will be said on this point shortly.

Essentially, the basic legal position of picketing, established early in this century, is undisturbed by the Act. "Peaceful persuasion" remains the central concept. Section 134 provides that:

> One or more persons . . . in contemplation or furtherance of an industrial dispute [are free to] attend at or near:
>
> *a* A place where a person works or carries on business, or
>
> *b* Any other place where a person happens to be, not being a place where he resides, . . . for the purpose of peacefully obtaining information from him or peacefully communicating information to him or peacefully persuading him to work or not to work

The new feature of the above is "not being a place where he resides"—intended to protect a person's home, an uncontroversial safeguard.

Our industrial history is undeniably chequered with instances of less than peaceful picketing. But the amount of unruly picketing as a proportion of total man hours spent in picketing is probably very small—though highly publicised. Tempers tend to blaze if in an embittered situation attempts are made to cross the picket lines with strike-breaking lorries. Much picketing is carried out slightly self-consciously and in an atmosphere of shop-floor jocularity. This has been very largely true of what might be described as the new form of *internal* picketing—the "sit-in" tactics employed by relays of picketing workers in engineering factories in the spring of 1972, in particular.

What revived the interest in the law of picketing was the widely diversified and sometimes mass-picketing carried out by miners during the bitter pre-Act strike of January and February 1972. Not only mines were picketed but coal and coke depots, even electricity power stations—not with the customary handfuls of men but thousands in the case of the Saltley fuel depot, Birmingham, where a riot was only narrowly averted. For miners to choke off the supply of what they produce—coal—is impeccably consistent with the "furtherance of an industrial dispute" but justification of mass-picketing and some of its uglier features can legitimately be called into question. ("Flying picketing" is not *per se* unlawful.)

The Government has undertaken to review the law of picketing. It is to be hoped that adequate time and study are given to this review. For example, what evidence is there to suggest that mass-picketing has come to stay? The miners' strike has been talked and written about as a "special case" [48]. Miners' mass-picketing seems much more likely to have been the result of long pent-up wrath and a mishandling of the situation by the Government, than an elaborately preconceived strategy which ante-dated the strike. Legislation to restrict the generality of the freedom to picket in order to curb picketing "excesses" could be highly damaging, not only to industrial relations but to the wider social, economic and political system.

Blacking and picketing require organisers. Prominent among these will be shop-stewards. Full-time union officers may visit the picket line to pass on information and boost the morale of those picketing but the continuing on-the-spot organisers must, in the nature of things, be the stewards. With such a critical role to play not only in blacking and picketing but all forms of industrial conflict activity, how does the law regard the shop-steward? (It is accepted that many stewards regard the law with sharp disapproval.)

As will be seen in Chapter 14, the Code of Practice not only endorses the legitimacy of the role of the steward in our industrial relations system but actually strengthens the steward's position at his place of work. Under section 167 of the Act, "official" in relation to an organisation of workers clearly includes shop-steward—although this title is not used because trade union representatives at the place of employment are not always known by that particular description.

As the steward (using this popular term for convenience) is a union official what should the formal authority relationship be between the union and such officials? This question has agitated many minds, not least union executives, ever since the shop-steward appeared in strength on the employment scene. Discussion has become more agitated in the past twenty-five years with the widespread development of workplace bargaining. Stewards commonly demonstrate *de facto* power which does not rest on formal *de jure* trade union authority. The Act is much concerned, the point is taken further in the next chapter, to bring about a greater congruence between power and authority. As far as stewards are concerned, unions on the whole have tended to skate round rather than into this particular issue.

What the Act has so far done, through three important judgements, is to provide authoritative analysis of the undeniably complex relationships, which different unions work out differently anyway, between the union as a corporate entity, its full-time officers, shop-stewards and rank-and-file members. Additionally, and more important, the House of Lords has ruled what the relationship is between a union and its stewards. In so doing the House of Lords reimposed a £55000 (contempt) fine on the T & GWU.

Dockland and the container dispute gave rise to the above rulings. Anti-blacking orders of the Industrial Court having been defied by Liverpool dockers the Industrial Court:

> . . . held that the union was accountable in contempt proceedings for its shop-stewards on the ground that they are its agents, and that merely advising them to comply with the orders was not enough to purge its contempt. The union had to take steps to ensure that its shop-stewards obeyed the Court—if all else failed by taking disciplinary measures against them [21].

The Court of Appeal overruled that judgement holding:

> The Transport and General Workers' Union . . . not liable for its shop-stewards when they act outside the scope of the authority delegated to them and take industrial action on behalf of the workers whom they represent [49].

Lord Denning, the Master of the Rolls, observed:

> The position of shop-stewards had never before been considered in our courts . . . .
> If he (the steward) was to have authority from the union so as to make it responsible for unlawful action by him, it must be found in the rules of the handbook or in the course of dealing. His Lordship had studied all those but found no authority in a shop-steward or a shop-steward committee to take industrial action on his own or their initiative. . . .
>
> A principal was not liable for the wrongs done by his agent unless the agent was carrying out a task or duty delegated to him by the principal, and did the wrongful act, not as a casual act of his own, but as part of the carrying out of that task or duty.
>
> In the present cases the union had at no time delegated the task or duty to the shop-stewards. They did the blacking on their own. The union was therefore not responsible for it.
>
> The shop-stewards acting as representatives of their work groups might be guilty personally of an unfair industrial practice within section 96; but they did not make the union responsible for it . . .[49].

The House of Lords (a *unanimous* decision of the five Law Lords) took a different view holding the union: ". . . responsible for the acts of its shop-stewards. . . ."

> Their Lordships decided that in accordance with union policy of devolution and consistently with its rules and practice, its shop-stewards had *a general implied authority* to act in the interests of the members they represented and in particular to defend and improve their rates of pay and working conditions; that they might do so by negotiation or by industrial action at the relevant place of work; and that they were not authorised to do any act outside union rules or policy. . . .
>
> They also concluded that as soon as the court orders were issued restraining the union itself, or by its officers, servants and agents from continuing such practices, the union became responsible for taking all possible steps to stop the blacking, including the unequivocal withdrawal of the shop-stewards' authority and, if necessary, disciplinary action. . . .
>
> What clothed a shop-steward in the eyes of his fellow members with authority to act on the union's behalf and assured him that if they did what he proposed it would receive "the fullest support and protection from the union" was that he held credentials given by the union . . . [52].

As the lawyers so rightly say: *res ipsa loquitor*, the thing speaks for itself——or does it?

A worrying feature of the House of Lords judgement in the opinion of some commentators is the "disciplinary action" a union may be expected to apply to its stewards. If some stewards in some situations were expelled from the union they would probably still provide leadership as unofficial leaders with their real power undiminished. The docks provide the obvious example—again. As Eric Wigham has pointed out [55], with the closed shop no longer lawful, a union no longer has the power to discipline members who kick over the traces by expelling them from the union and therefore from their jobs. More disorder may therefore be created if unions seek to discipline stewards by having the authority but not the power to do so.

The House of Lords judgement has not resolved the basic problems of what the union–steward–member relationship should be; probably no judgement can, but it provides a valuable contribution to the debate—and it is right that there should be a continuing debate on what is one of the central issues in industrial relations. Evidence that the debate continues appeared in press reports in November 1972 that the TGWU had modified the credentials issued to its stewards making it quite clear that stewards were not authorised to start or continue industrial action on behalf of the union.

13

New Rules for Organisations —as Organisations

REGISTRATION

> Registration is based on the principle that any organisation which is accorded special privileges under the law should be prepared to abide by certain minimum standards of conduct and administration governing its relations with its members [8, p4].

> Registration of trade unions has existed since 1871 but the Act incorporates a new system of registration which means surveillance of unions by the state [12, p1].

The first statement records the official Department of Employment view on registration; the second is the official trade union view expressed by the TUC. While the civil servants objectively state the factual registration position, the nature and extent of the "minimum standards" and "special privileges" are very much the stuff of subjective assessment. The TUC's references both to history and "a new system" are objectively correct. "State surveillance" is undisguisedly subjective in character.

Leaving aside for the moment "special privileges," the reference to (new) "minimum standards of conduct" seems to suggest that old ones were inadequate and/or insufficiently well observed. The body of evidence, as distinct from persuasive advocacy, to support the suggestion is somewhat meagre. Although unions are accused from time to time of bullying their members, Donovan considered that "the results of research justify the general conclusion that it is unlikely that abuse of power by trade unions in relation to individuals is widespread" [2, p270]. But Donovan continued "it does happen." Donovan therefore proposed some reforms to strengthen the position of the individual *vis à vis* a union explaining that "whereas the individual's statutory safeguards remain broadly as they have been since the passing of the Trade Union Act 1871, trade unions have meanwhile increased immensely in power" [2, p160]. The liberal Donovan Commission therefore proposed the creation of an Independent Review Body the functions of which would be:

> Adjudication in complaints by individuals of unfair treatment by unions, malpractices in union elections, etc. Settlement of disputes between Registrar and union as to its rules. Adjudication (concurrently with ordinary courts of law) in cases based on alleged breach of union rules or violation of natural justice [2, Appendix 9].

Similar ideas, if in somewhat different form, find expression in the Act.

Donovan was thus prepared to recommend the establishment of checks to the abuse, actual or potential, of union power in relation to individuals. Interestingly the *Consultative Document* which preceded the *Industrial Relations Bill* did not rest its registration case on the abuse of union power argument.

> In the Government's view, the substantial new rights which it proposes for trade unions should only apply to those which, by registering, accept statutory minimum standards in relation to their rules and the rights of their members [5, p11].

New minimum standards would, of course, impliedly check the abuse of power. More, probably most important from the Conservative viewpoint, the main abuse of union power in relation to the individual, the closed shop, was to be removed (at least in a form of words) in what became section 5 and the agency-shop provisions of the Act.

As discussed in earlier chapters, the new rights and special privileges established for trade unions by the Act are of a decidedly two-edged character. Registration creates organising, bargaining and security opportunities not otherwise available. Registration, while not providing legal immunity, establishes a greater degree of legal protection than non-registration. Registration therefore has far less to do with the checking of "union abuses against individuals" than with bringing trade unions within the law, meaning this particular law. To most unions this particular law seems bad law and registration must therefore be resisted. The TUC is right in saying ". . . registration lies at the heart of the Act" [12, p1] and because of its views on this it instructs affiliated unions to deregister or not to register [12, p64].

Union opposition to registration may sometimes be expressed in technical terms to the effect that the "minimum standards of conduct and administration" criteria of registration constitute unjustified state interference in the internal affairs of voluntary organisations with a long, proud and strongly democratic history. Sympathy can be felt with this argument. Historically, unions chose democratic forms of internal government and the oldest unions were democratic institutions well before this country became a broadly based parliamentary democracy. In fact, the trade unions, as major architect and builder of the Labour Party, played a vital part in the achievement of such a democracy. Trade unions collectively remain an important safeguard for the preservation of democracy by providing a check to the use of arbitrary power by governments or employers. It is significant that the trade unions of the Common Market countries particularly welcome British membership, because of the added trade union strength such membership brings. The likelihood of achieving effective union countervailing power against governments, Eurocrats, major employers and multinational companies will thus be much improved.

Powerful as these checks and balances arguments may be, they do not demolish the Donovan case that better safeguards need to be provided for individual members against the use of arbitrary power by unions. In some cases unions have grown into immense organisations in which the claims of bureaucracy and managerial efficiency increase the problem of democratic control. Some instances of union election ballot rigging have occurred. With union activists a much smaller proportion of union membership than card carrying members, it may sometimes be difficult to dislodge from control a particular caucus of leaders, that are possibly highly motivated politically and skilled in the art of union rules manipulation. Some union members, a relatively small number, have undoubtedly been harshly treated by their union executives.

While there are some technical difficulties in applying the guiding principles (which affect both registered and unregistered unions) to union practice and in applying minimum standards of conduct and administration to registered union practice, the union claim that unions now need a "state licence" to operate should be treated if not with complete scepticism then with considerable reserve. The central, as distinct from peripheral, objections to registration are to be found in political, ideological, psychological values rather than in technical requirements.

Unions which have chosen to remain registered have not found it difficult, technically, to do so. It may be that the Registrar will require these unions to modify some of their rules. If this is so, nothing has so far happened to suggest that changes are not likely to be feasible, technically, for these unions.

Commenting on his rules examination function:

> The Registrar's initial experience [to the end of March 1972] of a large number of rule-books . . . suggests, that taking the existing corpus of rules, by-laws, shop-stewards' handbooks, custom and practice as a whole, the Act's requirements would not be unduly difficult to meet in principle as far as many unions are concerned" [50, p10].

What then *are* these new guiding principles and new *rules* of conduct and administration? The principles and rules need separate consideration.

GUIDING PRINCIPLES

Section 65 establishes principles which "shall be guiding principles in the conduct of every organisation of workers, other than federations of workers' organisations." This means that the guiding principles apply to registered and unregistered trade unions and workers' organisations entered on the Special Register, such as the Royal College of Nursing. It is with the application and possible effects of the guiding principles that the TUC Handbook on the Act is much concerned. Rules and administration are not discussed as these affect only registered unions. Features of the TUC guidance on principles can be indicated here but readers are advised to refer to the TUC *Handbook*, for a proper appreciation of the TUC concern.

Section 65(2) requires that an applicant who is *prima facie* eligible for membership of a particular union, because he is qualified to do the kind of work he does, "shall not, by way of any arbitrary or unreasonable discrimination, be excluded from membership. . . ." Such a requirement may collide with the "TUC Bridlington Principles, which govern relations between affiliated unions" [12, p7]. (Collision between the AUEW and the Industrial Court occurred when it was held that Mr Goad had been unreasonably refused membership of the union—see Chapter 15.)

> Bridlington Principles . . . were drawn up because trade unionists recognised that, in situations where more than one union was capable of representing a particular grade of worker, it was necessary to prevent the indiscriminate proliferation of unions if stable and

> rational trade union structures and collective bargaining machinery were to be developed. Their existence has also prevented the instability that would occur in industrial relations if breakaway unions were formed, or if groups of workers were able to move on a whim from one union to another [12, p7].

Order, stability and rationality are consistent with the objectives of the Act and part of the remit of the industrial tribunals whose job it will be to consider complaints (section 107) brought by people who claim to have been "arbitrarily or unreasonably" excluded from union membership.

> . . . it is to be hoped that they (the tribunals) will recognise that the Bridlington Principles are not only fair and reasonable in themselves but are conducive to the maintenance of stable industrial relations [12, p8].

More sensitive recognition of the Bridlington Principles might have been achieved if trade unionists had not withdrawn their membership (arbitrarily? unreasonably?) from the tribunals.

In terms of admission to *a* union—as distinct from admission to union *A* rather than union *B*—much hinges upon the phrase "appropriately qualified for employment as a worker of that description" ((2)(b)) which a union represents. TUC guidance on this point is to the effect that unions should clarify their qualification for admission tests. Unless this is done it might, for example, be unfair "not to accept into membership individuals who would not normally be regarded as qualified" [12, p55] and to refuse the transfer of a member from the unskilled to skilled section of the union.

Freedom to join is paralleled by freedom to leave in the following terms:

> Every member of the organisation shall have the right, on giving reasonable notice and complying with any reasonable conditions, to terminate his membership of the organisation at any time (s65(3)).

Reasonable notice and reasonable conditions are not defined but remain to be determined by industrial tribunals if members should complain of unfair treatment. The TUC's view is that it would be reasonable for a member to give the same length of notice to terminate membership as the union is required under its rules to give him. "It would probably also be regarded as a reasonable condition that he should pay all arrears of contributions up to the date of termination" [12, p57].

"Freedom to participate" in a union's affairs is established for a member by the principles set out in section 65(4) (5) (6). The democratic safeguards contained in section 65(4) determine what a union shall *not* do:

No member . . . shall, by way of any arbitrary or unreasonable discrimination, be excluded from:

a Being a candidate for or holding office
b Nominating candidates for office
c Voting in any election or ballot
d Attending or taking part in the organisation's meetings

Office, candidates, voting and attendance at meetings relate to the organisation or "in a branch or section of it"—that is, the democratic process is to be observed at all levels and in all units of the organisation's activities.

Presumably it would not be unreasonable or arbitrary for a union to attach length of membership or past experience as shop-steward or branch officer as qualifications to eligibility as candidate for higher union office. Perhaps only paid-up members should have the right to vote. But would it be unreasonable to exclude from office, members of the Communist Party, Maoists or others who support quite different perspectives of democracy from social democrats? Protracted courageous action culminating in High Court proceedings in 1961 was required to dislodge the communists who had gained control of the ETU by ballot-rigging methods. It would be ironical, bitterly so to some, if the "democratic" Act facilitated a return to power of communist leaders.

There are, of course, countervailing factors including the encouragement given by the Act—and the Code—to greater membership participation in internal union affairs. TUC guidance (on the guiding principles) encourages the same democratic activity.

Section 65(5)(6) requires ballots to be secret and voting arrangements to be such that every member shall "have a fair and reasonable opportunity of voting without interference or constraint." As the TUC Handbook states:

> . . . it might be claimed that a vote taken on a show of hands at a mass-meeting was unfair because the atmosphere at the meeting was intimidating. This means that unions should ensure that such meetings are conducted in an orderly manner, and that there are adequate facilities to enable members to participate in them and express their views [12, p60].

Impeccable advice but onerous, too, when the setting is an emotional mass-meeting on a piece of waste land. In some situations management could conceivably help the union democratic process by providing facilities for meetings as the Code of Practice suggests. A mass-meeting in the canteen might facilitate the achievement of the "orderly manner" to which the TUC refers. There is reason to believe that people are less aggressive and display fewer mob characteristics when sitting down than standing up. Although other factors will be present, crowd behaviour on the football terraces is noticeably less orderly than in the "stands." Local drinking laws in parts of the USA which require alcoholic drinks to be consumed sitting down, are based on the belief that it is harder to throw a punch from a sitting than a standing position.

Sober necessity returns us to section 65. No union member is to be bullied by his union. Section 65(7) requires that the member shall not be subjected to "any unfair or unreasonable disciplinary action." Unfair and unreasonable are terms for adjudication. Additional to this general requirement is the specific duty on the union *not* to discipline (fairly or unfairly, reasonably or unreasonably) a member for having failed or refused:

a To take any action which would constitute *on his part* an unfair industrial practice, or

b To take part in a political strike or "an unfair industrial practice" strike, or

c To take part in "any irregular industrial action short of a strike"—in effect in support of political or "unfair" strikes (s65(7))

Such restraints are necessary to maintain the technical and philosophical consistency of the Act. It would obviously be inconsistent with the purpose of the Act if a union member could be disciplined by his union for not supporting an unfair industrial practice organised by that union. If the practice is "fair" then discipline can be applied but the discipline itself must be fair. In short there are two disciplinary contexts. An absolute prohibition is placed on the disciplining of members for failing to support unfair action. In other circumstances members may be disciplined provided this is done in accordance with the precepts of "natural justice." Section 65(8) deals with this second context.

Section 65(8) provides that except where a member is in arrears (covered by the rules) no member may be disciplined unless he:

a Has been given written notice of the charge and reasonable time to prepare his defence

b Is afforded a full and fair hearing

c Is given a written statement of the hearing's findings

d Has exercised any right of appeal available under the organisation's rules and the appeal has been heard—or the time allowed for appeal has expired

In the TUC's view unions which follow the TUC's Code in *Good Industrial Relations—A Guide For Negotiators* [43] "should encounter no difficulties" from section 65(8).

Section 65(9) requires that no person's membership shall be terminated without reasonable notice. Reason for the termination must be given. Section 65(10) provides that no member shall be restricted either by a union's rules, or in any other way, from "instituting, prosecuting or defending proceedings before any court or tribunal or giving evidence in any such proceedings." In sum, access to judicial bodies is not to be contracted away or impeded. Section 65(10) is an unimpeachable expression of individual rights in a free democratic society. Such rights may be abused by an "awkward squad"—barrack-room lawyer minority—who run to the law too soon and too often, but this is a small price to pay for the basic freedom. The TUC counsel that "there should be no delay in the operation of . . . (union disciplinary) procedures" [12, p58]. "Speed up of procedures" has frequently been urged by unions and their members in relation to the operation of employment grievance procedures agreed with employers. Perhaps it is no bad thing that internal union procedures should also be encouraged to function at a brisker pace.

Enforcement of the section 65 principles of good behaviour follows the familiar pattern of making contravention an unfair industrial practice. Potentially at risk are "any organisation of workers, or any official of or person acting on behalf of such an organisation" (s66). A member, ex-member (other than someone who has resigned voluntarily) and would-be member are eligible to complain of an unfair industrial practice to an industrial tribunal (s107). If the tribunal considers the complaint justified "the tribunal may, if it considers that it would be just and equitable to do so" grant a declaration of rights order to the complainant or award him compensation—*or both* (s109). As section 107 applies to "organisations of workers" which covers both registered and unregistered unions it may be appropriate to restate the basic rights of the individual.

Members of both registered and unregistered unions may complain to an industrial tribunal that guiding principles have been contravened by their organisation *or* that there has been a breach of the organisation's rules (s107(3)(a)(b)). (See also Chapters 2 and 5.)

If the union is *registered* the action complained of must have been "taken against the person who presents the complaint" (s107(3)). The unregistered union complainant is not restricted in this way and the complaint could therefore be of a general as distinct from specific to the complainant character. It must, of course, be remembered that the aggrieved member of the registered union has an additional champion to call upon, the Registrar. Furthermore, the Registrar himself could initiate an investigation into what he suspected were serious malpractices on the part of a registered union or a persistent flouting of the guiding principles. As the Registrar has no jurisdiction over unregistered unions, *any* member of such a union could seek a tribunal's help in stopping, for example, ballot rigging.

Making appropriate allowance for changes in terminology, substituting lock-out for strike and leaving aside TUC advice, what has so far been said, *in technical terms*, in this chapter applies almost equally well to employers' associations, registered and unregistered. (As with unions, federations are excluded.) The equivalent sections are 69 (guiding principles) 70 (the unfair industrial practice of contravention) 107 (complaints) 109 (remedies). In contrast to the trade union situation, relatively little is known about the way in which employers' "trade unions" behave towards their members, not least on disciplinary matters. Speculation would be idle but certain points may be made. Registration, as an issue, has evoked no apparent protest from employers' associations or their members. Politically and tactically it is obviously wise for the Government to apply the same guiding principles and registration rules to employers' associations and trade unions. Although the implications of the application of such requirements may be significantly different for the two sets of organisations it satisfies a rough sense of justice that technically employers' associations and trade unions are treated alike. (Well over 100 employers' associations were entered on the Permanent Register by the end of March 1972.)

RULES OF GOOD CONDUCT FOR REGISTERED ORGANISATIONS

Schedule 4 of the Act establishes the "rules" about rules and schedule 5 the "administrative provisions" which apply equally to registered trade unions and registered employers' associations.

Schedule 5 is much occupied with the financial and accounting integrity of the organisation, with annual returns to the Registrar, the qualifications, appointment, removal and functions of auditors and with the proper running of superannuation schemes. Such material is dull, largely uncontroversial—but important.

On the surface schedule 4 is dull but contains more volatile matter. Three sets of requirements are established for registration. One set relates "to property and finances of organisation," to the purposes for which members' money shall be used, the organisational benefits and the keeping of proper accounts and related matters. A second set of requirements concerns "members of organisation." These requirements make more specific the general duties contained in the guiding principles. For example, union rules must specify who is eligible for membership, a procedure for handling applications and appeals. Rules must be clear about contributions, the penalties for default. A disciplinary procedure must be devised which must include "provision for appeals against decisions of the committee or other body responsible for taking disciplinary action" (s4–16(*c*)).

The third set of requirements is arguably the most important of those contained in the schedule because the requirements concern the "constitution and management of organisation." Some of the requirements are conventional enough. The rules of registered trade unions and registered employers' associations must provide for the election and re-election of their governing bodies, the election or appointment and removal of officers, the manner in which business meetings are to be transacted, rules altered, elections and ballots held (paras 4, 5, 8, 9, 11).

Other requirements reflect the Government's concern to have an organisation's authority structure clearly identified, to bring about a greater congruence between authority and power, particularly within trade unions, and to have power wielded in a constitutional way—that is, formally authorised. The clauses themselves demonstrate these implicit objectives:

> Paragraph 3: If the organisation has branches, the rules must so indicate, and must also indicate the extent to which, and the manner in which, it has power to control the activities of its branches.

"Extent" and "manner" obviously permit flexibility, an essential quality given the variety of organisational forms among trade unions and employers' associations. "Power to control" is an interesting phrase particularly when placed in the trade union context. Historically rank and file members have established the formal authority relationships between the executive at the centre and the branches. Actual power relationships which of their very nature are dynamic, may not consistently coincide with authority relationships which tend to be more static, being set in an infrequently changed rule book. A union's essential power resides in its membership and thus flows upwards from the base of the power/authority pyramid to the union officials. ("I shall have to put your [management] proposal to my members" may be used as a delaying tactic by a union official but it is more likely to be an expression of the official's need to have his authority—and power—endorsed by his constituents.)

Even if a union can satisfy the "power to control" criterion of registration, perhaps not very difficult in a form of words, this cannot guarantee a continuing and corresponding match with the *reality* of the power situation. Too many people, including some managers, take the view that a union should be able to control its members, that a union can be managed by its managers. Transferring the managerial "frame of reference" to union organisation is misleading. In a company power *and* authority reside in the directorate and flow *downwards* through the hierarchy of managerial grades, whereas in the union power basically flows upwards from the members, not downwards from their managers. When a managing director says "jump," the foreman eventually jumps. Union officials, even the most senior, as the railway dispute in the spring of 1972 showed, must try to achieve what their members want them to achieve.

While the above arguments ignore or gloss over many issues it remains an incontrovertible fact that the management of a union rests much more on the consent of the managed than does the management of the management within a firm. In the important judgement referred to in Chapter 12 [49], Lord Justice Denning in effect held that a union does not control its shop-stewards, a view still held by many people, even though the House of Lords reversed that ruling on 26 July 1972 in the sense that the T & GWU was held to be responsible for its stewards and should therefore control them. Whether one favours the Court of Appeal's reasoning or that of the House of Lords, both rulings are pertinent to the next three paragraphs of Schedule 4:

6 If the organisation has officials who are not officers of the organisation (whether they are shop-stewards, work place representatives or other officials) the rules must make provision for their election or appointment and for the manner in which they can be removed from office

7 The rules must specify the powers and duties of the governing body of the organisation, of each of its officers and of officials who are not officers of the organisation

10 The rules must specify any body by which, and any official by whom, instructions may be given to members of the organisation on its behalf for any kind of industrial action, and the circumstances in which any such instructions may be so given

The message of these three clauses like other parts of the Act, is neat, clear and logical: "Power should only be used by duly authorised persons. If power is used in an unauthorised way then the offenders should be exposed to legal sanctions." Such a general proposition carries appeal but its application to the myriad rough and tumble situations of shop-floor life is a very different matter. Working men's reactions to what they believe to be unfair behaviour, are likely to be influenced much more by their own warm emotion than cold, precise, legalistic thinking. This is not to claim that there is no case for internal union authority/power structure reform, but to discourage optimism that legalism, via registration, will force unions to control their members. If schedule 4 does prompt registered unions to examine more closely their management structures this could be a gain for the industrial relations system—but a modest one.

That thought may be amplified and others crystallised.

Union branches of one or more unions may have authority but in many given situations the shop-stewards committee drawn from one union, and very commonly from several, has the power. The rules of one registered union can hardly be seen to apply, even under paragraph 10 above, to a multi-union shop-steward committee. This illustration again underlines the fact that this part of the Act in common with others, cannot be regarded either in isolation from other parts of the Act, or from many other features of industrial relations activities which exist independently from the Act. To some such messiness is no doubt a source of irritation, to others it is part of the fascination of the subject.

14

Industrial Relations Code of Practice

After twelve chapters of legally "induced" complexity you may well share the sense of relief I experienced on turning to examine the Code of Practice. A consideration of the main technicalities of the Act and some of the many implications and speculations to which they give rise is succeeded by a review of a layman's guide for laymen.

PURPOSE OF THE CODE

Simply to make the contrast, the Act may be described as being concerned with "the good, the bad and the ugly" in industrial relations behaviour, whereas the Code is concerned only with the good. In fact, the promotion of the good, as distinct from the prohibition of the bad, is its decreed purpose. Section 2 of the Act makes this quite clear. Section 2 charges the Secretary of State with the preparation of a code of "practical guidance" which in his opinion "would be helpful" in the realisation of the principles and purpose set out in section 1—namely, the promotion of good industrial relations. The principles are neatly summarised in the Code as:

> Freely conducted collective bargaining, orderly procedures for settling disputes, free association of workers and employers and freedom and security for workers [30, p2].

In the preparation of the Code, and therefore in its revision:

> The Secretary of State shall have regard to:
>
> *a* The need for those who manage undertakings to accept the primary responsibility for the promotion of good industrial relations, and

b The need for providing practical guidance with respect to disclosure of information by employers, and with respect to the establishment and maintenance of effective means of negotiation, consultation and communication at all levels between those who manage undertakings and the workers employed in them (s2).

Management's "primary responsibility" is the core element of the Code and "disclose and discuss" its "leit motif." But how are managements to be persuaded to take up their "responsibility" and to promote "continuous dialogue" with the workers they manage?

> The Code imposes no legal obligations. Failure to observe it does not by itself render anyone liable to proceedings. But section 4 of the Industrial Relations Act requires any relevant provisions to be taken into account in proceedings under the Act before the National Industrial Relations Court or an industrial tribunal [30, p3].

But what is meant by "taken into account?" The phrase would seem to include not only "worse than" and "as good as" but "better than" the Code's standards for judicial assessment and comment. In other words, some employers, for example, might earn pats of approval from their advanced disciplinary procedures while other employers have the finger of criticism wagged in their direction. Conceivably an employer held to have dismissed a worker unfairly could find himself attracting local disapproval because his dismissal procedure was well below the standards required by the Code. The Industrial Relations Code is thus not strictly analogous to the Highway Code as only non-compliance with the latter is taken into account in "proceedings."

Eventually, in the light of the CIR's report, the Code will be amended so that general guidance can be given about disclosure of information for collective bargaining purposes as required by Section 56.

Whether any party's industrial relations practices are as good as or worse/better than those required by the Code they can become part of the public record. This risk of potential exposure may well encourage sensitivity and concern, particularly among managers to ensure that their company's procedures and practices will, if challenged, be found to match the Code's requirements.

During the short time that the Code has been in operation there are substantial grounds for believing that many managers, and many more than would otherwise have been the case, have been engaged in this reform process. To this extent the Code is being successful. Its influence can improve the climate of industrial relations. But its influence cannot work in isolation from other factors which may worsen the climate such as Court rulings which unions consider unjust, a high level of unemployment and fights over pay with the Government.

Even so, interesting and important as the docks container, railway and mini-general strike disputes may be, most managers are not directly affected in their daily working lives by the sort of dramatic events that occurred during the spring and summer of 1972. What is of closest concern to most managers is keeping their own particular industrial relations "patches" in reasonable order, interpreting, as the Code does, industrial relations in the widest sense to include not only relations with unions but human relations. Employees, not union members, are the common factor for all employers and in very many firms, all too many perhaps, there is no union presence. For very many managers therefore the bible at their elbow will be the Code rather than the Act. Some managers would say: "If we observe the Code we need not become involved with the Act," and for many situations this is likely to be true. True or not, overnight improvement in deficient employment policies and practices cannot be expected. Direct enforcement of the Code is not allowed for, labour inspectors have not been appointed. But, and this is another important but, the values which the Code embodies and the practices it recommends seem more likely than not to exert a steadily growing influence on employment behaviour in general and managerial behaviour in particular.

AUTHORSHIP

Are the values and recommendations therefore of the right kind? The attempted answer must be related to the authorship and the influences brought to bear on the authors. Formally the author of the Code is the Secretary of State for Employment. His civil servants may therefore be said to have drawn up this document. The Code is not the product of a tripartite working party of government, employer and union members. Had such a working party been appointed in 1970 it would probably still be sitting, unless it had disintegrated, with little to show for its endeavours. When the *Consultative Document* on the Code appeared in June 1971 the Department of Employment invited comments from all and sundry on its proposals. The draft Code which appeared in January 1972 was a tauter and more practical document which owed nothing, at least overtly, to the trade union movement for the changes made. Committed to non-co-operation the TUC made no formal submissions for change to the

Department of Employment but produced its own rival code [43] before the official draft Code appeared.

One of the most significant and quickly spotted additions to the *Consultative Document* which appeared in the Draft and Final editions of the Code was its final paragraph which reads:

> No disciplinary action should be taken against a shop-steward until the circumstances of the case have been discussed with a full-time official of the union concerned (para 133v).

The TUC Code includes:

> No disciplinary action should be taken by management against a trade union workplace representative until the circumstances of the case have been discussed with a full-time official of the union concerned [43, p16].

Other points of affinity between the two Codes can be readily identified, particularly concerning: the need for industrial relations training for managers, the importance of status quo provisions and the recognition that management and unions have both common and divergent interests. In the absence of formal representation by the trade union movement in the drafting of the Code, Department of Employment officials have seemingly been alert and responsive to trade union aspirations.

It is well we should remember that the authors of the Code are civil servants. Parliament was not empowered to devise or amend the Draft but to ratify or withhold ratification from the proposals presented by the Secretary of State. Such a process is open to the criticism that the legislature are expected to "rubber stamp" the ideas of the executive—an undemocratic shift in the locus of power. This is an arguable point but the danger to the democratic authority of Parliament can easily be exaggerated. Revision of the Code entails a different procedure. When revision is contemplated the Secretary of State is required to consult with the CBI and TUC before preparing a Draft of the revised Code (s3(3)). The Draft must then be sent to the CIR "for their consideration and advice." In short, once the directly involved power groups have had their chance to influence the Department of Employment's ideas, the independent agency is asked to comment on the resultant Draft. The Secretary of State is not required to accept the CIR's advice but he is under a duty to have the advice published (s3(4)). It would seem unlikely therefore, that a revised

Draft Code would diverge widely from views expressed by the CIR. Parliamentary ratification of the new Code would then be sought (s3(5)).

To pursue the matter of authorship a little further. It would be self-evidently wrong to have adopted as an official Code either a TUC or CBI Code. A joint CBI/TUC Code assuming it ever emerged, would have a better claim to adoption but the "community interest" element in such a Code would probably be weak. A formally achieved tripartite Code would be best but its realisation unlikely for some time. Inevitably, and particularly if one accepts that something needs to be done quickly rather than talked about interminably, authorship of the Code moves to a public agency. And what better than the Department of Employment with its long experience of handling employment problems under all kinds of Government, and expanding expertise in industrial relations. However, the upshot is that civil servants inform Parliament of what Parliament should approve and instruct the Court and industrial tribunals on how they should interpret the "good" of good industrial relations. Whether the executive should have this kind of mentor/magisterial relationship with the legislature and the judiciary is the starting point for a discussion which is not the subject of this book.

What really matters for present purposes is not so much the character of the authors and their constitutional position but what they have to say. Popular mythology decrees that civil servants will tend to be stodgy and conventional in their thinking and somewhat inflexible in their insistence that they and other people observe the rules and "stick to the book." Does the Code reinforce the myth? Before answering that question some general comments need to be made.

"The Code applies wherever people are employed" [30, p3]. Given the immense variety of employment situations that exist and the inherent dynamism in all of them, the drafting of a General Code could be a tall order for anyone. It would be all too easy for a Code to comprise a variegated bundle of platitudes, pious resolutions and clichés, tedious to read, easily forgotten and therefore without positive influence. Weaknesses of this kind were discernible in the *Consultative Document* but the Draft which followed, as hinted above, removed most of these. Anyone's "general code," because of its general nature, would be open to snide attacks. Few such have been made. Criticisms have been small scale and moderate. This reaction suggests two main eventualities: that the Code is innocuous and, therefore, ignored; that it is fair and likely to become slowly but increasingly effective. From the evidence of personal discussions, particularly with managers, and of commentators, the latter explanation appears by far the more valid.

It is not proposed to summarise the contents of the Code with which most readers are assumed to be reasonably familiar. In any event, the Code itself is a summary, not an exposition, of good practice. It would seem more sensible, therefore, to select and discuss particular features from the Code.

SELECTED FEATURES

Except perhaps on points of detail the Code is likely to present few problems to firms with sophisticated labour relations policies and practices. Indeed such firms may well be a little patronising in their attitude to the Code with its conventional wisdom—as such firms see it. Many more firms, however, are likely to pay more attention than in the past to their grievance and disciplinary procedures and facilities to be given to shop-stewards including shop-steward training. Some employers and therefore their employees may well be helped by the educational aspect of the Code, notably on "Employment Policies." Some firms, probably the smaller ones in particular, will carry on as though the Code had never been published. But it would be an incautious person who wagered that the overall effect, over time, of the Code would be negligible. The more likely result is the general raising of employment and industrial relations practices and standards to a position nearer to that of the high fliers which can't be bad [83].

A number of interesting responsibilities are placed upon management in the Code:

4 Where trade unions are recognised . . . management should . . .
iii Make clear to employees that it welcomes their membership of an appropriate recognised union and their participation in the union's activities.

The key word is "welcomes" which, if less positive than "encourages," is much stronger than the neutral stance of some employers: "It's up to the workers themselves to decide whether or not they want to join one of the unions we recognise."

Paragraph 31*v* under "Recruitment and Selection" has already been referred to in Chapter 7 in the context of the closed shop. This paragraph constitutes a tactful hint to management that a *prospective* employee should be left under no possible misapprehension about trade union strength, practices and values in the department he may be joining.

To return to responsibilities:

7 All managers should receive training in the industrial relations implications of their jobs. This is as necessary for line managers, including supervisors, as for personnel managers.

Amen to that. Paragraph 7 helps to strengthen the push given to industrial relations training which is likely to become a growth industry. (In the context of the Code and by implication in the total context of employment, industrial relations is taken to include human relations—that is, to include the sociology and psychology of work, motivation, and so on.) Paragraph 7 indicates that the supervisor is part of line management; paragraph 8 points out the supervisor's "key position to influence industrial relations" and the consequent responsibility on management to select, train and keep adequately informed, the right person to occupy the role of supervisor. And—footnote 5:

> In this Code supervisor means a member of the first line of management, who is responsible for his work group to a higher level of management.

So we have a clear declaration of public policy that the supervisor is part of management. For too long and in far too many instances supervisors and foremen, in particular, have felt themselves to be in a vulnerable no-man's land position enfiladed by shop-stewards and inadequately supported by higher management. A form of words will not in itself resolve the ambiguities in the position of particular supervisors but the Code's formula in conjunction with other factors should stimulate some managements into thinking more carefully about the nature of the supervisory activity.

One of the sentences of the Code which carries many and subtle implications according to the weight attached to the sentence by the reader is contained in paragraph 9:

> In particular, management should recognise the employee's need to achieve a sense of satisfaction in his job and should provide for it so far as practicable.

Job satisfaction literature had been expanding before the appearance of the Code but paragraph 9 may well swell that expansion. Who knows, ideas such as McGregor's *Theory X* and *Theory Y*, Maslow's *Hierarchy of Needs*, Likert's *People Oriented Rather Than Production Oriented Management*, Blake and Mouton's *Managerial Grid*, Herzberg's *Job Enrichment* and much else besides may have been present—or absent—in the minds of the authors of paragraph 9. Job satisfaction is a quicksilver concept, attractive but elusive. It obviously means different things to different people but, less obviously perhaps, it can mean different things to the same person over time. Bright young girls with one or two "A" levels may be highly dissatisfied with the lack of intellectual challenge in their work as clerks. The same girls having become middle-aged matrons will probably be much more content with the same sort of work.

Job satisfaction may contain many elements being drawn from two sources: the job and the person. Jobs may range from the simple to the complex—people are more likely to be complex than simple. The mix of the two can be volatile. Even so, certain elements can be identified as warranting specific attention, while allowing that more research is needed. A reasonable correspondence between a person's skills, knowledge and the job's requirements is obviously important. A fair effort/reward relationship has to be established. The nature and variety of tasks within the total job activity is a necessary consideration. A person's motivation is relevant and motivation can be influenced not only by the recognition, status, responsibility and blame given or not given to him at work, but by what happens to him at home, at the football ground, at the union branch. Personal values play a part. Some managers would not work for firms with selection practices that include the "vetting" of wives, believing such suitability screening to be an unjustifiable invasion of privacy [51].

From this sketch it seems obvious that even with much more sensitive analysis and concern than in the past, the most we can hope to achieve, at least in the short run, is some probably slight and unquantifiable improvement in job satisfaction. This may contribute to a reduction in industrial conflict (seeing that phenomenon as an expression of job dissatisfaction) absenteeism, labour turnover—and so on. Strong optimism would appear misplaced. Employee expectations in relation to job satisfaction are steadily rising while the intrinsic content of too many jobs appears to be shrinking under the pressures of technological change. At this point a retreat call must be sounded to what otherwise might become a foray into a "quality of life" discussion.

Fortunately, for practical day-to-day purposes, paragraph 9 provides an escape route. Job satisfaction should be provided "so far as practicable." Practicable in whose judgement? Presumably managements are not expected to be the sole arbiters of "practicable" but in many cases they will be unless challenged by the workforce—and challenge is largely influenced by the extent and character of worker organisation. Technical constraints on "practicable" may be enormous, especially when they spring from heavy capital investment. It will probably be very much easier to reorganise the work of office cleaners so as to bring them greater job satisfaction than a group of operators working on heavy presses. The Mrs Mopps are likely to be unorganised and not overbothered about job satisfaction—the heavy press operators may well be union members and "press" their steward to win extra pay for lack of job satisfaction as manifested in heavy and boring work.

Responsibilities rest not only on management but on employers' associations, the individual and trade unions. To ensure their organisation is effective unions should:

> Employ enough full-time officials to maintain adequate contact with management *and with their members in every establishment where the union is recognised* . . . (13(i))

In the italicised words can be discerned a reflection of the Act's concern, probably shared by the Department of Employment and seemingly by the House of Lords, to edge more authority and power back into the hands of the union professionals and away from the "amateur" shop-stewards. The historic House of Lords ruling on 26 July 1972 provides a major illustration of this "constitutional" concern to shift the distribution of authority within the union in the direction of its full time officers [52].

Predictably the Code shares the sensitivity of the Act to the position of the "professional employee." (A Special Register was created to meet the needs of professional institutions.) To indicate the nature of the personal dilemma that may arise where an individual is both a trade unionist and "professional employee" an oversimplified illustration may be given. Should a nurse go on strike? Paragraph 22 of the Code constitutes an attempt to resolve the possibly competing claims on the individual of loyalty to the professional ethic and loyalty to the union. From paragraph 22 and its associated paragraphs 21 and 23, it seems clear that greater weight should be given to professional than to trade union duty where the special health and safety needs of others are involved.

The section on "Employment Policies" contains sensible advice and for some managements, particularly in the less-sophisticated firms, it may perform a useful educational service.

> In recruiting and selecting employees management should: . . . *consider* filling vacancies by transfer or promotion from within the undertaking (31(ii))

In other words before buying from the external labour market management should give some thought to the use of the internal labour market. Both the advice, and the process if undertaken, are entirely consistent with the furtherance of job satisfaction. Considerable dissatisfaction can arise if present employees are passed over for promotion because "new blood" is thought to be necessary to the firm. This is not an anti-new-blood argument, it is only anti the ill-considered transfusion of such blood.

Paragraph 42 is important for its public policy endorsement of the desirability of eroding the status, conditions of employment and facilities differentials that too often exist between staff and works personnel. It is a matter of history rather than present-day rational justification that the blue-collar worker is required to clock-on and work forty hours while the white-collar worker is off the clock for his thirty-five hour working week. Paragraph 42 may do something to reduce the elements of the "class system" in the employment situation and promote the idea that all employees are entitled to basic "employee citizenship" rights and conditions, differentials of whatever nature being related to the requirements of the job and not to the fact that one employee wears a boiler suit and another an office dust jacket. Some staff workers may, of course, be prompted by paragraph 42 to join or become active in unions to maintain or have re-established differences they believe to be merited.

Two points are selected for brief comment from "Communication and Consultation":

> Major changes in working arrangements should not be made by management without prior discussion with employees or their representatives [52]

"Major" and "working arrangements" beg questions but the Code would seem to acknowledge the desirability of some form of status quo arrangement indicating that change should not be imposed but achieved by consent.

For many years, one might say from the Whitley Committee of 1917 onwards, public policy has recommended, even required in the public sector, the separation of joint negotiation and joint consultation processes. Paragraph 70 of the Code marks a sharp departure from this practice as it confers public "blessing" on the fusion of the two processes where fusion seems appropriate. In other cases, careful linkages should be established between the processes.

"Collective bargaining" compresses a good deal of sensible advice, particularly to management, on what to do if a union seeks recognition and how to set about the design of orderly bargaining structures. Paragraph 78x contains the hint, for example, that it might be better to have separate rather than common bargaining arrangements for the supervised, the supervisors and those managers who negotiate on behalf of the firm.

"Employee Representation at the Place of Work" legitimises the position of the shop-steward and adds weight to the desirability of constitutional behaviour. For example, management can "encourage union members to vote in elections of shop-stewards" by providing facilities for elections "in the establishment" (para 108). Trade unions should:

> . . . seek agreement with management on the issue of *joint* written credentials setting out the relevant *rights and obligations* of the stewards and of management (para 110(ii))

(The TGWU have reached such agreements since the code became operational.)

Facilities for stewards, too commonly a fuzzy area in collective agreements, are recommended in paragraphs 116 and 117. "As a minimum," stewards should be given reasonable time off for their industrial relations functions and maintained earnings while performing those functions. Additional facilities might include: lists of new employees, accommodation for private meetings, access to a telephone, the provision of noticeboards, office facilities "appropriate to the circumstances." In some firms these facilities provisions which (stand in direct line of descent from CIR [53] and Donovan thinking) could constitute a powerful prod to management to come to terms with the steward's position in a rational constructive way rather than keep attempting to fight off the steward's influence.

A similar prod is contained in paragraph 118 which sees shop-steward training as a joint management–union responsibility. The special protection afforded stewards in "Disciplinary Procedures" has already been mentioned above (133v). In sum, it would need a determined application of crooked as distinct from straight thinking to maintain that the Code was hostile to the steward's position. It is my impression from discussions with hundreds of managers in the past twelve months that many firms are using the Code as a checklist to identify the additional facilities that need to be given to the stewards. In situations where facilities have been rudimentary and grudgingly conceded, stewards are presented with a bargaining counter, the Code, if they choose or are permitted by their unions to use it. To ignore the Act but use the Code may not be a logical stance for a union or its stewards to adopt but it could be a productive one—for workers, the management and the enterprise concerned.

"Disciplinary Procedures" (paras 130–3) are important not only in their own right but for their relationship to the unfair dismissal provisions of the Act. Before an employer claims before an industrial tribunal that the dismissal was fair, he would be wise to check that his disciplinary–dismissal arrangements are consistent with the Code's standards. For example, the following basic issue has been all too often neglected in the past:

131 Management should make known to each employee
i Its disciplinary rules and the agreed procedure
ii The type of circumstances which can lead to suspension or dismissal

The example is only part of the much bigger point that the Code's publication has stimulated a great deal of managerial activity directed towards analysing and overhauling procedural arrangements, shop-steward facilities and employment practices generally. Managers who previously have shown little interest in or have had little to do with the untidy world of industrial relations have found themselves discussing with their more knowledgeable colleagues the circumstances under which employees can be disciplined and dismissed, the firm is prepared to recognise a white-collar union, new facilities are to be given to blue-collar union stewards—and so on. Senior managers or directors who have been involved in industrial relations in the past but with a sense of irritation and off-handedness rather than constructive commitment, are being prompted to accept industrial relations as one of their major concerns instead of a tiresome subsidiary activity. In short, the Code is helping to inject increasing professionalism into industrial relations, an injection strongly urged by Donovan.

It would be a pity if this reform momentum was lost because the Act which brought the Code to life was repealed. But encouragement can be derived from the assumption, not unduly optimistic, that the TUC's *Good Industrial Relations* guide for negotiators could contribute materially to a Labour Government's Code, which itself would draw upon the experience gained from the operation of the present Code. Whatever the final effects of the legally "induced" convulsions of the summer of 1972 prove to be, and whatever the outcome of the next General Election, there is every reason to believe that some sort of Industrial Relations Act and some sort of Industrial Relations Code will persist as an important part of our total industrial relations activity. More will be said on this point in the final chapter.

15

Straitjacket or Framework

Three strands of objectives are intertwined in this chapter: an attempt to take stock of what the Act accomplished in the first twelve fractious months of its life, an appraisal of the Act in general terms and a tentative prediction about the possible future movement of public policy on industrial relations.

Within the compass of one chapter only certain highlights and key areas of activity can be selected for discussion. To a certain extent the pattern of the discussion will follow the general chapter structure of the book.

INSTITUTION

Crucial to the operation of the Act is the role of the Industrial Court and particularly its effect on trade union behaviour. In the same way that employers have sometimes grudgingly yielded increasing degrees of recognition to trade unions, so have trade unions, in the main, come increasingly to recognise that the Industrial Court is an institution whose power and influence cannot be ignored. The TUC soon acknowledged that boycotting the Court, which in specific cases could be viewed as defiance of the law, was inadequate as a policy. To claim, however vehemently, that the Industrial Court was "not a proper court" hardly constituted an effective strategy. Early in May 1972, against a background of the railway dispute and the £50000 fine on the TGWU for contempt, a special meeting of the TUC General Council decided that unions should defend themselves before the Industrial Court or industrial tribunals.

Some unions, most notably the AUEW, spurned this "ignoble" art of self-defence. At the time of writing, March 1973, the AUEW was still pursuing its pristine policy of not appearing before the Court—at some cost to its members. On balance, however, the unions have chosen to be pragmatic rather than doctrinaire, "defence" being interpreted and established in a variety of ways. At a basic level a trade union can defend itself against charges of unfair industrial practice, appearing before the Court to explain its point of view and to contest an "injured party's" claim for a declaration, compensation or, most important, for an injunction. In this way, unions can possibly ward off the threat of legal "sanctions."

Lines of defence may be extended to include appearances before the Court (and/or co-operation with the CIR) to thwart the attack of competitors—that is, rival unions and rival staff associations. In this context, APEX, ASTMS, the Union of Post Office Workers, the EETPTU (Electrical, Electronic, Telecommunications and Plumbing Trade Union) have all appeared before the Court to protect, and successfully at that, their members' interests against raiding new unions, seeking recognition and bargaining rights. Some unions have chosen to become registered, to accept suspension and possible expulsion from the TUC in order to protect their members' best interests by seeking approved closed-shop agreements which the Court will defend.

If experience is encouraging the unions to respond more flexibly to the Court's existence and operation, there is also some evidence to suggest that the Court itself is reacting more imaginatively and sensitively to the industrial relations environment than critics sometimes allow. Although from its inception the Court has exercised its conciliatory function as it is required to do by its own rules [64], this activity has been obscured by the public's attention being inevitably focused on the confrontations.

Some employers have come to learn that claims for legal redress are not freely conceded, some new unions have learnt that the Court is not an automatic ally in their attempts to establish beachheads in what other interests regard as their negotiating territory. Employers and unions together have been persuaded by the Court, or have persuaded themselves under the Court's encouragement, to reach voluntary solutions to their problems. It has been common for the Court to hold private preliminary meetings between the parties before setting the date for a formal hearing, with a view to narrowing the issues in dispute and promoting a voluntary settlement. One close observer of the Court's operation has claimed that only about 10 per cent of the Court's first year of work concerned complaints of unfair industrial practice and that a good number of these had been withdrawn or settled by conciliation [65].

In relation to confrontation-type issues, there has been a softening in the Court's response in which the House of Lords ruling on a "union and its stewards" [52] has played a vital part. In effect, the House of Lords decision results in the institution rather than named individuals being held accountable for industrial relations sins. The Industrial Court has gone on to say that in any future contempt proceedings, officials of organisations will not be imprisoned for contempt of court, the penalties being applied to the financial resources of the organisations, through sequestration if necessary. Categories of contempt are to be established which could materially affect, in the sense of reducing, the amount of money to be paid. It seems that although it will still be possible for unofficial leaders of industrial action to be sent to jail for contempt, such seclusion will be very difficult to achieve.

The Industrial Court has also indicated that interim (restraining) orders will be used only with the greatest circumspection and that time will be allowed for the organisation concerned to impress upon its membership the need for compliance with an order. In short, these developments suggest that the risk of the labour injunction being freely used to limit severely "the right to strike" has been materially reduced. More will be said on this point later.

Thus, during the first few months of the Court's life the ground rules for the Court's operation have steadily become clearer. It has also become clear that the Court is not the hammer of the unions, although it has pummelled one or two, but, it can be argued, essentially at their invitation. Nor is the Court the provider of the panacea for our industrial relations ills. It was never intended to be but misconceptions about its cure-all function persist. Whether it will survive a change of government is a matter of guesswork. New courts of law are not lightly created or abolished because they become enmeshed with the general legal system. Even if the Court is abolished, the House of Lords confirmation of the Court's view that a union is accountable for its shop-stewards, would presumably carry authority unless Parliament changed the law.

There is a good case for modifying the Court's jurisdiction because many people, rightly in my view, believe the Act itself should be modified. But, whatever one may think of the Court, it seems undeniable that the friction surrounding its early work generated not only heat but light—notably light on the problems of the "container revolution" and the distribution of power and authority within unions.

INDIVIDUAL RIGHTS

After twelve months' operation, it is possible to outline some of the dimensions of change brought about by the provisions affecting the rights of individual workers. From 28 February to 29 December 1972, 7374 complaints of unfair dismissal were received by Department of Employment conciliation officers [66]. Of these 6863 were referred by the tribunals for conciliation while 511 requests for help were made direct to the Department before applications were made to the tribunals. Of these total cases, 1196 were settled by conciliation while many others were still being dealt with by this process when the above figures were published. Unfortunately, as the Secretary of State for Employment confessed: ". . . we shall not be able to provide details of the results of references to the tribunals until the end of the year, since these records have become computerised (laughter...)" [67].

Even so, from this background and from the information given in Chapter 6, it seems odds on that after a year's experience of the unfair dismissal provisions, the total of dismissed workers who are given back their jobs or compensation in lieu will be numbered in four rather than three figures. Whatever the sense of injustice that may be felt by some employers or workers whose claims and counter-claims have not been upheld, on balance the above changes constitute a valuable reform advance on the pre-Act position. Whatever the *x*-number successful claimant workers for a given period proves to be, there will probably be an even greater *y*-number, but an unknown number, who are more fairly treated if dismissed or better protected by being kept on because of the case law on unfair dismissals. The disappearance of such protective provisions from our labour law seems highly unlikely.

Other individual rights conferred by the Act occupy a more dubious position on the scale of worthiness.

From 28 February to 29 December 1972, conciliation officers received 278 complaints (the great majority being referred from tribunals) relating to the infringement of rights about trade union membership and activity [66]. Measured by volume, complaints on unfair dismissal apparently constitutes a much greater "injustice area" than infringement of union membership rights. Some section 5 cases have been decided by industrial tribunals and the following is illustrative of the sensitivity of that area of social behaviour where individual and collective values clash.

Because a worker would not join an unregistered union, his union workmates refused to work overtime if the "nonner" worked overtime. The nonner complained that the employer had committed the unfair industrial practice of discriminating against him by denying him overtime because he wished to exercise his statutory right not to join a union. The tribunal upheld the complaint making an order declaring: ". . . to deprive Mr Jones of an equal right to overtime with that of every other employee in his section is an unfair industrial practice . . ." (*on the part of the company*). "The effect of that declaration, or how effect can be given to it in practice, is a matter for further consideration by the company with or without consultation with Mr Jones or others" [68, p255]. The rest of the declaration indicates both an awareness of the company's problem of balancing individual and group rights and the paramountcy, from the Act's perspective, of individual rights. "If Mr Jones remains employed by the company and, for economic reasons, the company decides that it must continue to act contrary to our declaration, then it may be that the only thing that Mr Jones can do is to apply to us for compensation." Mr Jones' dismissal by the company or by himself might warrant compensation for unfair dismissal.

In a rather different context, the Industrial Court ruled [69] that employees who were officials of a *registered* union were not entitled to conduct union activities (established as a right for registered unions under section 5(1)(c)) on an employer's premises, *if* the employer had not given his consent to such activities—for example, the distribution of literature, the collection of subscriptions, the use of a noticeboard. The background to this case is the continuing attempt by the registered Telecommunications Staff Association (TSA) to win recognition from the Post Office in face of opposition by the unregistered but recognised Union of Post Office Workers (see page 168).

And what of the rights of the individual worker in relation to a trade union? Here the test case has tested the resolution of the individual concerned (a not inappropriately named Mr Goad), the resolution of the AUEW, with its policy of boycotting the Court, and the authority of the Court itself.

Having allowed his membership of the AUEW to lapse because he disagreed with an unofficial strike, Mr Goad later tried to rejoin the union. His application was refused and the industrial tribunal ruled that he was entitled to reinstatement. The tribunal's ruling proved unenforceable, Mr Goad sought help from the Industrial Court which ordered that he ought not "as a union member . . . to be arbitrarily or unreasonably excluded from branch meetings" [70]. This order was not observed, the union ignored an order to appear before the Court and, in due course, was fined £5000 and later a further £50000 for contempt.

Mr Goad may or may not be a "village Hampden" [71] defying a tyrant but if the Court ruling, which resulted from Mr Goad's activities, prompts the AUEW to reconsider its policy of non-appearance before the Court, Mr Goad will have done the union a service. As Sir John Donaldson put the point: ". . . a refusal to obey a Court order is not 'non-cooperation,' it is simple law breaking" [70].

The Act which created the Industrial Court and many of its powers is certainly open to sharp criticism, as has been indicated, but the best route to its reform surely lies through the ballot box, the many forms of political influence open to a large organisation, and subtler tactics than self-wounding confrontations with the Courts. The actual danger inherent in the AUEW's example of disregarding the law it dislikes may be exaggerated because the example is unlikely to be followed as TUC and other union responses to the Court's position have demonstrated. But, as a general proposition, the potential dangers inherent in all interests observing certain laws and ignoring others of which they disapprove cannot be argued away. And, it is not difficult to envisage that the AUEW policy could be counter-productive to the promotion of trade union and labour movement interests.

COLLECTIVE BARGAINING

By the end of February 1973, one of the fears voiced by many commentators had, fortunately, not been realised. Little litigation of disrupting consequence had arisen concerning the operation of the closed shop. The potential danger of such disruption remains. As intimated earlier, management and unions in local situations appeared to have found ways to safeguard the status quo of union security arrangements. (In a related context, even that august giant the ICI, issued with their unions a joint statement to the effect that the Act would not disturb their mutual relationships.) Incomes Data Services identified four main approaches to the handling of sections 5 and 7:

1 A joint statement on continuation of previous bargaining machinery and arrangements
2 A voluntary agency shop-agreement or an unofficial agency shop with unregistered unions
3 Avoidance of over-emphasising workers' rights not to belong to a union
4 Aiding unions to persuade employees to remain or become members of recognised unions by providing them with better recruitment facilities [72, p6]

All these approaches have an air of subterfuge about them, particularly where terms like "voluntary agency shop" or "unofficial agency shop" are employed. If union policy changed to one of registration this would significantly reduce the number of hole-in-the-corner arrangements on union security but would not of itself re-establish union security at its pre-Act level. In essence, what is needed by many employers, unions and this tension-laden aspect of industrial relations, is the restoration of the closed shop to its former pre-Act position.

Agency shop-agreements, consistent with the Act's requirements, have been reached but are relatively few in number because of their restriction to registered union situations. NUBE have concluded several agency-shop agreements.

Expectations that the Act would prompt the emergence of new unions, some from the chrysalises of staff associations or house unions, have been partly realised. So far, however, these new organisations have not had the disruptive effect on bargaining structures that was once feared. Their attempts to achieve recognition by using the Act's procedures have been largely unsuccessful. Numbers of staff associations have run into difficulties in attempting to satisfy the Registrar, in order to remain registered, that they are financially independent of their parent companies. If the amount of overt conflict arising from interunion rivalry for membership has not been as great as originally anticipated, the potential for serious clashes in the growth area of union membership, the white-collar sector of private employment, remains significant. Clashes tend to be sharp where a heightened interest in trade unionism is shown by professional workers and is expressed by the creation of a new union which is then seen as a threat by long-established white-collar unions attempting to penetrate the ranks of engineers and managers. Such a clash occurred at C A Parsons between TASS the technical section of the AUEW and the new union for professional engineers UKAPE. After an Industrial Court order had achieved a truce, the CIR was able to complete its investigations into the dispute about bargaining rights.

Eventually, in October 1972, the CIR recommended [73] that TASS should be recognised as sole bargaining agent for technical staff up to but not including assistant managers. The claim by UKAPE and its associates for negotiating rights for a bargaining unit from the "level at which a new graduate would normally start his career" was not accepted.

An application by UKAPE (United Kingdom Association of Professional Engineers), APST (Association of Professional Scientists and Technologists) and ASEE (Association of Supervisory and Executive Engineers) to the Industrial Court (all three being registered trade unions) for a CIR investigation of their claim for a separate bargaining unit for senior qualified engineers and technologists employed by Rolls-Royce at Derby was refused by the Court. "The President said that there was so little evidence of any failure to serve their best interests by their present recognised unions that it would be wrong to order a reference to the commission" [74]. The "present recognised unions" were APEX, ASTMS and TASS who opposed the application, as did the employer (although TASS did not appear before the Court).

Despite these rebuffs, UKAPE and similar unions will doubtless soldier on but in relation to the Act's significance for the issues outlined above, three important points may be made. A cessation of interunion hostilities can be achieved while competing claims are independently examined. The ground rules on recognition and bargaining unit matters are becoming clearer and firmer because of the developing case law. These two facts together should help other managements in comparable situations to design adequate recognition and bargaining structure policies.

INDUSTRIAL ACTION

A tough thread binding together the *Donovan Report*, *In Place of Strife*, *Fair Deal at Work* and *the Industrial Relations Act*, in some form of loose association, has been the recognition that something should be done about strikes, a recognition in itself that there is a strike problem. But what are the dimensions of that problem? Space limitations permit only a brief indication of one or two of the parameters.

International strike statistics are notoriously difficult to handle in terms of making fair comparisons. Even so, the following data [75, p899] based on ILO information is sufficiently accurate to prompt valid discussion points on the "what to do about strikes" issue.

DAYS LOST THROUGH INDUSTRIAL DISPUTES PER 1000 PERSONS EMPLOYED
(mining, manufacturing, construction and transport industries)

	YEARLY AVERAGE		
	5 years 1962–66	5 years 1967–71	10 years 1962–71
Italy	1388	1608	1498
[1]United States	790	1648	1219
United Kingdom	228	596	412
Japan	250	194	222
West Germany	34	78	56
[2]Sweden	26	62	44

[1] Figures cover also electricity, gas and sanitary services
[2] All industries included

The countries selected for this excerpt from the table in the Department of Employment *Gazette* include most of the major industrialised countries of the free West—and a number of our most important competitors in export markets. (France has been excluded because of incomplete data.)

With the exception of the Japanese experience, it is clear that increased militancy in the later of the two five-year periods was not confined to the UK. While it may give us some satisfaction that our record is better than that of the USA and Italy, we have no cause to feel smug about our position compared to the more peaceful industrial relations of those major industrial competitors of ours—Japan, West Germany and Sweden.

While it is easy to exaggerate expectations concerning the influence of the law upon strikes, the above table legitimately prompts the question: should we eschew the strike laws of the USA and Italy and adopt features from the strike laws of Japan, West Germany and Sweden? To attempt to answer that question adequately is material for a separate book. Some brief comments may, however, be ventured now.

It is ironic perhaps, that we should appear to have adapted within the Industrial Relations Act, American practices of cooling-off orders in relation to serious disputes. Clearly, the Heath Government's wish is that our gentlemen's collective agreements should develop contractual force. This may bring about the American-type strike which follows the expiry of the contract. While West German constitutional law does not guarantee the right to strike, it does guarantee the freedom to organise and protects that freedom from attack. Readers who wish to know more about comparative labour law systems and, in particular, about *Laws Against Strikes* are recommended to read the Fabian pamphlet of that title [76]. An obvious point but one that merits emphasis is that the labour laws of any one country, if they are to be understood properly, must be set in the very complex and dynamic networks of elements that have shaped a particular country's culture, history, political, social and economic systems. The low strike incidence in West Germany and Japan may have as much or more to do with the cultural values of those countries as with their formal systems of strike laws.

But have the Industrial Relations Act's restrictions on the strike and other forms of industrial action brought about changes in our patterns of industrial conflict? It is too soon to say and, in any event, it may prove very difficult to unravel cause/effect relationships. Presumably the hope of the legislators would be the eventual substitution of "due notice" official strikes for "no notice" unconstitutional strikes. Some evidence that this may happen can be adduced from various sources—for example, the TUC's advice to unions to give due notice of industrial action [12], advice which has been passed on by unions to their members; rulings from the Industrial Court on instances where due notice had not been given and, as a consequence of the ruling, due notice has then been given. (ASTMS were involved in one such case early in December 1972, concerning a strike against Horizon Holidays.) While more in the nature of a pointer than evidence, there appears to have been a drastic reduction in the amount of news space devoted to unofficial strikes.

A feature of the Act's anti-strike provisions which, quite understandably, worries many people, particularly labour sympathisers [76] is the resurrection of the labour injunction which until the enactment of the Norris La Guardia Act in 1932 virtually crippled industrial action by American unions. The classic work on the subject was written by Frankfurter and Greene in 1930, *The Labour Injunction*, and it is still widely cited. Two of the many anti-injunction points are indicated here:

> The basic concepts applicable to the grant of inter-locutory injunctions (the preservation of the status quo and the "balance of convenience") were unsuited to labour disputes because the suspension of a strike always affects the strikers adversely while allowing the employer to continue his operations and so defeat the strike; that a judge cannot weigh the tangible interests of an employer in his property and business against the intangible interests of strikers in the continuance of their strike . . . [76, p52]

The above are powerful arguments but one must remember that their setting was America at a time of union weakness before the dawn of the New Deal, and not Britain of the 1960s and 70s when unions enjoy great organic strength in an economy increasingly vulnerable to industrial action. Furthermore, under the Industrial Relations Act, the injunction is granted only if certain tests have been met, conciliation attempted, and, as far as strikes are concerned, granted only in relation to unfair industrial practice strikes (not all strikes) and national emergency disputes. In the 1920s in the USA virtually any union activity, let alone a strike, which interfered with an employer's business, could be restrained by the courts and "the grant or denial of an injunction bore no relation to the merits of the underlying social and economic dispute" [77, p101]. Up to a point, this last comment tallies with the granting of restraining orders under the Industrial Relations Act—but only up to a point, for the unfair industrial practices which are restrained are so defined as to incorporate, if only very broadly, social and economic issues. As for the merits of these issues, their identification and evaluation sometimes becomes the concern of the CIR. In the case quoted on page 173, TASS was restrained from taking industrial action while the CIR investigated the social and economic merits of bargaining rights of rival unions at C A Parsons.

While it is not possible to be assertive on this point, the British experience of the injunction under the Act might turn out to be less a case of "stop the action—full stop" than "stop the action and then we will try to probe to the causes of the dispute." From the foregoing, it should not be assumed that I favour the use of the labour injunction but as a proposition one would have to allow that there may well be a legitimate place for this form of legal restraint in industrial relations, not least perhaps in its application to militant employers. In the nature of things it is much more difficult to identify employer militancy than worker militancy but the Act does technically permit a restraining of certain types of lock-out.

POWER IN SOCIETY AND DIRECTION OF REFORM

Mid 1972 resounded with impassioned but sometimes rational debate. "Abrasive," "confrontation," "polarisation of society," "government by consent," "a threat to democracy," appeared among the words and phrases used with considerable, perhaps excessive, frequency. In retrospect, it will probably seem a good thing that as a society, we did discuss with great concern the limits and nature of legitimate protest against an act, the introduction of which, it was widely claimed, did not rest on the consent of the people. Late in July, *The Times* could thunder in an extended leading article "Yes, we are in danger" [78] because the trade unions were setting themselves above the law. A few days later *The Times*, in another lengthy leading article, suggested "How the Law should be changed" [79].

The future may show that the social, economic and political ferment generated by the Act in its initial operation was part of the price society paid for the beginning of a continuing systematic intervention by the State into the procedural features of collective bargaining.

Much of the Donovan analysis of Britain's industrial relations ills centred on the tensions arising from the badly matching "two systems" of industry-wide and workplace bargaining. Another Donovan-type inquiry might do well to focus on the tensions arising from two sets of values: individualism and collectivism. Professor Wedderburn has argued, and he is supported by many others, that the Act represents "a philosophy of extreme individualism which inhibits collective organisation . . ." and has urged that "the duty of a labour law system is *first* to the individuals in the collective majority; and only *second*—not to be forgotten, but *second*—to individuals who wish to opt out of collective labour relations" [56, p288, 290].

One simple but recent illustration of the clash between individualistic and collective values may be given. On 2 December 1972, TASS was reported by the press as saying that "whereas weekly hours and related conditions were previously a collective concept, flexitime created a situation where people worked an individually chosen working week," a change which threatened to undermine collectively negotiated employment standards. Any government proposing to revise the Industrial Relations Act would do well to keep these two systems of values constantly in mind.

Revision, repeal, replacement of the Act—which is it to be? Repeal would need to be followed by replacement which would entail revision. To repeal the Act without replacing it would be to put the unions at far greater legal risk than they are under the Act. This is because the Act repealed parts or the whole of earlier laws which protected trade unions. A new Act would, therefore, be essential to protect the unions from attack at common law and particularly from the law of tort. It seems hardly likely that the ramshackle edifice of acts from 1871 to 1913 would be re-erected. In fashioning a new union protecting framework, it seems fairly obvious that even a Socialist government, as the most likely repealer, would retain, perhaps with modifications, those features of the Act which experience had shown to be of advantage to work people and possibly the unions. In this respect, the unfair dismissal and disclosure of information provisions come to mind—both sets of provisions are to be found in Labour's Industrial Relations Bill of 1970.

Even if the Conservative Party remain in power, revision of the Act seems certain. The Heath Government have promised to amend the law but have insisted that the Act first be given a reasonable opportunity and period to operate. When revisions are being contemplated I, personally, hope that the straitjacket around the closed shop is removed and far less importance attached to the individualism expressed in section 5 and related sections. Restrictions on strikes and blacking need liberalising not least because of further restrictions on the right to strike that may emanate from any Government's counter-inflation policies. The registration principle also requires re-examination.

Industrial relations constitute a subsystem of larger economic, social and political systems. The interaction of these systems should be taken into account when changes in the law are being contemplated. In relation to multi-national companies, unions need more power than they have. On the other hand, a civilised society ought to establish better ways of mediating between the claims of miners and power workers and the needs of lonely but unorganised old-age pensioners, deprived by industrial action of light, heat and mobility if living in a multi-storey flat. It may be that, as Professor Phelps Brown has suggested [80], the days of traditional and free collective bargaining, not only in Britain but Western Europe and

North America, are close to cessation—that the distribution of wage and salary income will need increasingly to be achieved on a tripartite basis of employer, union and public agency responsibility. The CBI–TUC conciliation service initiative, taken in August 1972, may be a struggling bipartite harbinger of such arrangements.

Whatever the deficiencies of the Industrial Relations Act, and I have tried to indicate what are, in my opinion, the more serious of these, we can be grateful to it for two things. It has caused many more of us than would otherwise have been the case to re-examine the assumptions and values which influence our behaviour. In the light of the above and other remarks in this chapter, it will be interesting to see whether the views of Mr Chapple, general secretary of the EET–PTU will come to hold more sway than ideological opposition to the Act. The following are excerpts from a speech which Mr Chapple claims he was not allowed to make at the TUC 1972 congress when unions were suspended from membership—a speech which is printed in the September 1972 issue of *Contact* [81] the EET–PTU journal.

> Haven't the milestones of this so called free collective bargaining been appeals to Governments yes, even Tory Governments, for help and intervention against employers—for subsidies to keep shipyards and factories open where, despite the freedom of the trade unions to negotiate, plants are closing?
>
> Are we really saying that we don't want an Act which provides workers with protection from unfair dismissal?
>
> Are we saying we don't want an Act which forces employers to bargain with unions for the first time in their history?
>
> It is contrary to 100 years of TUC policy for us not to make use of what is to our advantage under the law and to oppose and to seek to change that which is damaging.

The second result for which we can feel grateful is the injection by the Act of increased professionalism into management's handling of industrial relations. The issue is not simply one of "how does one comply with the Act?" but "how does one set about doing a more competent manpower management job?" (The CIR has recently attempted to provide some of the answers with its "industrial relations training" and the "managerial industrial relations role" reports) [82]. Over time, the impetus for change created by the Act will decline but the odds are that because of this legislation, replaced and revised or just revised, the inputs of managerial expertise and resources into the many and varied activities of industrial relations will stabilise at a higher level than would have been achieved had there been no Act.

Appendix 1

Unfair Industrial Practices and Breaches of Duty

The Act defines the unfair industrial practices for which registered and unregistered organisations and individuals may be open to complaint to the Industrial Court or an industrial tribunal. The following list is for ease of reference; the relevant chapters in the guide describe the circumstances in which unfair industrial practices and breaches of duty may take place, and the qualifications which attach to them. The list is in three sections: unfair industrial practices which may be taken by:

1 An employer or employers' association
2 An organisation of workers or any person
3 Employers or workers, or organisations of either

BY AN EMPLOYER OR EMPLOYERS' ASSOCIATION

It is an unfair industrial practice:

1 To infringe an employee's right to join a registered trade union or to take part in its activities (s5(2))
2 To infringe an employee's right not to join a registered trade union or unregistered organisation of workers (s5(2))
3 To refuse to employ an individual because of his membership or non-membership of a union except where there is an agency-shop agreement or an approved closed shop (s5(2))
4 To dismiss an employee unfairly (s22(1))

5 To fail to negotiate seriously with a registered trade union (or joint negotiating panel) where the Industrial Court has made an order that the union or panel is to be the sole bargaining agent for the bargaining unit; or to negotiate in respect of the employees in the bargaining unit with any other registered or unregistered organisation of workers (s55(1))

6 To conduct or threaten a lock-out to induce or attempt to induce anyone to refrain from making an application to the Industrial Court about the recognition of a sole bargaining agent or the withdrawal of such recognition (s55(8))

BY AN ORGANISATION OF WORKERS OR ANY PERSON

It is an unfair industrial practice:

1 To induce an employer not to perform his duty to enter into an agency-shop agreement after a ballot has shown a majority of employees to be in favour of one (s13(2))

2 To induce an employer to enter into an agency-shop agreement after an application has been made for a ballot (s16(2))

3 To organise or threaten a strike or irregular industrial action short of a strike to induce an employer:

a To discriminate against any employee (or individual seeking work) because of his membership or non-membership of a trade union

b To induce or operate an agreement for a pre-entry closed shop

c To join in an application for an approved closed shop

d To dismiss an employee unfairly (s33)

4 To organise or threaten a strike or any irregular industrial action short of a strike to induce an employer:

a Not to negotiate with a registered trade union or joint negotiating panel which the Industrial Court has designated as sole bargaining agent or

b To negotiate in respect of the designated bargaining unit with any other registered or unregistered organisation of workers (s55(3))

—if an order withdrawing recognition exists, for anyone, by organising or threatening industrial action, to induce or attempt to induce an employer to disobey it (s55(7))

BY EMPLOYERS OR WORKERS, OR ORGANISATIONS OF EITHER

It is an unfair industrial practice:

1 To induce a registered trade union or employer or an individual to refrain from making an application for a ballot to establish or continue an agency shop (s16)

2 For a party to a collective agreement to break any part of the agreement which is a legally enforceable contract (s36(1))

3 For a party to a collective agreement of which the whole or part is a legally enforceable contract, made after the commencement of this Act, not to take all reasonably practicable steps to prevent or end an action by its agents or members (or anyone purporting to act on its behalf) of a kind which some legally enforceable term of the agreement binds the organisation not to take (s36(2))

4 To organise or threaten industrial action in furtherance of a recognition dispute while the issue is before the Secretary of State (i.e. he has been given notice of intention to apply to the Industrial Court), the Industrial Court or the CIR: and for six months after the CIR has reported on it (s54(4))

5 For two years after the CIR reports to the Industrial Court on a recognition reference, for anyone to organise or threaten industrial action to induce an employer to recognise or bargain with any registered or unregistered organisation or workers not recommended by the CIR (s55(6))

6 For any registered or unregistered organisation of workers or employers, or anyone acting on its behalf, to act or threaten to act in contravention of the Act's guiding principles about its conduct (s66 and 70)

7 For anyone, other than a registered trade union or registered employers' association or an authorised individual acting on their behalf, to induce or threaten to induce a breach of contract in pursuance of an industrial dispute (s96)

8 To organise or threaten industrial action for the purpose of furthering any act which is an unfair industrial practice (s97)

9 For anyone, in pursuance of an industrial dispute, to organise or threaten industrial action for the purpose of inducing another person, who is neither a party to the dispute nor materially supporting a party to it, to break a contract made with a party to the dispute (other than a contract of employment) or preventing him from performing it (section 98)

BREACHES OF DUTY

It is a breach of duty:

1 For an employer, after a ballot in favour of an agency shop, not to take all action necessary to enter an agency-shop agreement and to observe that agreement during its currency (s13(1))

2 For an employer to refuse or fail to disclose to representatives of recognised registered trade unions certain information needed for the purposes of collective bargaining, or not to confirm such information in writing on request (s56)

3 For an employer in certain circumstances not to provide his employees with specified information about the undertaking in which they are employed (s57)

[*Source: Industrial Relations, A Guide to the Industrial Relations Act 1971*, Department of Employment and the Central Office of Information 1972]

Appendix 2

Application Concerning Sole Bargaining Rights

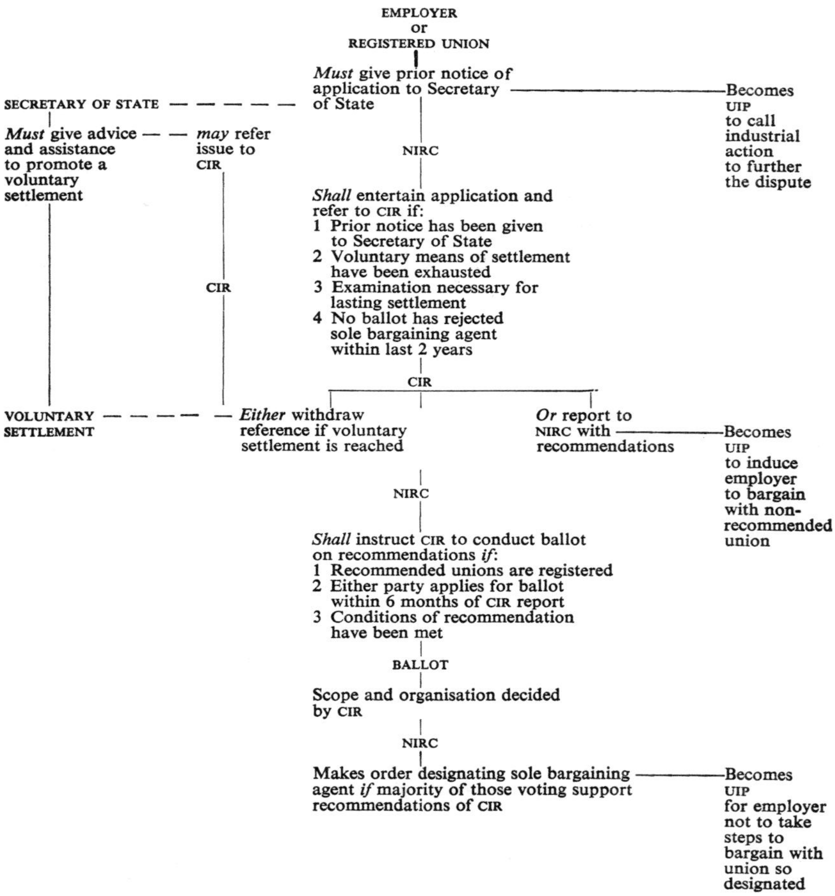

[Source: *Industrial Relations Problems and the Industrial Relations Act*, D J Hall, Kogan Page]

References

1 Committee of Members of the Inns of Court Conservative and Unionist Society, *A Giant's Strength*, Christopher Johnson, London, 1958

2 Royal Commission on Trade Unions and Employers' Associations, report, Cmnd 3623, HMSO, 1968

3 *In Place of Strife—a Policy for Industrial Relations*, Cmnd 3888, HMSO, 1969

4 *Fair Deal at Work*, Conservative Political Centre, London 1968

5 Department of Employment and Productivity, *Industrial Relations Bill—Consultative Document*, DEP, 1970

6 Conditions of Employment and National Arbitration Order, SR & O 1940, number 1305

7 Industrial Disputes Order, SI 1951, number 1376

8 Department of Employment and the Central Office of Information, *Industrial Relations Act 1971*, *Registration*, Department of Employment, 1971

9 Department of Employment and the Central Office of Information, *Industrial Relations, A Guide to the Industrial Relations Act 1971*, Department of Employment, 1971

10 *The Times*, 27 May 1971

11 J Henderson, *The Industrial Relations Act at Work*, The Industrial Society, London, 1971

12 Trades Union Congress, *TUC Handbook on the Industrial Relations Act*, Trades Union Congress, London, 1972

13 R J Harvey, *Industrial Relations*, Butterworths, London, 1972

14 *The Times*, Law Report, 1 December 1971, National Industrial Relations Court, Statement by the President, The Hon Sir John Donaldson upon the opening of the National Industrial Relations Court

15 *The Times*, Law Report, 12 June 1972, National Industrial Relations Court, Churchman and Others *v* Port of London Joint Shop Stewards' Committee and Others

16 *The Times*, Law Report, 20 April 1972, National Industrial Relations Court, Heaton's Transport (St Helens) Ltd *v* Transport and General Workers Union; Craddock Brothers *v* Same
17 *The Times*, Law Report, 16 June 1972, Court of Appeal, Churchman and Others *v* Steer and Others
18 Panel on Tolpuddle Martyr Gate, Tolpuddle, Dorset
19 The *Financial Times*, 26 April 1972
20 *The Times*, Law Report, 18 May 1972, National Industrial Relations Court, Panalpina Services Ltd *v* Transport and General Workers' Union
21 *The Times*, Law Report, 12 May 1972, National Industrial Relations Court, Heaton's Transport (St Helens) Ltd *v* Transport and General Workers' Union; Craddock Brothers *v* Same
22 *The Times*, 11 February 1972
23 Commission on Industrial Relations, Report Birmid Qualcast, Cmnd 4229, HMSO, 1970
24 Commission on Industrial Relations, Report Shipbuilding and Shiprepairing, Cmnd 4756, HMSO, 1971
25 Commission on Industrial Relations, Report The Associated Octel Company Ltd, Cmnd 4246, HMSO, 1969; Report General Accident Fire & Life Assurance Corporation Ltd, Cmnd 4247, HMSO, 1969; Report W Stevenson & Sons, Suttons Cornwall Ltd, Cmnd 4248, HMSO, 1969; Report BSR Limited, Cmnd 4274, HMSO, 1970
26 I Macbeath, *The Times Guide to the Industrial Relations Act*, Times Newspapers Ltd, London, 1971
27 The Industrial Tribunals (Industrial Relations, etc) Regulations 1972 (SI 1972, number 38)
28 C E McCormick, "The Redundancy Payments Act in the practice of the Industrial Tribunals," *British Journal of Industrial Relations*, volume VIII, number 3, November 1970, London School of Economics and Political Science
29 Ministry of Labour, *Industrial Relations Handbook*, HMSO, 1961
30 Department of Employment, *Industrial Relations Code of Practice*, HMSO, 1972
31 Department of Employment and the Central Office of Information, *Industrial Relations Act 1971*, *Rights of the Individual*, Department of Employment, 1972
32 Ministry of Labour, *Dismissal Procedures—A Report*, HMSO, 1967
33 *The Times*, Law Report, 19 May 1972, Court of Appeal, Secretary of State for Employment *v* Aslef and Others
34 *The Times*, 26 February 1971

35 A Flanders, *Industrial Relations: What is Wrong with the System?* Faber and Faber, London, 1965
36 W E J McCarthy, *The Closed Shop in Britain*, Blackwell, Oxford, 1964
37 R O'Brien, *Plant Procedures and Agreements—a Case Study in Conflict at Work*, edited by S Kessler and B Weekes, British Broadcasting Corporation, London, 1971
38 Commission on Industrial Relations, Report, Clayton Dewandre Co Ltd, Cmnd 4640, HMSO, 1971
39 Research Papers Royal Commission on Trade Unions and Employers' Associations, Research Paper 2 (Part 1) *Disputes Procedures in British Industry*, A I Marsh, HMSO, 1966, Research Paper 2 (Part 2) *Disputes Procedures in Britain*, A I Marsh and W E J McCarthy, HMSO, 1968
40 T S Eliot, *The Waste Land in Selected Poems*, Penguin Books, 1948
41 National Board for Prices and Incomes Report number 110, *Pay and Conditions in the Clothing Manufacturing Industries*, Cmnd 4002, HMSO, 1969
42 E G A Armstrong, "Minimum Wages in a Fully Employed City," *British Journal of Industrial Relations*, March 1966; *Birmingham and some of its Low-Paid Workers*, The Manchester School, December 1968
43 Trades Union Congress, *Good Industrial Relations—A Guide for Negotiators*, Trades Union Congress, 1971
44 TGWU, *The Ford Wage Claim*, Transport and General Workers' Union, 1970
45 Ford Motor Co Ltd *v* Amalgamated Union of Engineering and Foundry Workers (1969) 2 QB 303; (1969) 2 A11 ER 481
46 *The Times*, Law Report, 30 May 1972, Court of Appeal, Heaton's Transport (St Helens) Ltd *v* Transport and General Workers' Union; Craddock Brothers *v* Same; Panalpina Services Ltd and Another *v* Same
47 Interim Report of the Joint Special Committee on the Ports Industry Joint Special Committee Secretariat, c/o National Ports Council, London, 25 July 1972 and Further Statement and Explanatory Notes 15 August 1972
48 J Hughes, and R Moore, (edited for the NUM) *A Special Case? Social Justice and the Miners*, Penguin Books Ltd, Harmondsworth, 1972
49 *The Times*, Law Report, 13 June 1972, Court of Appeal Heaton's Transport (St Helens) Ltd *v* Transport and General Workers' Union
50 Registry of Trade Unions and Employers' Associations, *Report of*

the Chief Registrar of Trade Unions and Employers' Associations for the Year 1971, HMSO, 1972

51 E Mumford, "Job Satisfaction: A Method of Analysis," *Personnel Review*, volume 1, number 3, summer 1972, Gower Press

52 *The Times*, Law Report, 27 July 1972, House of Lords, Heaton's Transport (St Helens) Ltd *v* Transport and General Workers' Union; Craddock Brothers *v* Same; Panalpina Services Ltd *v* Same and Another

53 Commission on Industrial Relations, Report, *Facilities Afforded to Shop-Stewards*, Cmnd 4668, HMSO, 1971

54 Department of Employment, *Contracts of Employment Act 1963, A revised guide incorporating changes arising from the Industrial Relations Act 1971*, Department of Employment

55 E Wigham, "Ruling the unions are unable to enforce," *The Times*, 1 August 1972

56 K W Wedderburn, "Labour Law and Labour Relations in Britain," *British Journal of Industrial Relations*, July 1972

57 D Kujawa, *International Labor Relations Management in the Automotive Industry, A Comparative Study of Chrysler, Ford and General Motors*, Praeger Publishers, New York, 1971

58 P Plouviez, "Getting in on the Act," *Socialist Commentary*, June 1972

59 V Hanna, "The formula that makes 'you're fired' a sweeter sound," the *Sunday Times*, 12 November 1972

60 *Industrial Tribunal Reports*, volume 7, part 9, HMSO, 1972

61 *Industrial Relations Act, IDS Report Supplement number 4*, Incomes Data Services Ltd, London, 1972

62 Commission on Industrial Relations Report number 30, *Approved Closed Shop Agreement British Shipping Federation/National Union of Seamen*, HMSO, 1972

63 Commission on Industrial Relations Report number 31, *Disclosure of Information*, HMSO, 1972

64 *The Industrial Court Rules 1971*, SI 1971, number 1777, cf Rule 71

65 G Scott, *New Law Journal* reported in *The Times*, 1 December 1972

66 Department of Employment *Gazette*, July, October 1972, and January 1973, HMSO

67 *The Times*, 2 August 1972 (Parliament, 1 August 1972)

68 Industrial Tribunal Reports, volume 7, Part 8, HMSO, 1972

69 *The Times*, Law Report, 7 July 1972, National Industrial Relations Court, The Post Office *v* Ravyts and Others

70 *The Times*, Law Report, 8 November 1972, National Industrial

Relations Court, Goad *v* Amalgamated Union of Engineering Workers (Engineering Section)

71 T Gray, *Elegy in a Country Churchyard*, an allusion to defiance of arbitrary power

72 Industrial Relations Act, *IDS Report Supplement number 1*, Incomes Data Services Ltd, London 1972

73 Commission on Industrial Relations, Report number 32, C A Parsons and Co Ltd, HMSO, 1972

74 *The Times*, Law Report, 18 July 1972, National Industrial Relations Court, United Kingdom Association of Professional Engineers and Others *v* Rolls-Royce & Associates Ltd and Others

75 Department of Employment *Gazette*, October 1972, HMSO

76 O Kahn-Freund, and B Hepple, *Laws against Strikes*, Fabian Research Series 305, Fabian Society, London 1972

77 A Cox, *Labor Law Cases and Materials*, The Foundation Press, Brooklyn 1958

78 *The Times*, 28 July 1972

79 *The Times*, 3 August 1972

80 E H Phelps Brown, *Collective Bargaining Reconsidered Stamp Memorial Lecture 1971*, University of London, The Athlone Press, 1971

81 *Contact*, volume 4, number 3, September 1972, Electrical Electronic Telecommunication, Plumbing Trade Union

82 Commission on Industrial Relations Report number 35, *Williams & Glyn's Bank Ltd*, HMSO, 1973

83 Department of Employment *Gazette*, January 1973, HMSO

84 Commission on Industrial Relations Report number 33, *Industrial Relations Training*, HMSO, 1972; Report number 34, *The Role of Management in Industrial Relations* HMSO, 1973

Index